IMAGES
of America

FORREST CITY AND
ST. FRANCIS COUNTY

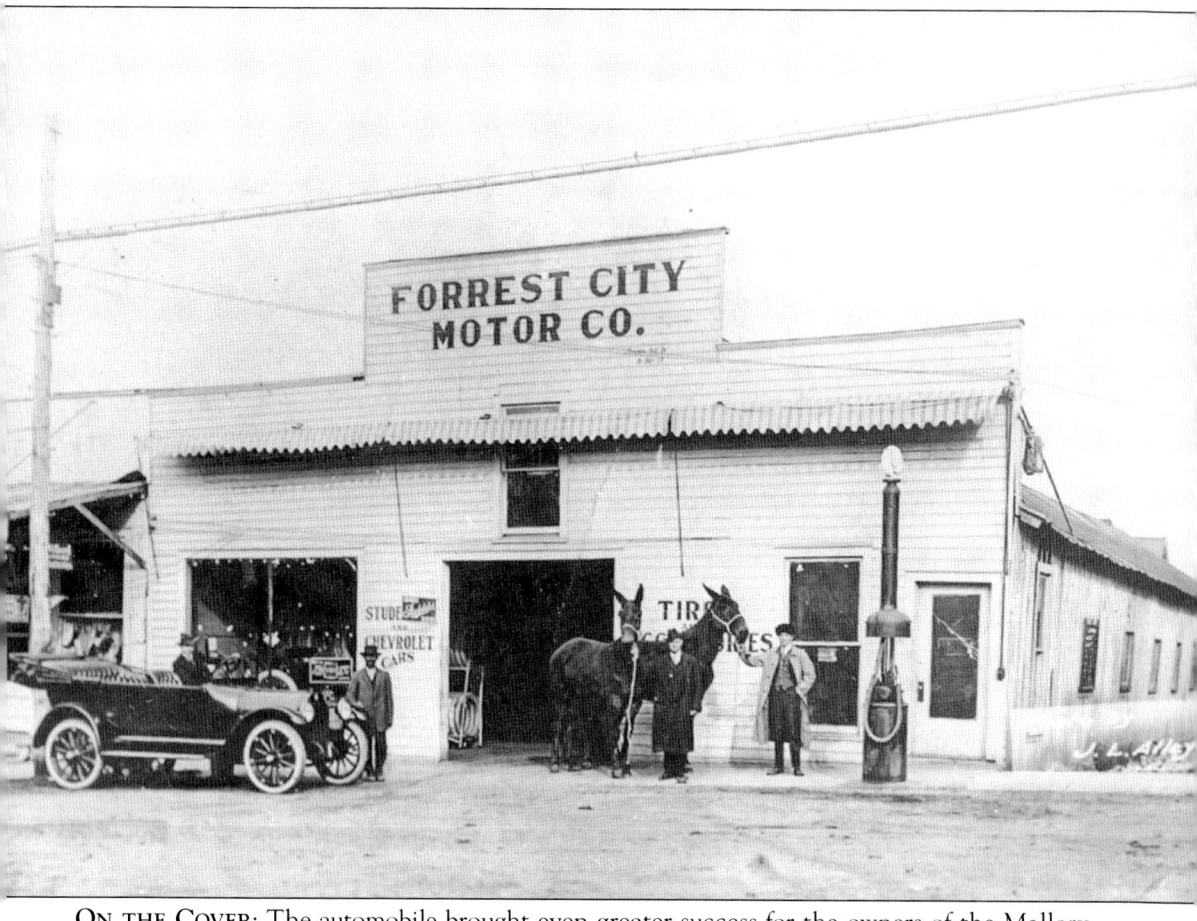

On the Cover: The automobile brought even greater success for the owners of the Mallory-Eldridge Livery Stable. In the early 1900s, the business was already thriving as a stable that rented and sold mules, horses, and buggies. The company wanted to change with the times, however, so it began to sell such makes of automobiles as the Gardner and Overland. Rolfe C. Eldridge Sr. (overcoat), Josh Mallory, Rufus Scott (cap), and John Jones stand in front of the old livery stable in this 1918 photograph. The frame building was destroyed by fire but rebuilt in 1929. (Courtesy of the St. Francis County Museum.)

IMAGES
of America

FORREST CITY AND ST. FRANCIS COUNTY

H. Wayne Parker and Wendy Kittler
of the St. Francis County Museum

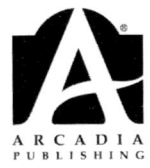

Copyright © 2008 by H. Wayne Parker and Wendy Kittler of the St. Francis County Museum
ISBN 978-0-7385-5422-8

Published by Arcadia Publishing
Charleston, South Carolina

Printed in the United States of America

Library of Congress Catalog Card Number: 2008922666

For all general information contact Arcadia Publishing at:
Telephone 843-853-2070
Fax 843-853-0044
E-mail sales@arcadiapublishing.com
For customer service and orders:
Toll-Free 1-888-313-2665

Visit us on the Internet at www.arcadiapublishing.com

*To Judge Gazolla Vaccaro,
the founder of the St. Francis County Museum*

Contents

Acknowledgments		6
Introduction		7
1.	Early History of St. Francis County	9
2.	Settlement and Civilization	25
3.	Agriculture	63
4.	People	83
5.	Education	105
6.	Disaster Strikes	119

ACKNOWLEDGMENTS

There are so many people and businesses that need to be mentioned, foremost the generous God that I serve; my mother, Mary Courtney Parker; my father, Howard W. Parker (how I wish he could have seen this book); and my family members, who are always there when I need them. I also thank Shelley Gervasi for putting up with my crazy moods at work, Judge Vaccaro for help with the introduction, the *Times-Herald* for allowing us to reprint many of the images from its 1905 book, and the complete board of the St. Francis County Museum for allowing us to move and copy so many great photographs and artifacts. I am grateful to the family of Claude O'Dell for the use of his photographs. This book could never have been made without Jerald Burns's expertise in scanning all of the images. And most of all, to my dear friend Wendy Kittler: this book would have been impossible without you. You are a wonderful friend, and I love you like a sister.

—H. Wayne Parker

I would like to acknowledge the following: the Lord; Jerald Burns (both for scanning the photographs and for being my dad); Nellie Higgins, Dr. Dale Morris, Warren Faupel, and Edith Dodson for providing photographic information; George King, Claud O'Dell, and Jerald Burns for images; the *Times-Herald* for continually supporting the museum; Mary Ann Burns (the best mom in the world); and my wonderful family—Brian, Brianna, Madeline, and Mason Kittler. Shelley, you rock! To my brother Allan: it is your turn. To my "brother from another mother" Wayne: love you. Without people like Dr. J. O. Rush, Dr. Julius Bogart, Dr. Alley, Rush Harris, and Gazolla Vaccaro, we would not have any history to pass on. Thank you. May those reading this book make a decision to preserve and pass down their remembrances.

—Wendy Kittler

IN MEMORIAM

It breaks my heart that my friend and coauthor, H. Wayne Parker, is not here to share in the fulfillment of this project. When I first met Wayne, we discussed what fun it would be to write a book. He knew it was a personal dream for me—one of those lifelong dreams that few people get a chance to tackle. He was thrilled when Luke Cunningham from Arcadia Publishing called looking for writers about the county. I would not have attempted it if Wayne had not been willing to go through it with me. It was a joy to work as the assistant curator of the St. Francis County Museum with Wayne serving as the curator. We worked on many projects and exhibits together, and he was crazy enough to trust my intuition and creative processes. He is the only person I have found that would bounce ideas back to me as fast as I could throw them. He encouraged me to be myself. The exhibits we created together will remain some of my fondest memories. More than a creative partner, Wayne was one of my best friends. Sometimes we got on each other's last nerve, but we had too much fun to stay that way for long. He treated my family like his own, and we will never forget that. In his lifetime, Wayne had been to more places, seen more things, and met more people than I will ever imagine. May the Lord bless his memory and his family.

With great respect from a friend,
Wendy Kittler

INTRODUCTION

St. Francis County had been inhabited by Native Americans for 12,000 years before the first white man explored the area. They were the builders of great mounds some 7,000 years before the Egyptians were building pyramids. No one knows when they arrived, but there is evidence of Native American settlements in eastern Arkansas as far back as 650 CE. The Parkin Archeological State Park is a 17-acre Casqui village believed to be the site visited by the expedition of Hernando de Soto.

Spaniard Hernando de Soto was most likely the first white man to visit what is now eastern Arkansas. His expedition crossed the Mississippi River in May 1541. Some historians put the river crossing near Helena; others say it was near Memphis. Regardless, the expedition traveled north and west for several more weeks in search of gold. They found swamps, mainly between the Cache and White Rivers, and decided to return down the St. Francis River, crossing near Madison. De Soto explored much of Arkansas during the next few months, but he never found any gold and never left the state. He chronicled a meeting with the Native Americans at a settlement near present-day Parkin in the summer of 1541. The men erected a giant cypress cross in the region and were generally welcomed by the Native Americans. De Soto died of a fever and was secretly buried in May 1542, reportedly in Helena, to hide the body from the natives.

There were no other written accounts of Europeans in the region until around 1673. At this time, Jacques Marquette and Louis Joliet, French Catholic missionaries, came from Illinois down the Mississippi River, entering the Arkansas River. In 1682, Chevalier de la Salle reached Native American villages on the Arkansas River and took possession of all lands drained by the Mississippi River and its tributaries. The land was called Louisiana in honor of the French king. In 1686, Arkansas Post became the first white settlement in the state.

The French never settled the land on a large scale and had trouble with Native American tribes, especially the Chickasaws. In early 1679, the French built a fort near Wittsburg on the St. Francis River in Cross County but later abandoned it. Arkansas became a Spanish territory, but Napoleon Bonaparte forced Spain to cede the land to France.

In 1803, the territory became part of the United States with the Louisiana Purchase. At this time, fewer than 500 white settlers were living in what would be Arkansas. St. Francis County was officially approved by the Arkansas Territorial Legislature on October 13, 1827. The county was named for the river, but no one knows exactly who named the river. Most historians agree that it was probably named by French Catholic missionaries in the late 17th century. There is evidence of an early Jesuit mission near Helena where the St. Francis River drains into the Mississippi. The land itself was taken from part of Phillips County. At the time, St. Francis County included parts of what are now Cross, Lee, and Poinsett Counties. The county seat started at the home of William Strong, one of the early settlers and the county's first sheriff. It was soon moved to the newly created town of Franklin near Old Military Road.

In 1838, Cross County was formed from part of St. Francis County, placing Franklin in the extreme northern part of the county. In 1840, the county seat was moved to Madison near an old Native American village on Crow Creek. The center of government was transferred once more in 1855 to the bustling community of Mount Vernon, where a courthouse and jail were constructed. After a fire in 1856, the county seat was moved back to Madison. There it remained until 1874, when the citizens of St. Francis County voted to make Forrest City the permanent seat.

The county has had its share of difficulties, but its residents are anxiously awaiting a revival of this once-great land. As tourists begin to look for a more natural land in which to explore and relax, St. Francis County becomes a logical destination. People from Memphis and Little Rock seek to retire here to be close to nature. Even a few people from Hollywood have hunting resorts. If we, the residents of the county, will take pride in what we have to offer, our land will flourish once again. It is only by studying our past that we can positively influence our future.

One

EARLY HISTORY OF ST. FRANCIS COUNTY

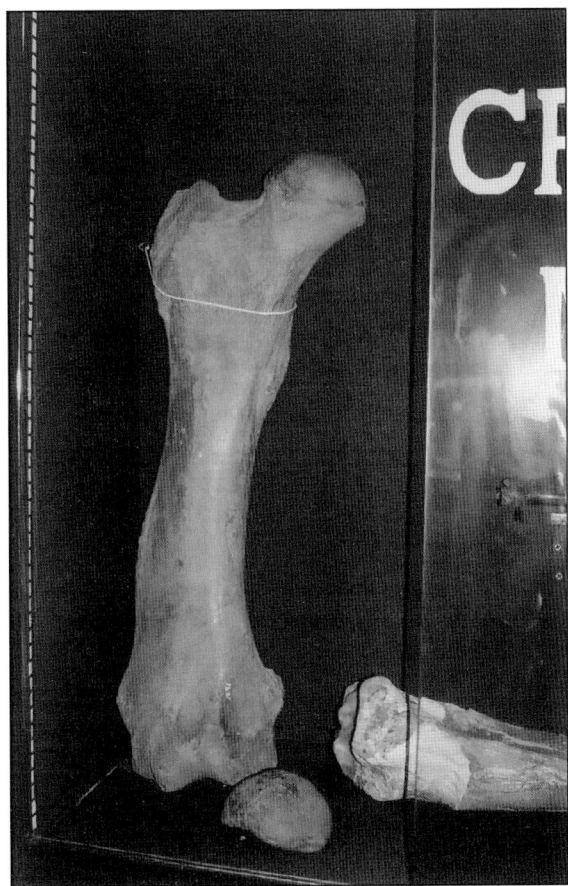

Crowley's Ridge is a geological anomaly. It is named for Benjamin Crowley, whose friends once traveled past Memphis and through Wittsburg. They told others they were going to "Benjamin Crowley's Ridge." This ridge served as a natural bridge off of the glacier that stretched into the South during the Ice Age. Even Forrest City natives find it flabbergasting that several mastodon bones have been found in the last century. The remains of one mastodon were unearthed in 1949 by city workers who were excavating for sewer improvements. The St. Francis County Museum is indeed blessed to have a group of mastodon bones as part of the Dr. J. O. Rush Collection. Gazing at the immense femur bones of this prehistoric creature gives visitors a new appreciation for the size of the animal. The excavation tools chipped one long bone, though it was repaired with plaster at the initial placing in the doctor's exhibit.

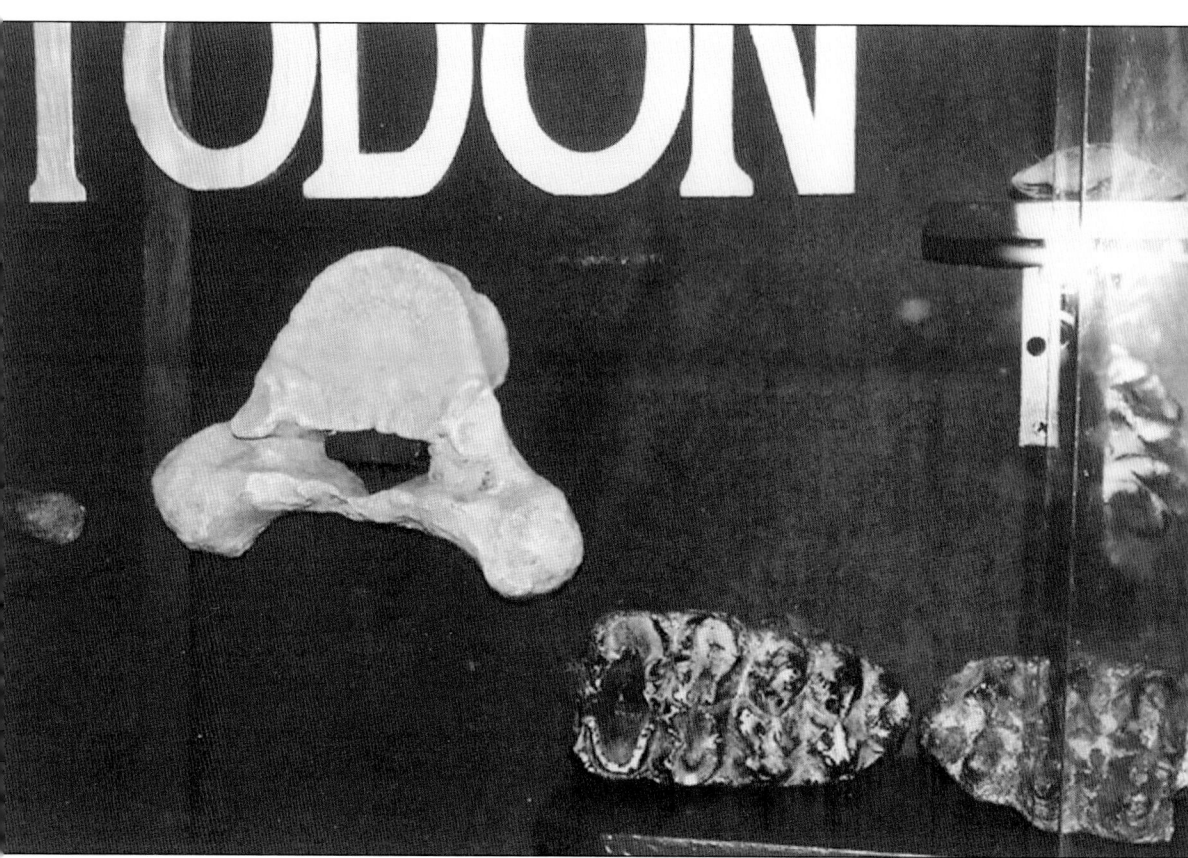

Although the femur bones are the most impressive because of their size, the teeth and vertebrae of the mastodon provide evidence of the animals' daily habits. Mastodons were plant eaters. Also included in the exhibit are pieces of the ball-and-socket joint and several small bones. These continue to be favorites with visitors both young and old.

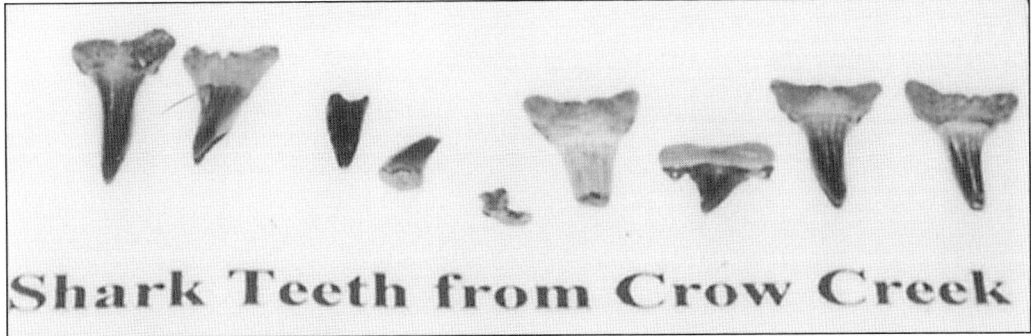

While it is difficult to imagine mastodons roaming this now-fertile Delta farmland, the shark and ray teeth routinely pulled from the earth give yet another perspective on the geological history of Crowley's Ridge. At one time, this entire area was covered by the Gulf of Mexico. Although these Crow Creek teeth are relatively small, amateur archaeologists have brought in examples of sharks' teeth greater than an inch wide.

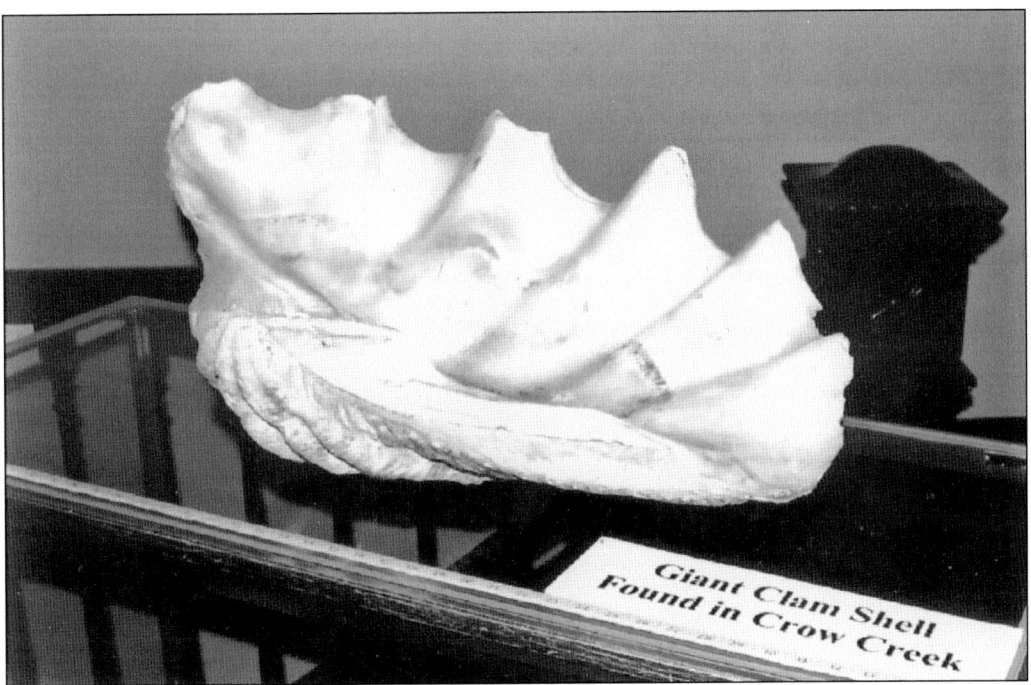

This half-shell further demonstrates the sea life that once flourished here. Also found in Crow Creek, it weighs in at 65 pounds. Just imagine the size of this monster if both halves had been located! Also included in the shell exhibit are examples of petrified wood and other natural artifacts, including an 8-inch-wide brain coral fossil found by John Colvin.

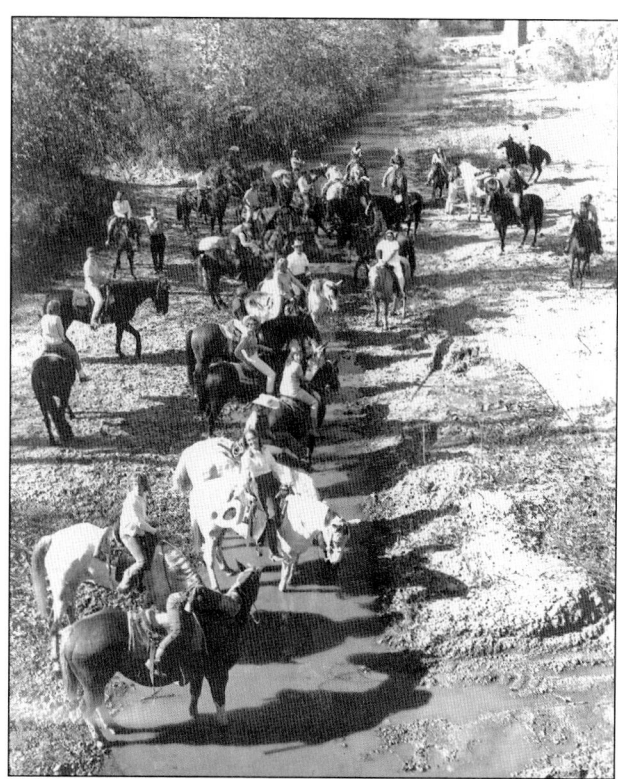

Crow Creek, the site of many great fossil finds, is a winding stream that sometimes meanders and weaves its way down to a mere trickle. In some spots, a wide riverbed still peeks out to share some history. Here riders explore the creek by horseback in the 1970s.

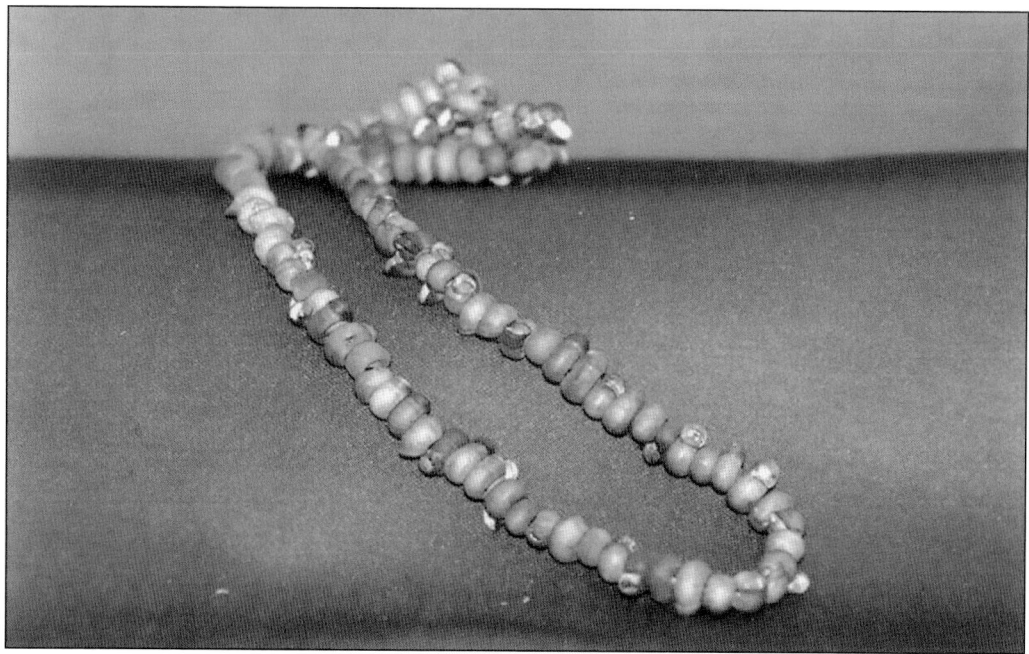

The children on today's playground still look for aquatic fossils. These shells are believed to have been traded as money by the Native Americans who inhabited the region. Rocky areas and bare patches of land continue to yield fossil plant life and the occasional shell. This string of shells is part of the Dr. J. O. Rush Collection.

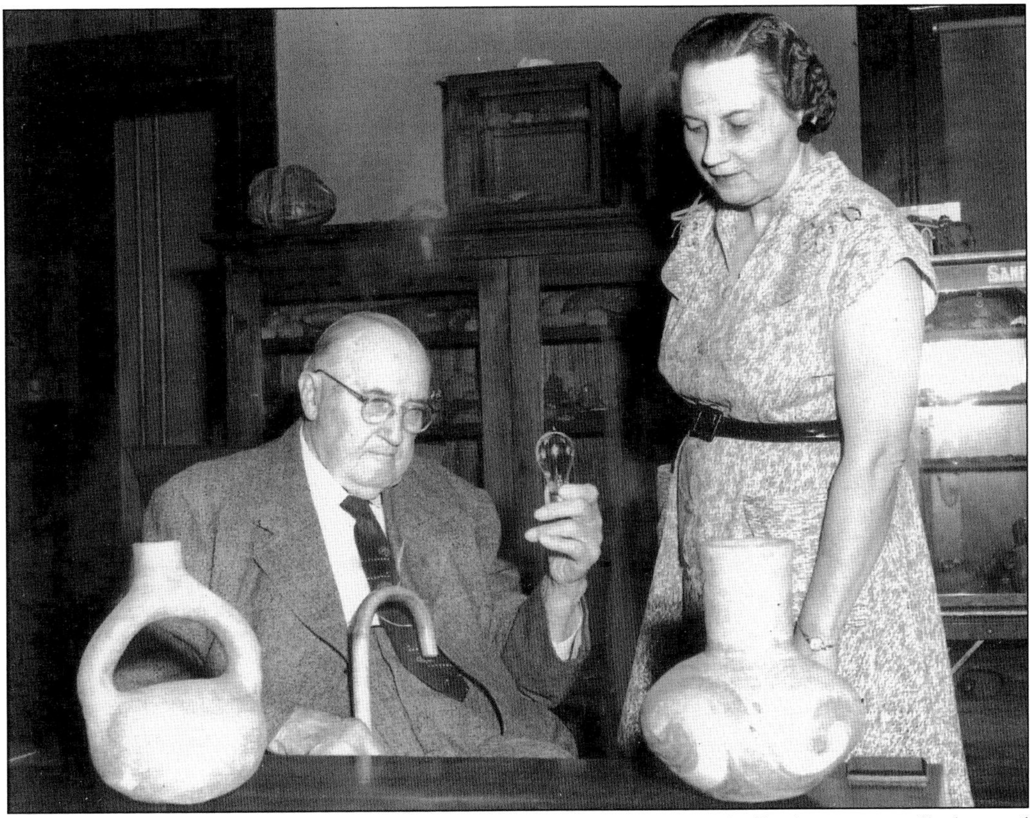

Dr. Rush, pictured with his daughter Annie Gates, views a light bulb that reportedly burned for 40 years. The doctor is seated in his waiting room, which doubled as his museum collection. Upon the deaths of David and Annie Gates, the artifact collection was sent to Arkansas State University for cataloging, appraisal, and preservation. Great care has been taken to display the artifacts closely to their original conditions. Other museums have on display in a gallery the same number of pieces this site has in just one case.

This unique double-necked pot was made in the Mississippian Period and is the only one of its kind in the collection. This simple, yet fluid, artifact demonstrates the use of art in utilitarian objects. While practical, the Mississippians had an artistic flair and style not present in all Native American art. For example, the Toltec Mound site in Scott, Arkansas, displays a simple, unadorned type of pottery that is much more focused on its intended use. The mound builders preceded the Mississippian culture, which produced distinct artistic tendencies.

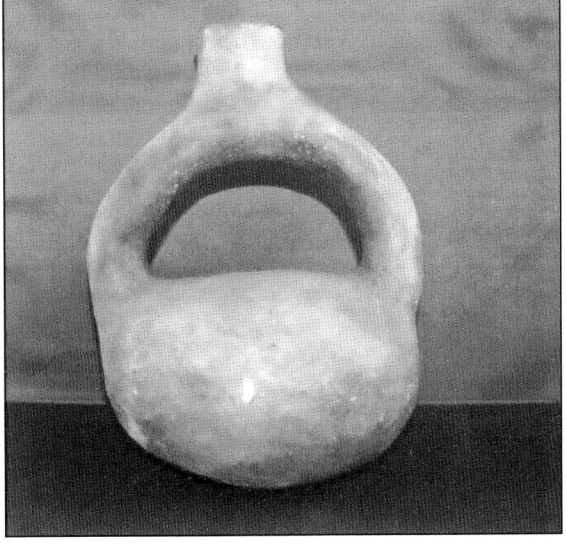

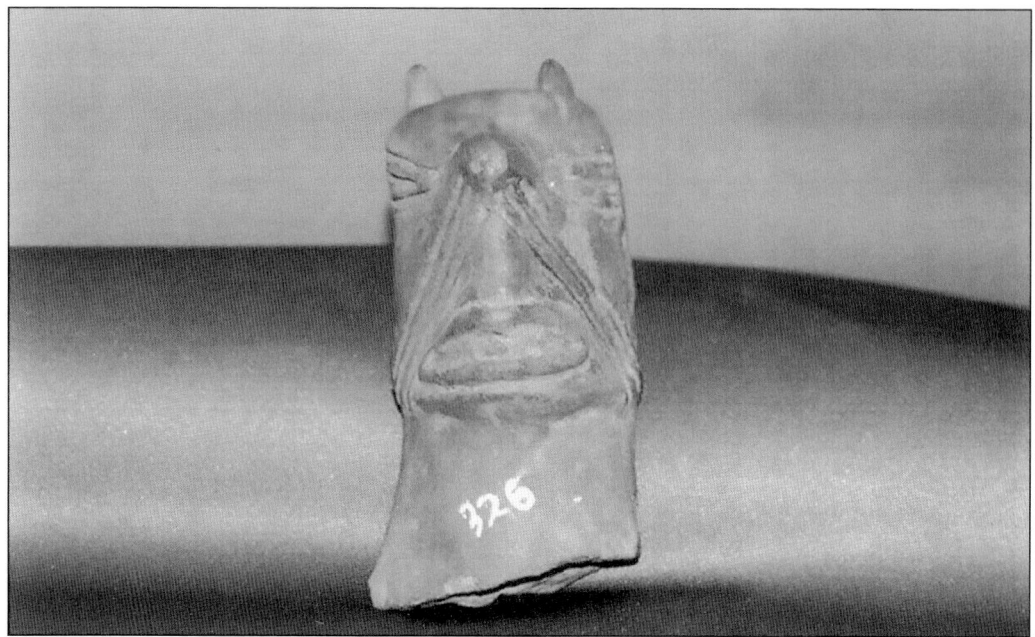

During the Mississippian Period, Native Americans worked with effigies in artistic, religious, and utilitarian works. This effigy is one of several in the Dr. J. O. Rush Collection. Other effigies in the museum represent dogs, turtles, and other small animals. For more information on effigies in Arkansas Native American works, please visit www.encyclopediaofarkansas.net and the Parkin Archeological Site.

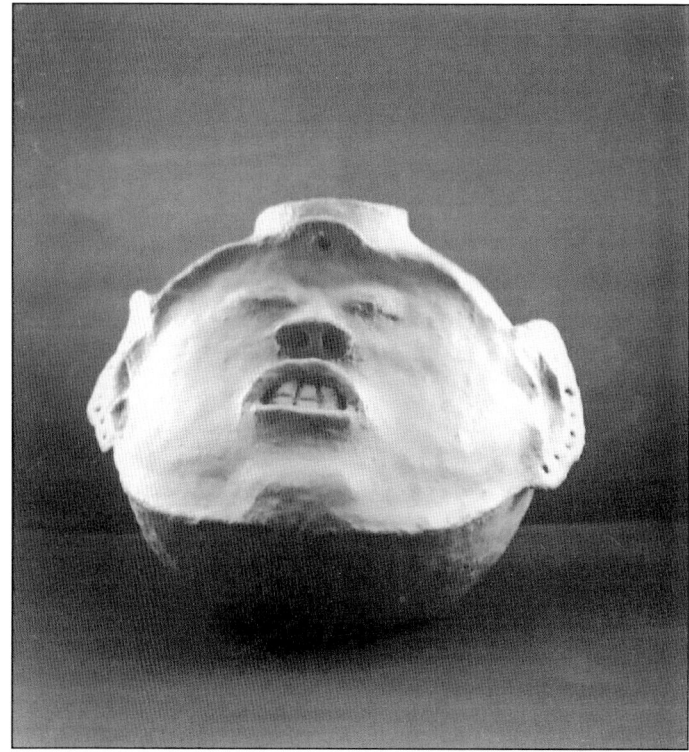

Head pots are found in several native cultures around the world, but the Mississippian Native Americans were the only ones to design the entire pot in the likeness of a head. Others just put facial features on the front, while the Mississippians wrapped the design around the pot to include the ears and shape of the head.

Created at approximately the same time as the head pot, this swirled pot uses the characteristic red and white glaze from that period. The red glaze is a brick color, and the white glaze resembles chalk. This pot is representative of many in the collection.

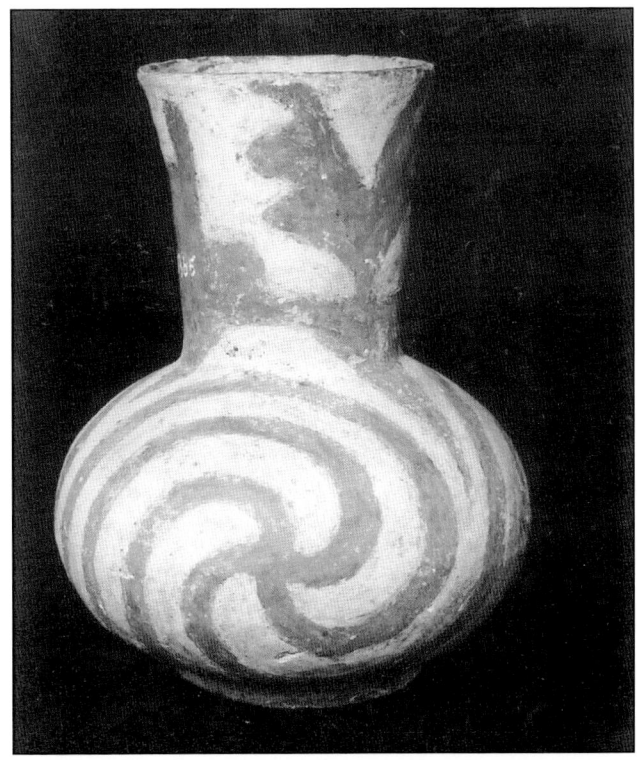

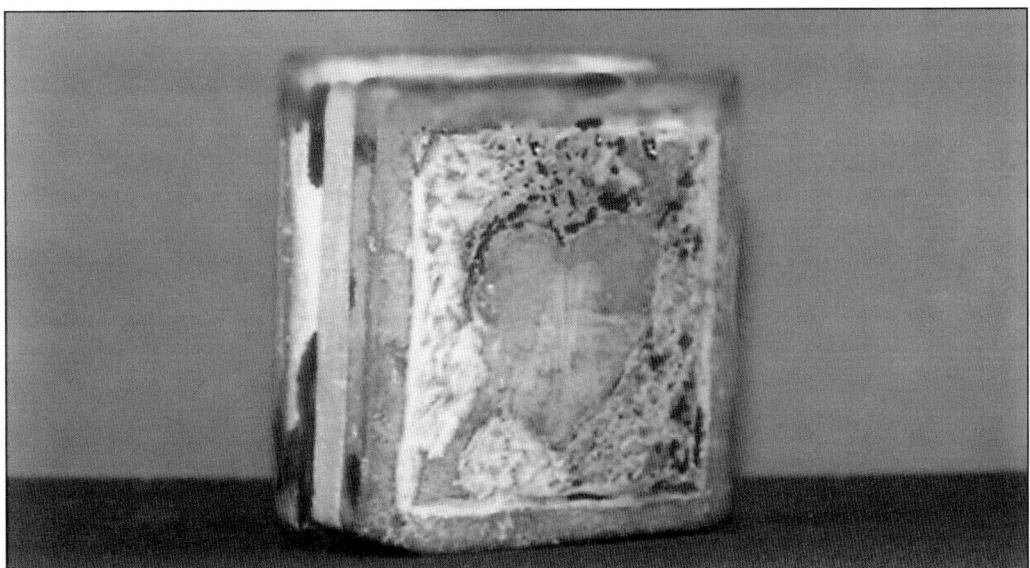

This Bible was hand carved from a black stone. It reportedly belonged to a Spanish soldier from the time of Hernando de Soto. In 1541, de Soto's men crossed into Arkansas a little below Helena, which is south of St. Francis County. The men wintered in Hot Springs and spent considerable time exploring eastern Arkansas. This artifact is currently under study to verify its history. One side bears a rough-hewn heart with a dagger through it, while the other side has a simple cross. The edge has been carved to resemble a spine. The present belief is that it was carried by soldiers to evangelize the Native Americans.

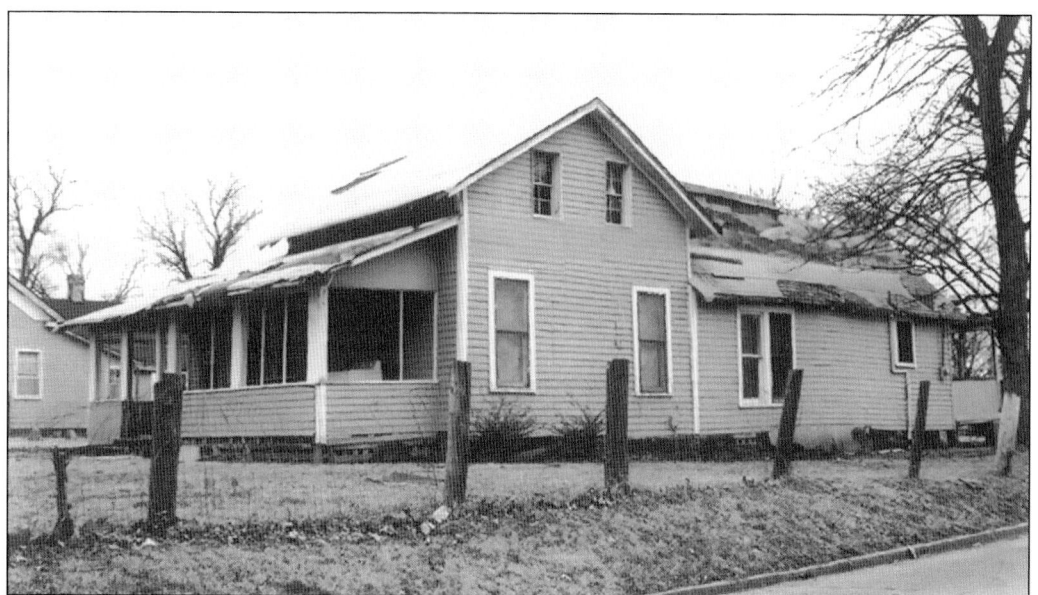

This house may appear to be just an insignificant building in need of repair, but it has a rich history. Located in the heart of old-time Forrest City, it is believed to be one of the oldest standing homes in the county. Additions have been constructed over the years, but in the two-story part, one can see the remnants of a simple log cabin. A look underneath the house reveals logs greater than 18 inches wide, still maintaining their bark after all these years. The home reportedly belonged to Dr. Julius Bogart, who moved his practice from Wheatley.

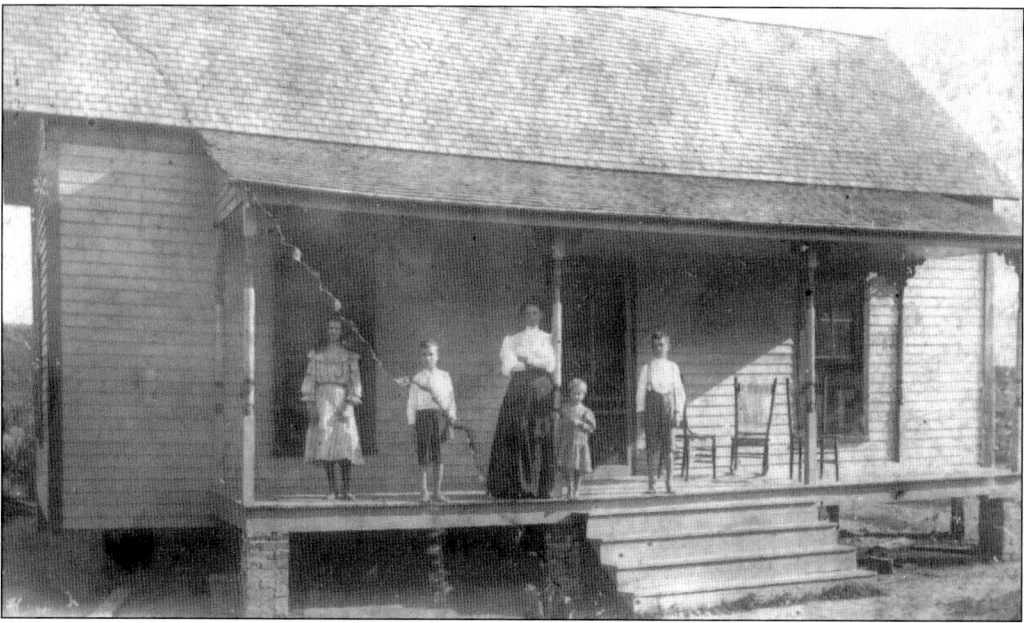

Mittie Thomas (center) is shown with her family—(from left to right) Annie, Charles, Lillian, and Van—at the start of the 20th century. This is also one of the oldest extant houses in town. Annie later married Cyrus Dodson and lived at Dodson's Corner, halfway between Palestine and Forrest City on the Broadway of America, Highway 70. Annie ran a dairy, a sweet potato farm, and a service station during her life.

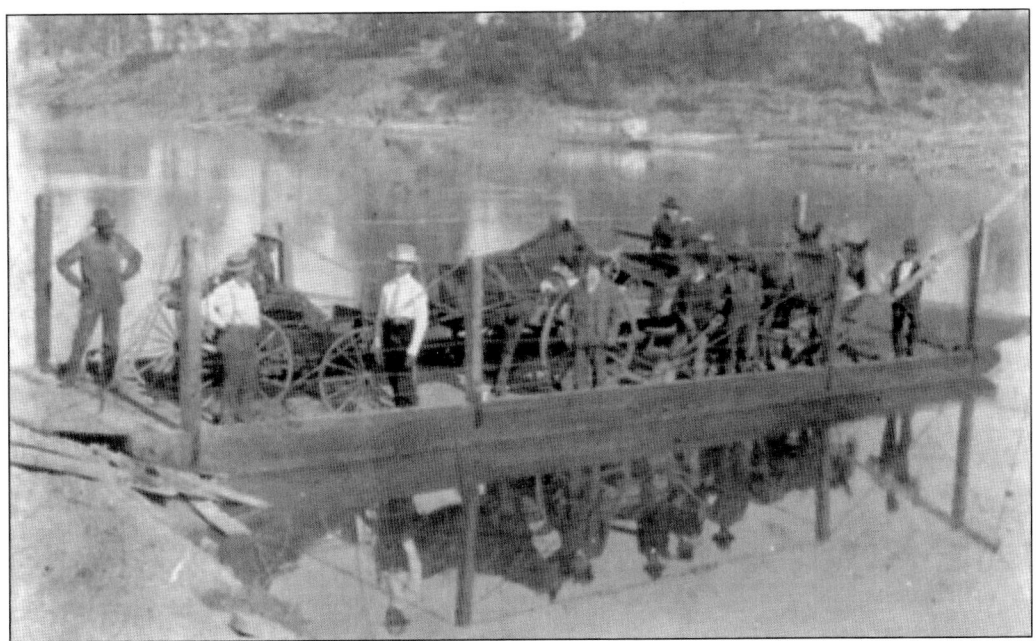

The ferry across the St. Francis River at Madison is pictured during a time of prosperity. Before roads and bridges were established, the ferry was the only way to cross the then-wide river. (At this time, riverboats could still navigate the channel.) This photograph is one of the most popular ones at the St. Francis County Museum.

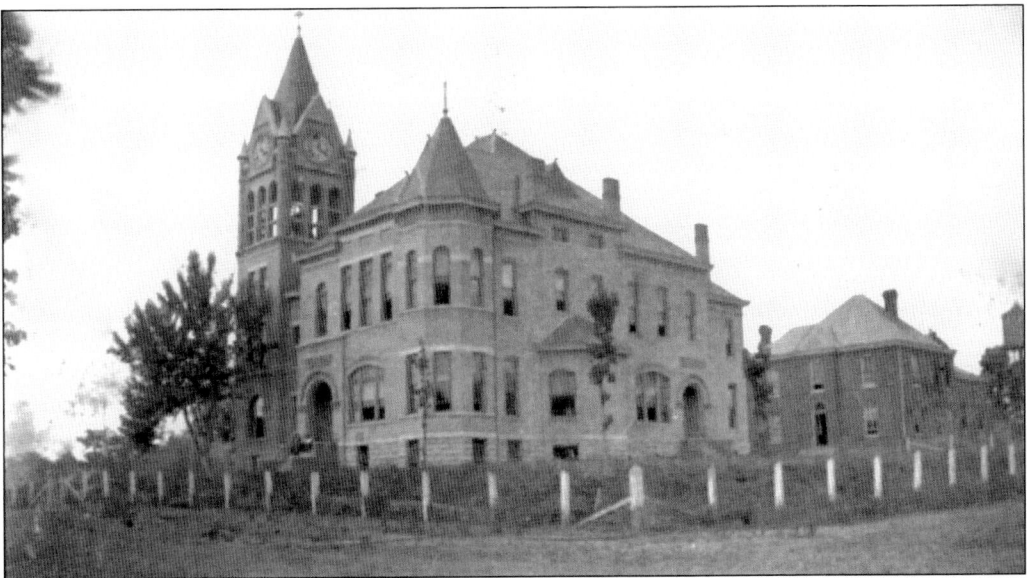

The county seat was eventually moved to Forrest City, creating animosity between Madison and Forrest City residents. The records were moved out of Madison under cover of darkness—but legally, a 1905 history book declares. For a while, the records were kept in a spare room of the Fussell-Graham-Alderson Company (FGA). In 1897, the new county courthouse was completed in Forrest City. Of course, the records had burned twice, so not many remained. (Burning the records to avoid paying property taxes was in vogue at the time.) Unfortunately, few documents exist dated before 1862.

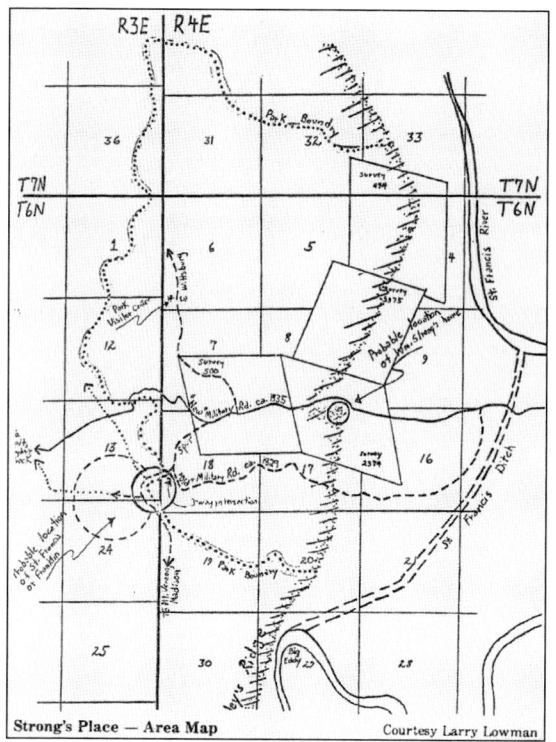

Strong's Place — Area Map   Courtesy Larry Lowman

William Strong was the first judge of the county and a rather infamous character. Both revered and reviled, he had an undeniably positive impact on the county, which then included much more land than today. The William Strong Home at Colt is the site for many community activities. The small circle on the map represents Strong's most well-known house, the boardinghouse he owned on Military Road. Strong reportedly had servants slip items in the saddlebags of boarders, and then he would accuse the boarders of stealing. The diamonds on the map mark Spanish land grants, which were surveyed out before the Louisiana Purchase. After the purchase, lines were north-south and east-west. The larger, dotted circle is the probable site for the town of St. Francis, also known as Franklin.

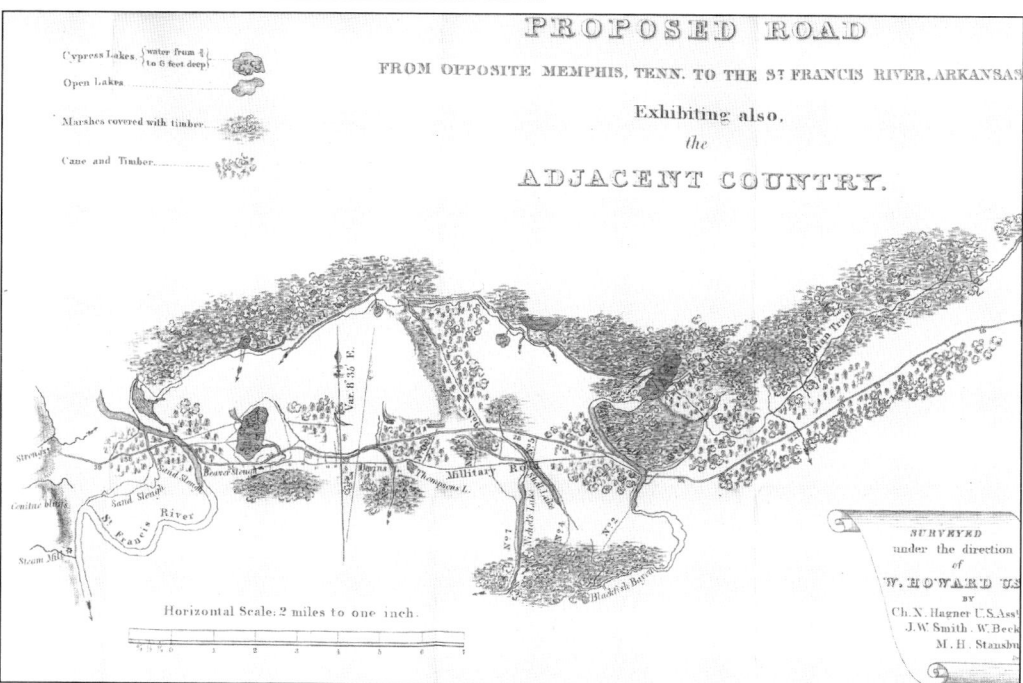

The military knew that as it removed the Native Americans, it would have to make a route to the reservations. William Strong lobbied to have this trail developed into a full-scale road. It was the main east-west path through eastern Arkansas, while the St. Francis River carried the north-south traffic.

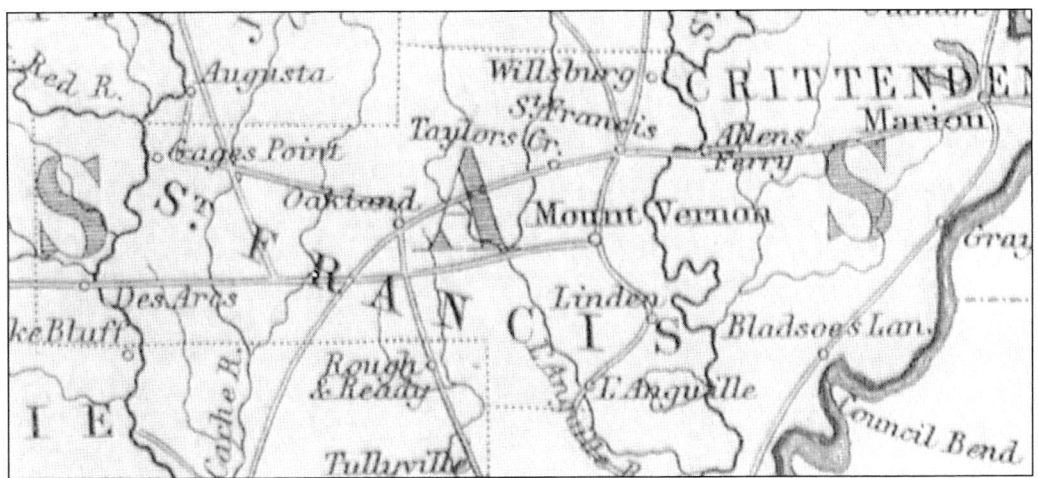

This map is believed to have been made during the Civil War era. Note that at that time Des Arc was actually part of St. Francis County. Wittsburg, Taylor's Creek, Mount Vernon, and St. Francis are discussed in depth in Richard Ellis's *Pinetree Times* book. This map predates the first division of the county.

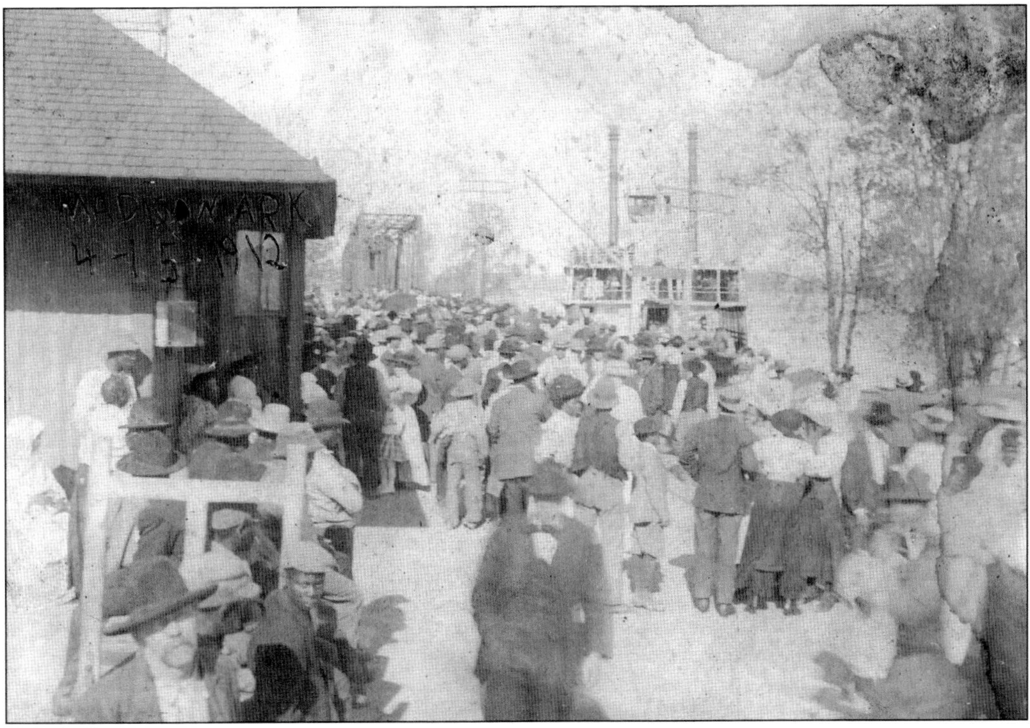

Until the late 1800s, Madison was the largest town in the county. It flourished because of its location on the St. Francis River, which at that time was large enough to accommodate riverboats. This photograph was taken on April 15, 1912, during that bustling time when the river ruled, before the advent of the train through the county. Note the excitement in the crowd members' faces, and the mixture of people as they wait for the boat to dock.

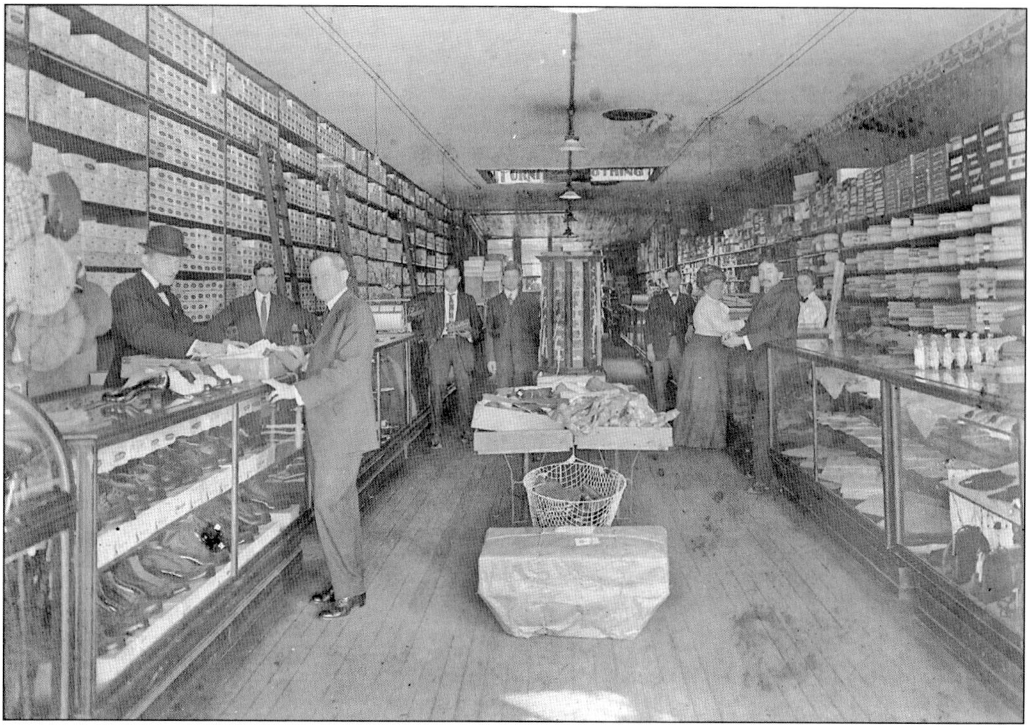

These elegant wood cases hold wares such as shoes, hats, and other dry goods for sale. The woman's dress would have been appropriate for the beginning of the 20th century. The photograph is labeled "FGA," for the Fussell-Graham-Alderson Company.

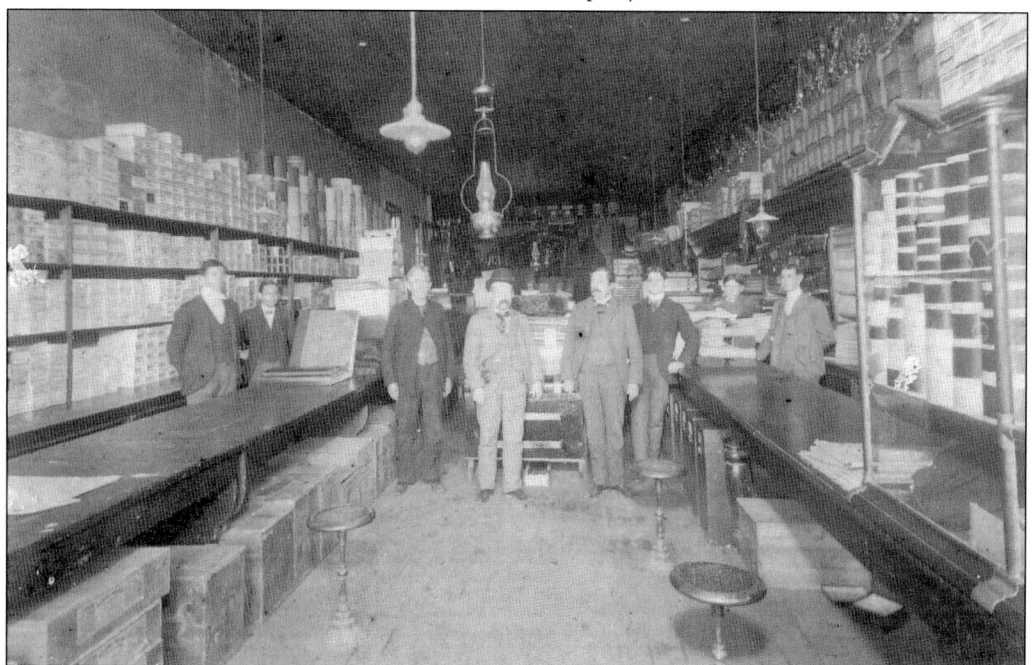

Boxes line the shelves and floor in this early-1900s store. Note the three hanging light fixtures near the front; they appear to be oil lamps.

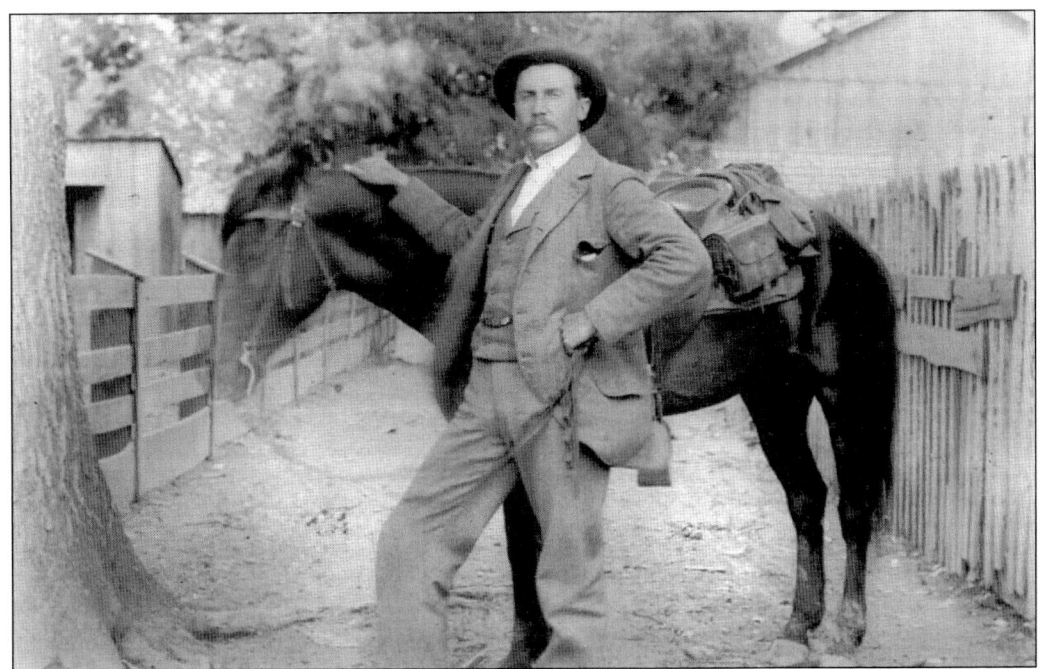

Dr. J. O. Rush poses with his horse in 1885. As the railroad doctor, he owned a home and ran an office close to the tracks. The doctor's farming estate, which he called Rushmore, was located roughly two miles east of Forrest City. His medical practice continued to flourish, and in 1906–1907, he built his 7,000-square-foot office and house just a few hundred feet from the tracks. Dr. Rush continued to make house calls, riding his horse or using his buggy, and often traveling into the country via handcar on the rails. The doctor is considered one of the town's founding fathers and its prime historian.

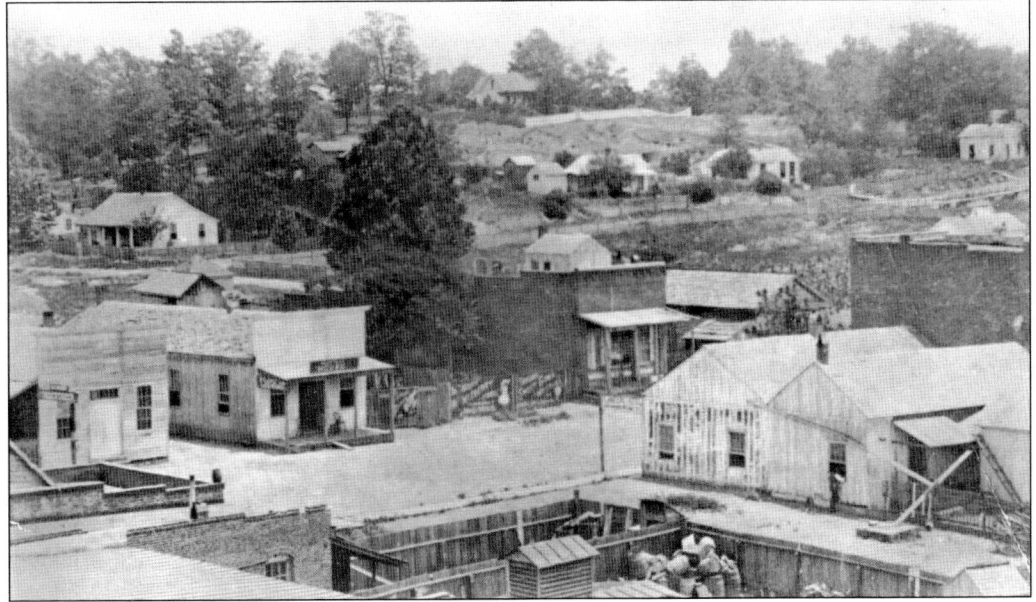

This view of North Izard Street south of the railroad was taken in 1886 and is part of the Bogart Collection. The buildings appear to be under construction.

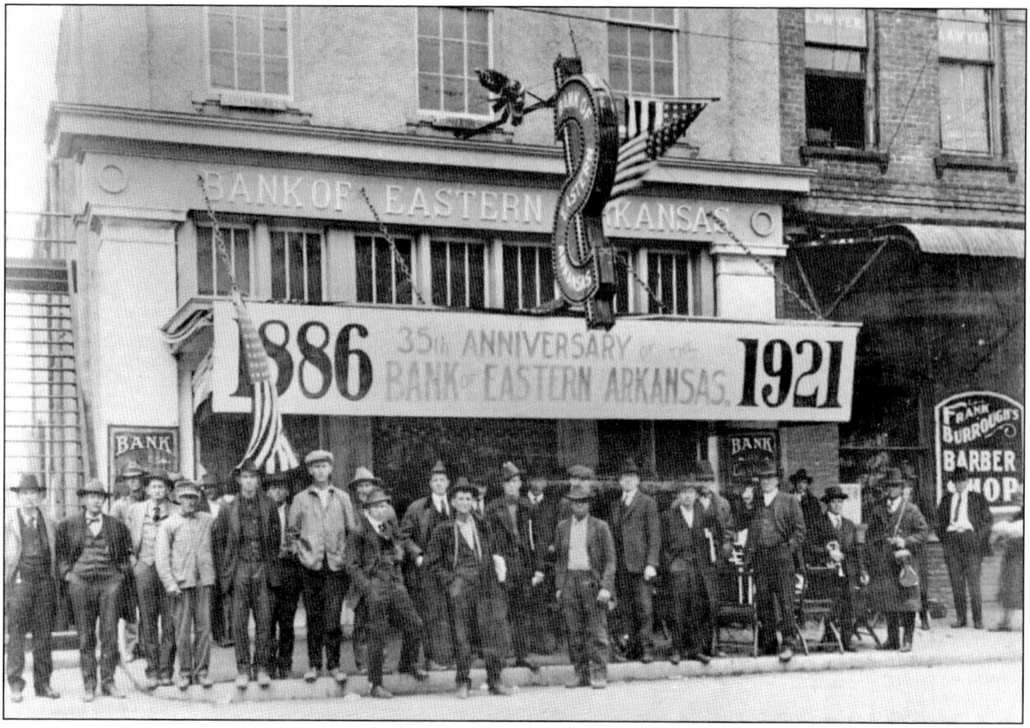

The First National Bank of Eastern Arkansas is one of the grand establishments of the modern era. Founded in 1886 as the only bank between Helena, Arkansas, and Poplar Bluff, Missouri, it provided a place for settlers to protect their savings, which had previously been hidden away. When the Depression hit, this bank was one of only a handful that remained solvent. First National is shown here in 1921, when it was celebrating its 35th anniversary.

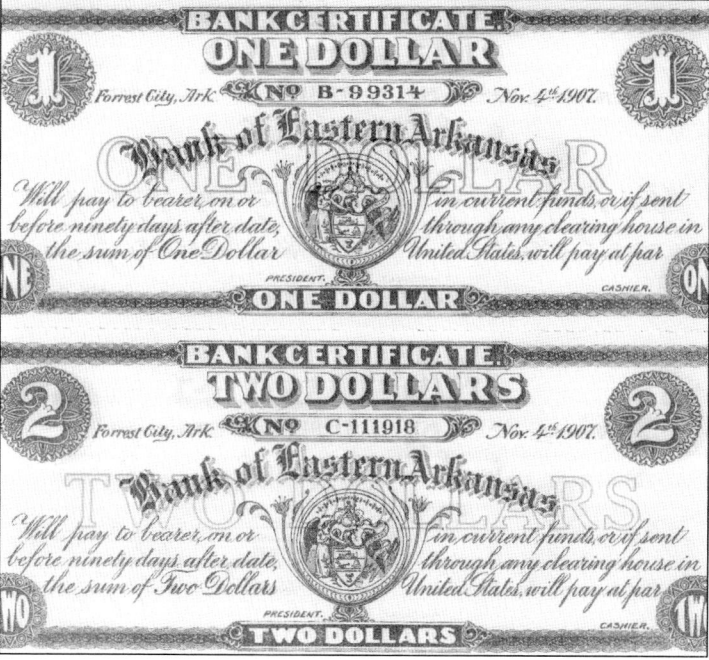

Another centerpiece of the St. Francis County Museum is the collection of Forrest City money. This is real currency, some of which has not circulated. During the Depression, William Campbell reportedly displayed a large box of money so that when frenzied customers came in he could reassure them that of course their bank would not run out. He was able to convince them. This was a true feat at a time when most farmers and businessmen still worked out of shoeboxes and Mason jars.

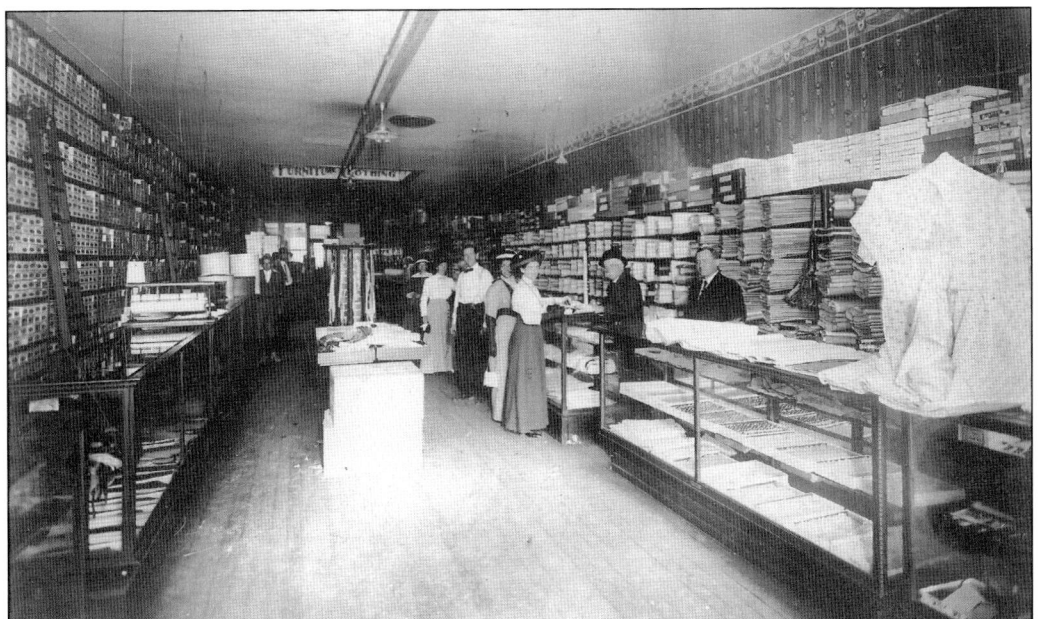

The St. Francis County Museum has several photographs labeled with the name M. C. Hambleton. The period dress leads one to suspect this photograph was taken during the last years of the 19th century. A larger number of women are shopping in this image compared to the others, and it appears that fabrics and women's wares are for sale in this department. M. C. Hambleton's later became the Fussell-Graham-Alderson Company.

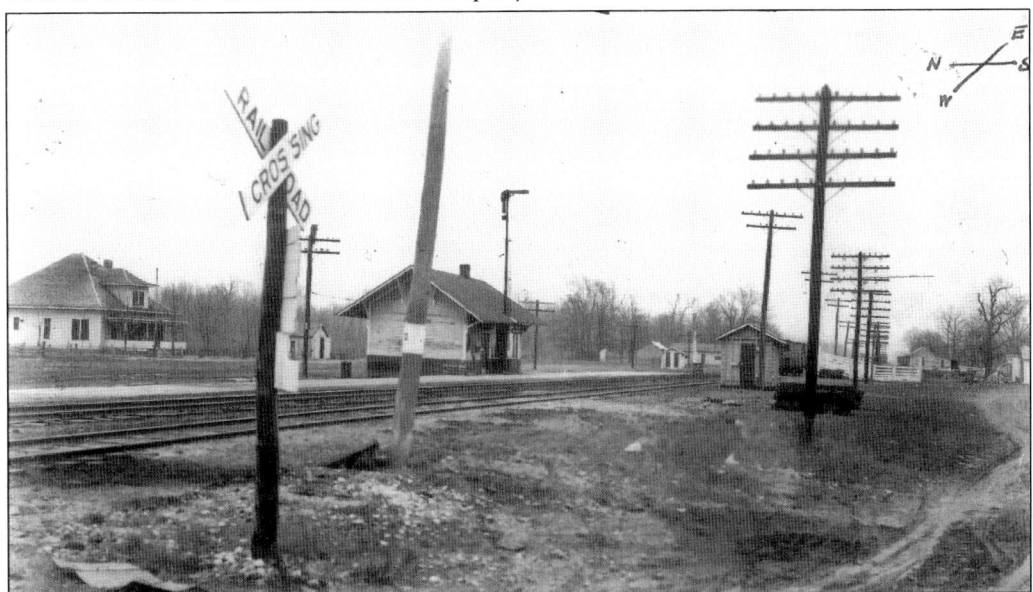

Goodwin is a small town on the west side of the county, located between Wheatley and Palestine. Still standing, one residence is known as the Dusek House (far left) because of its original owners. It represents the flourishing railroad days. Since the waning of the railroad, however, Goodwin has lost much of its population. This farming community is quietly waiting for its revival. The new tourism industry of "edutainment" offers a glimmer of hope because many tourists are beginning to come to the area for wildlife sightings, hunting, and farm and Delta tours.

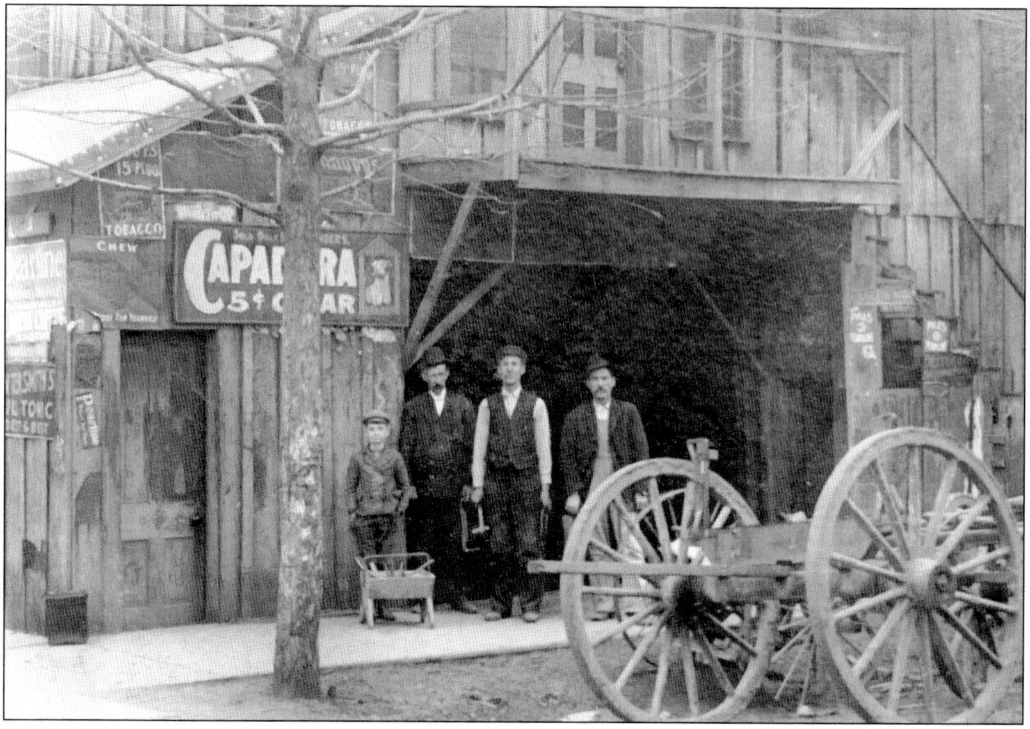

According to family lore, this young man (far left) was Vance Stancel's great-grandfather. The blacksmith shop was a necessity in frontier life, and this shop was located in the heart of the city.

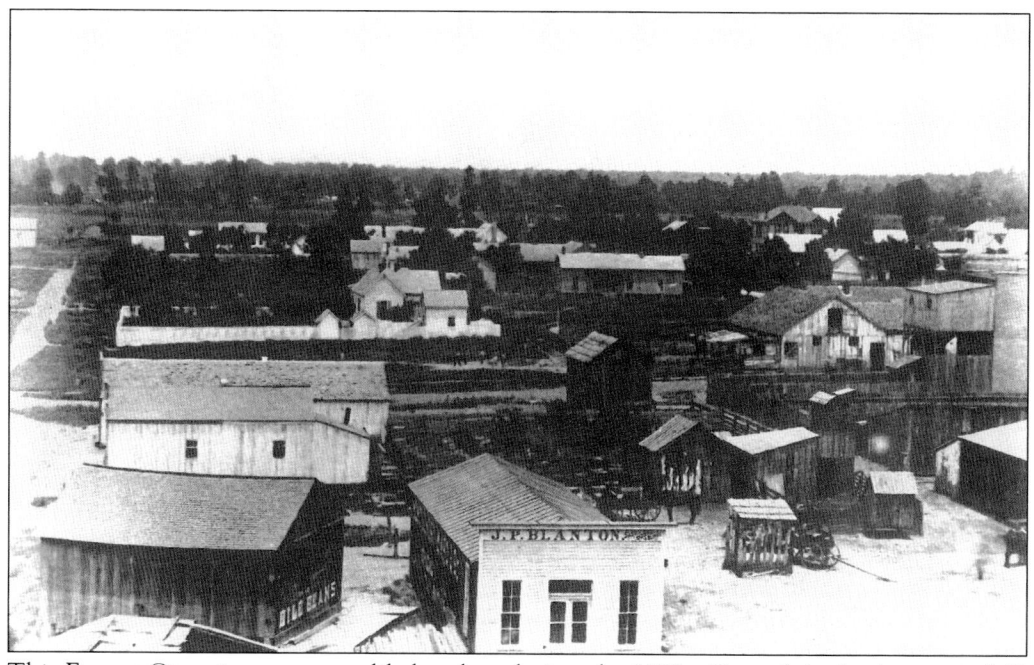

This Forrest City view was most likely taken during the 1870s. One of the businesses is J. P. Blanton's (bottom center). The growing residential district appears in the background.

Two
SETTLEMENT AND CIVILIZATION

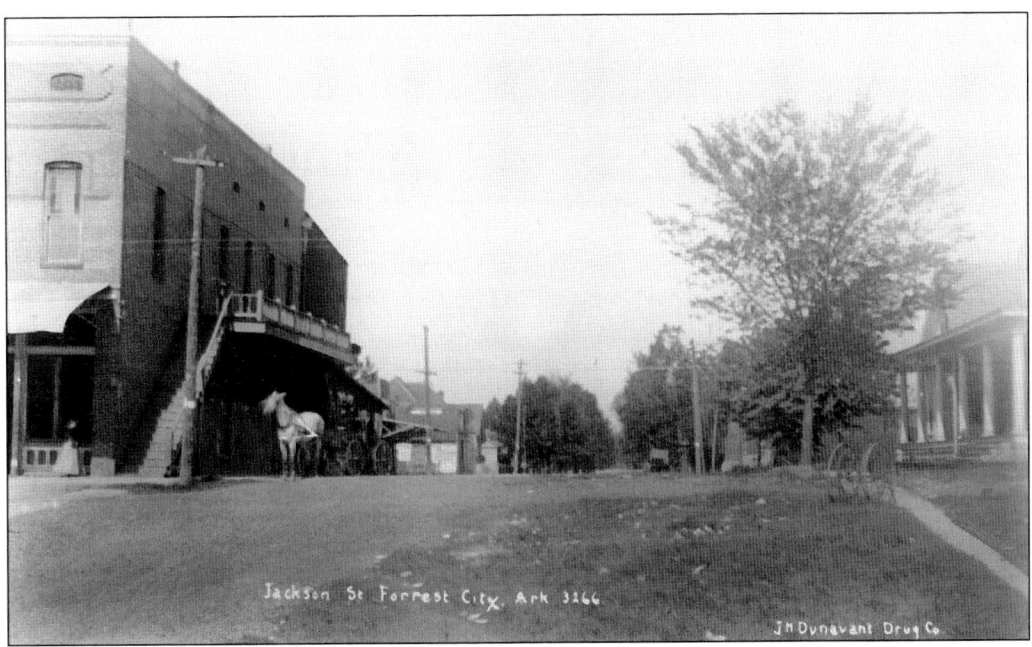

This photograph was taken after 1906, as evidenced by the completed Rush-Gates House to the right. The doctor's home stood on the corner of Front and Izard Streets, immediately across from the courthouse on one side and the opera house on the other. The home still includes its original hitching block, which assisted ladies in stepping down from buggies. At one time, every residence was required have one. The horse at left patiently waits for his master to return from shopping or visiting the doctor.

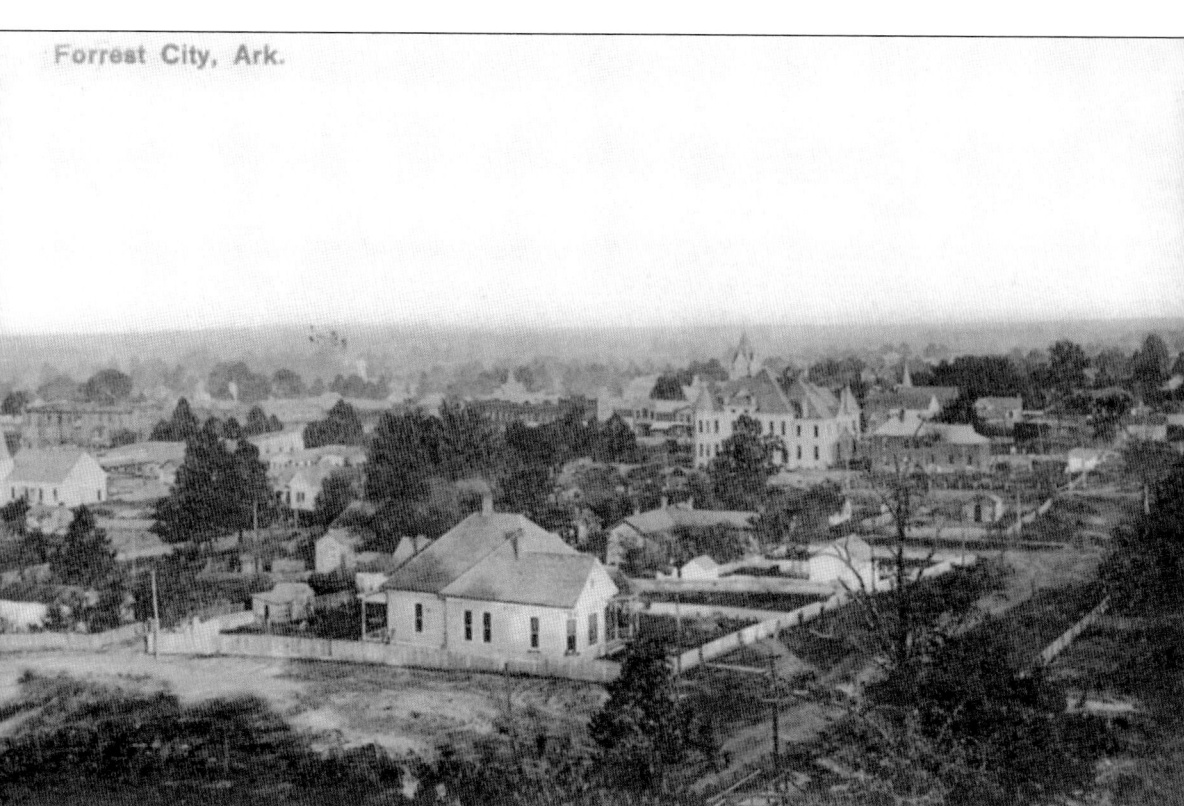

This wonderful view looks north from Judge Norton's house in the courthouse area. It appeared in the 1905 *Forrest City Times* art souvenir book.

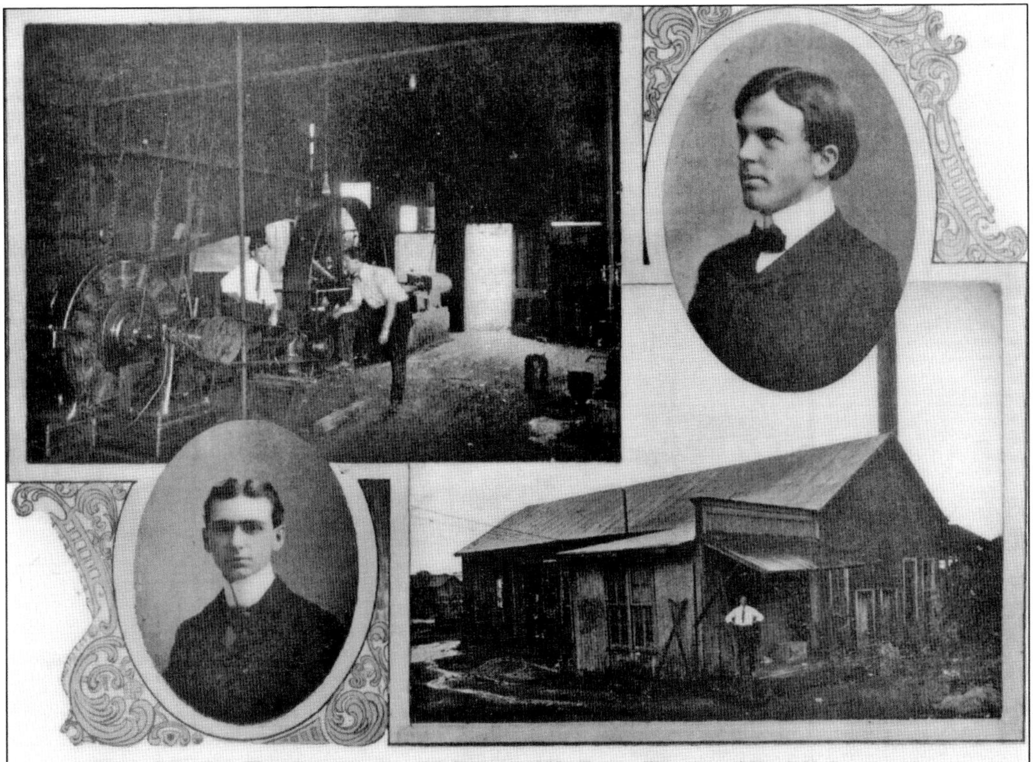

Plant of the City Electric Company—with Portraits of Mr. Eugene Williams and Mr. J. M. Covey, owners.

The Rush-Gates House was the first in Forrest City to be built specifically for electricity. The lights were turned on in the morning, and when the plant manager went home at 6:00 p.m., the electricity went with him. The plant was run by Eugene Williams (left) and J. M. Covey. Constructed in 1906–1907, the J. O. Rush home still bears some of its original light fixtures.

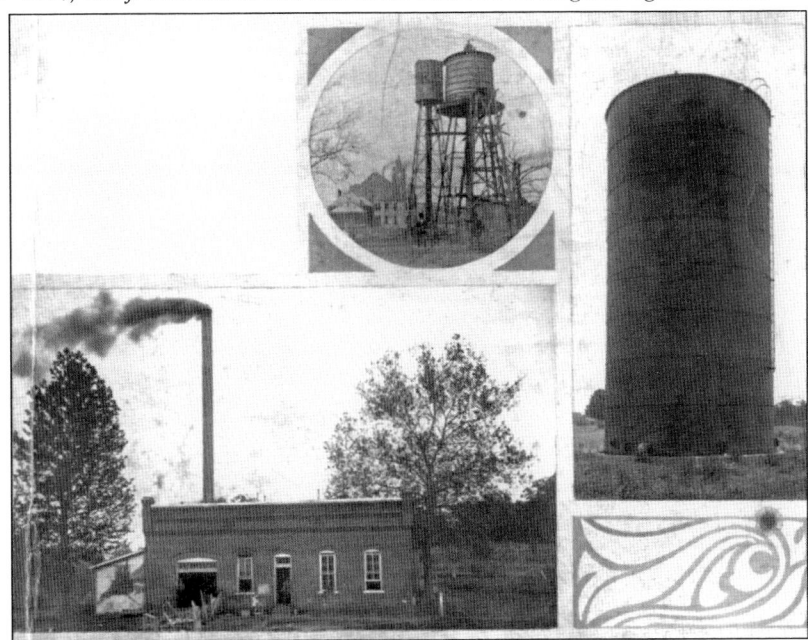

This water plant provided water for the burgeoning town. The tower in the image (at right, center) is also visible in the view of Dr. Rush standing by his tent office (see page 83). The standpipe was located on Crowley's Ridge, a quarter-mile east of town. The two other photographs show the new waterworks in 1905.

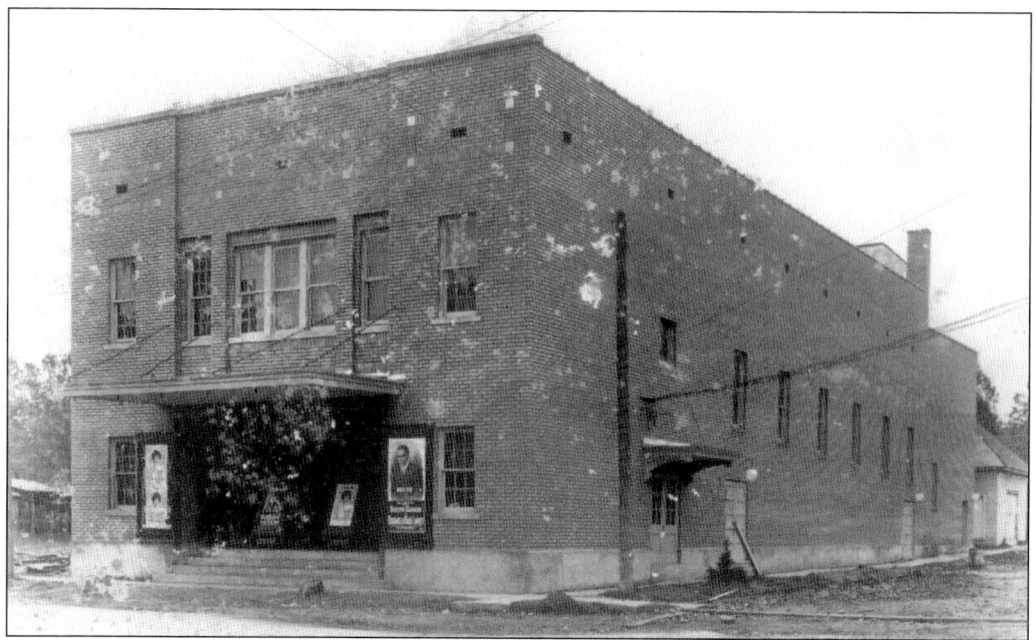

The Imperial, pictured about 1930, was among a handful of theaters in Forrest City. Today the Vaccaro family continues the entertainment tradition with the Broadway Twin Cinema. In a small, rural town, a theater is an important place. At one time, "Peacock the Mover," John C. Peacock, worked as the Imperial projectionist. Peacock also rescued Dr. Julius Bogart's roll-top desk from being scrapped. He took it to Jerald Burns, who restored the historically valuable desk piece by piece. Peacock the Mover was featured in the 1954 green book entitled the *History of St. Francis County, Arkansas*.

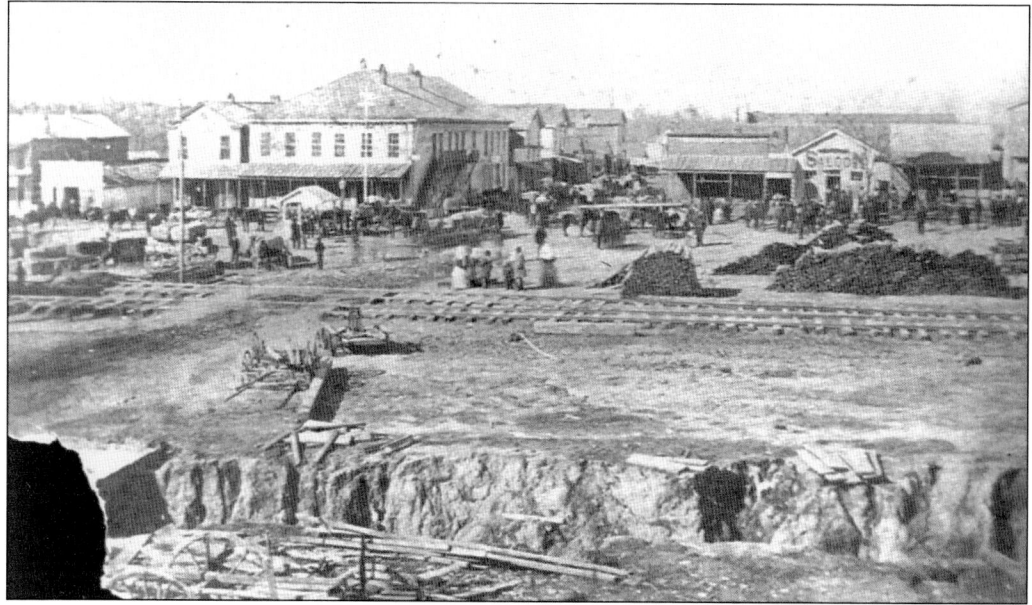

Historian Margy Cannon graciously donated this photograph, displaying one of the earliest known street scenes in the county. The railroad tracks have been laid, and much construction is going on around them.

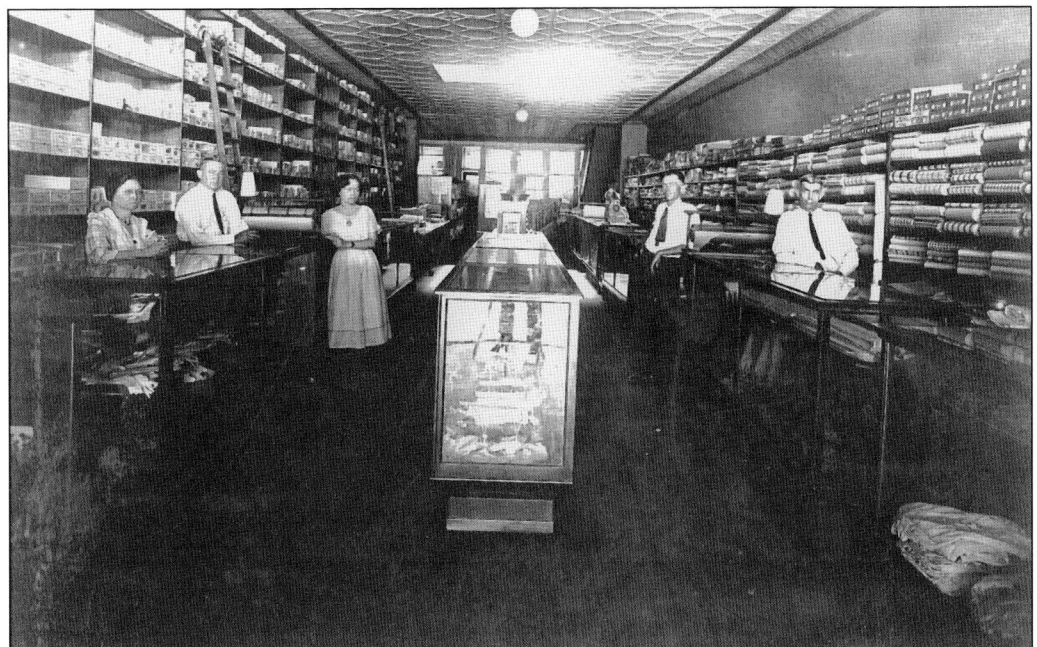

This photograph may depict the same store as in the previous M. C. Hambleton image, but the clothing reveals that it was taken approximately 30 years later. Pictured from left to right are ? Hunt, M. C. Hambleton, Alberta Ovenly, unidentified, and a Mr. Stubbs.

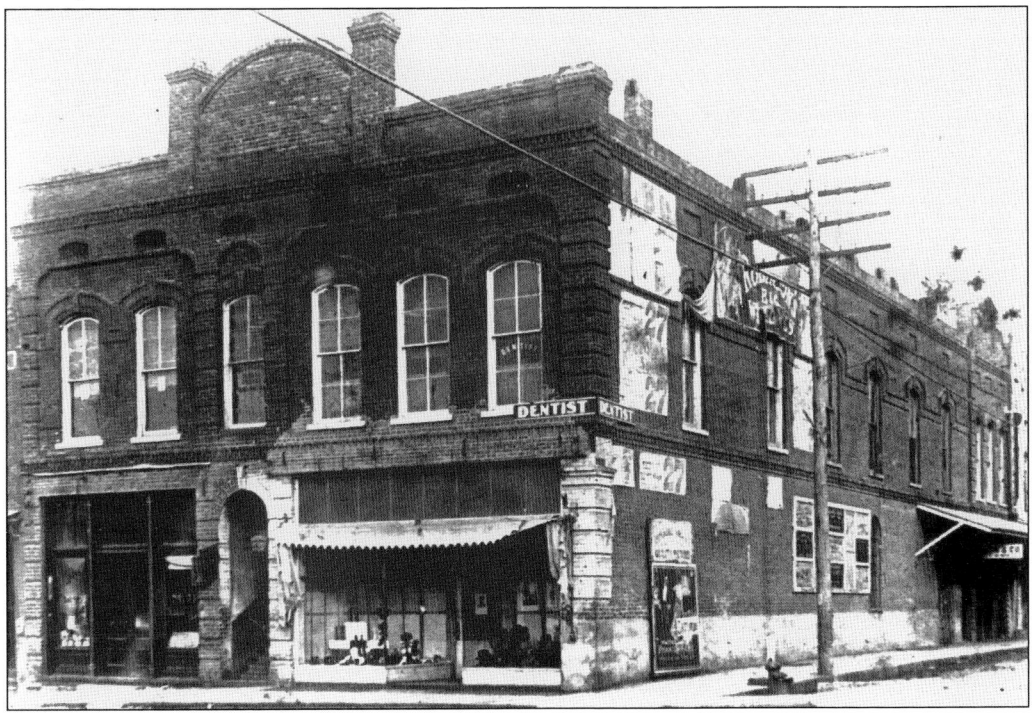

As shown on the sign, this downtown Forrest City storefront was occupied by a dentistry practice. Locals believe it was that of Dr. John Burke. This building is also visible in the Front Street image on page 31.

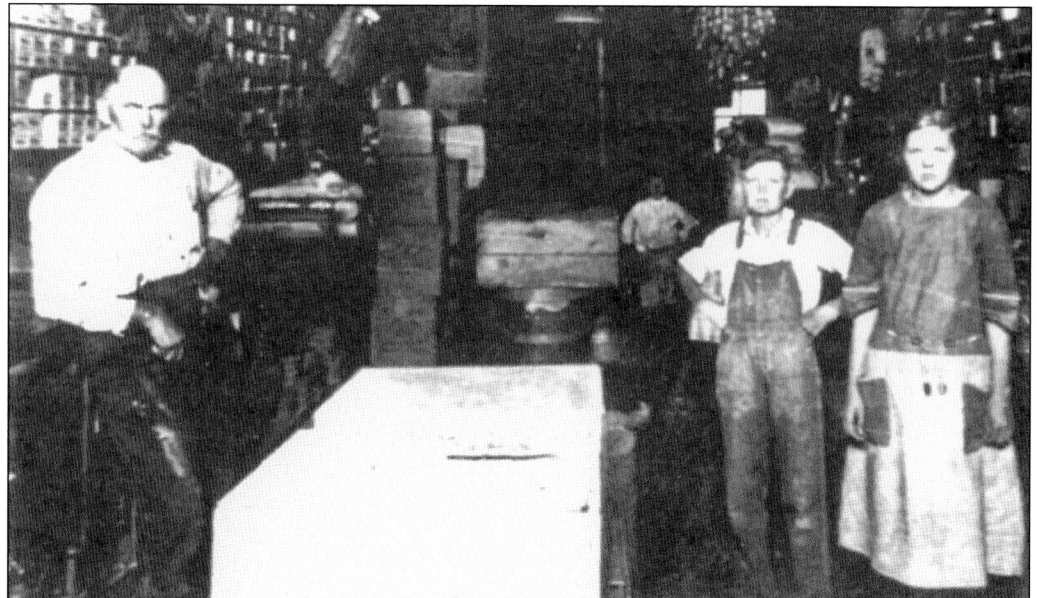

One of the first settlers in Palestine, D. K. Burns owned a general store on Main Street. He is pictured here with his three children—(from left to right) Donald King, Abe, and Marie. The store flourished until a fire occurred on Main Street; afterward, the Burns family decided to focus on the cotton gin and the rice crop.

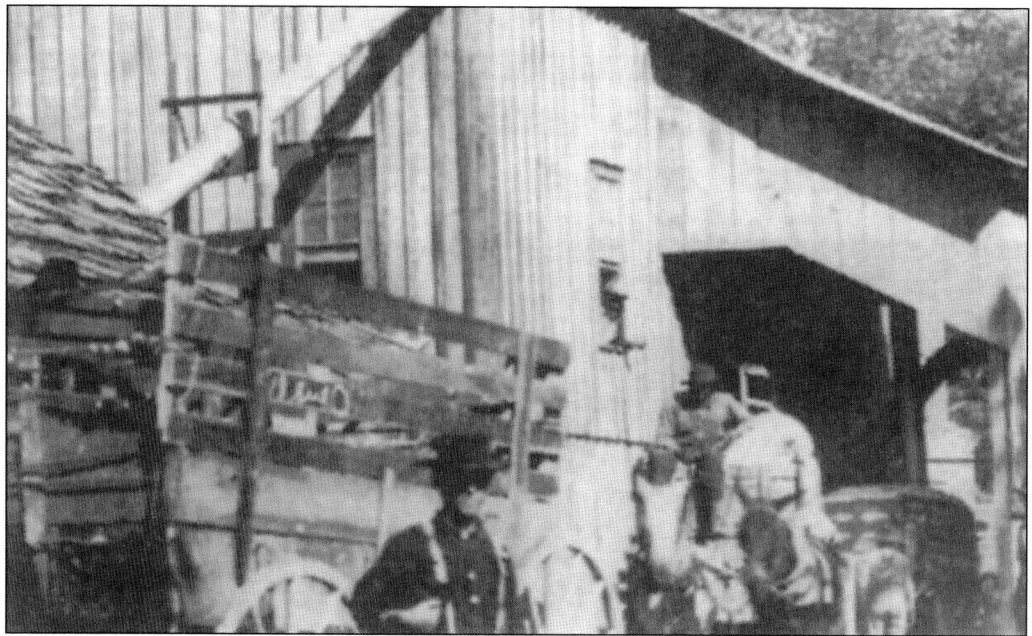

D. K. Burns bought a half-interest in the cotton gin from Sam Sulcer in 1896 and then bought the remaining part 10 years later. Located in the heart of Palestine, the gin remained a local landmark through the 1960s. Highway 70, the Broadway of America, originally ran through town on what is now Wood Street, and Burns Street was one road over. Children from the 1950s recall cotton trailers lining the streets to enter the gin. Though still owned by the family, the Burns Gin is no longer in operation. Donny and Pam Burns continue to farm the land.

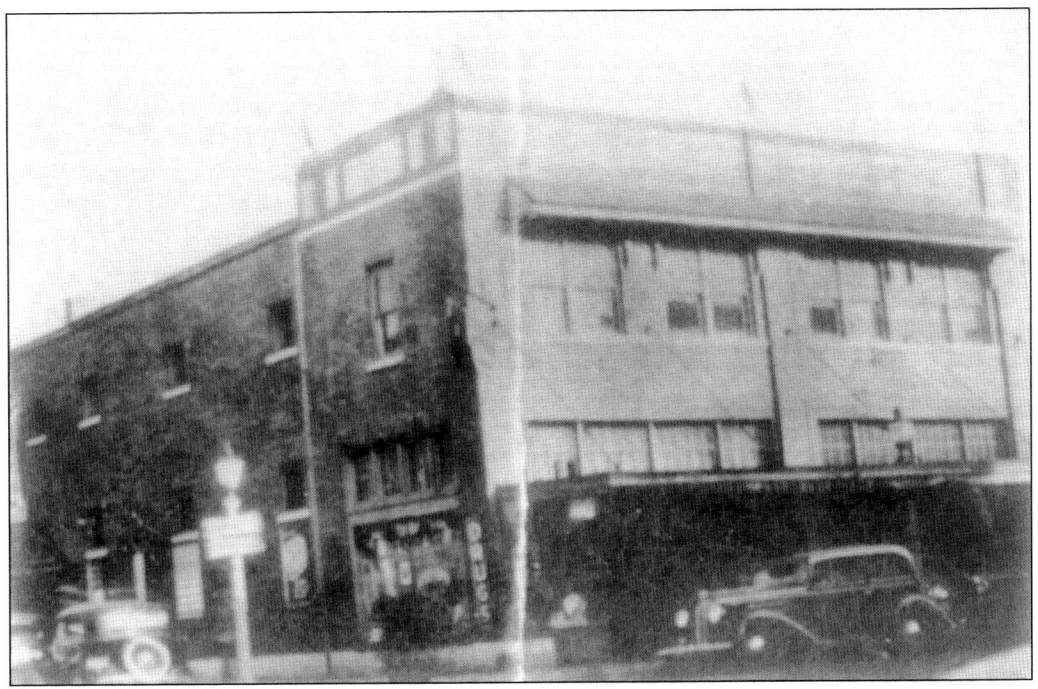

A quaint streetlight stands guard at the corner of Broadway and Washington Street in this photograph.

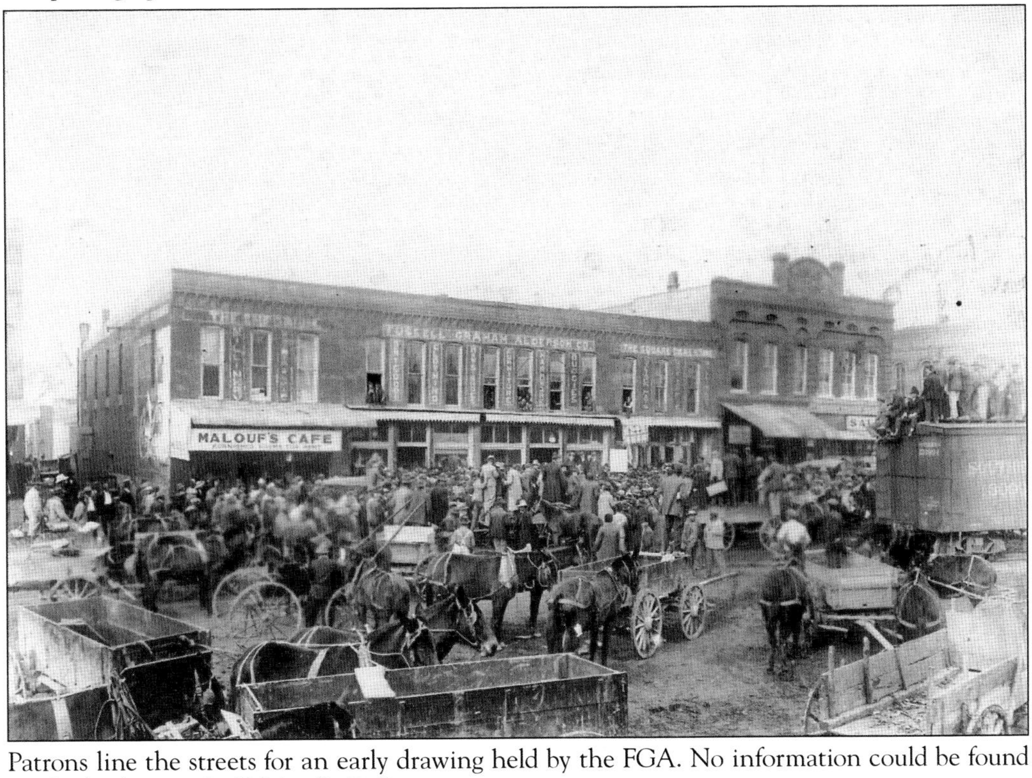

Patrons line the streets for an early drawing held by the FGA. No information could be found on the background of Malouf's Café.

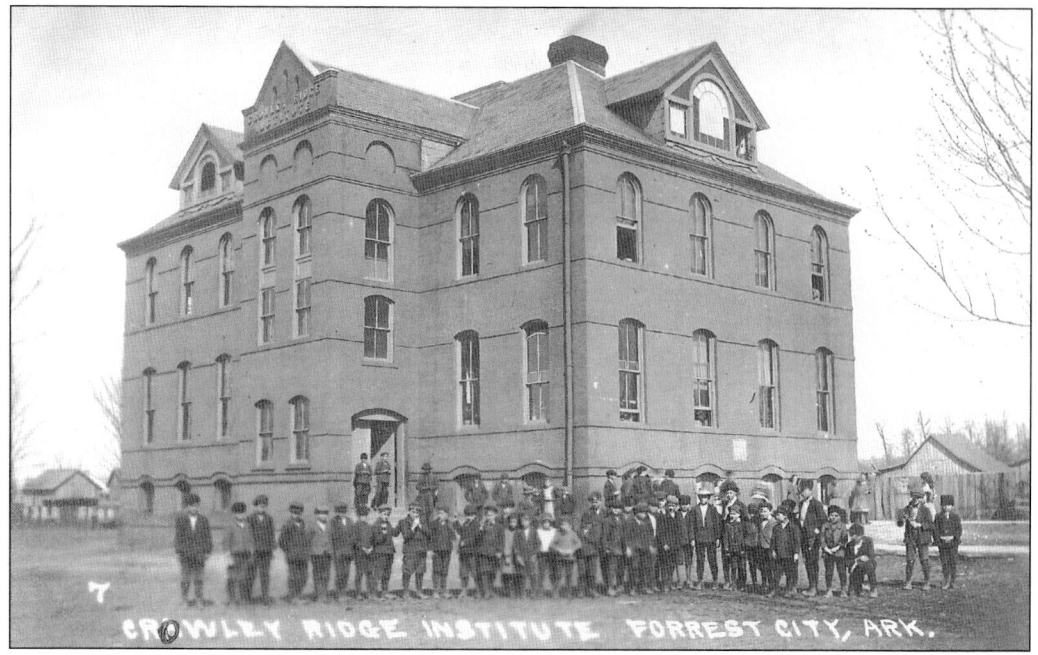

One of the most well-known schools of its time was the Crowley's Ridge Institute. Amazingly, during the summer of 2007 as the roof of the St. Francis County Museum was being replaced, Lance Cooper discovered a set of blueprints belonging to the institute. While Cooper was replacing part of the eave that had never been restored, he noticed a rolled-up paper peeking out. Museum workers compared the prints to photographs of the institute and conferred with local architect Bob Beavers, who believes that they belong to the school's addition, which was constructed almost 100 years ago. Cooper Roofing also discovered a 1912 lithograph at the museum in much the same way. These artifacts have been added to visitor displays while awaiting preservation.

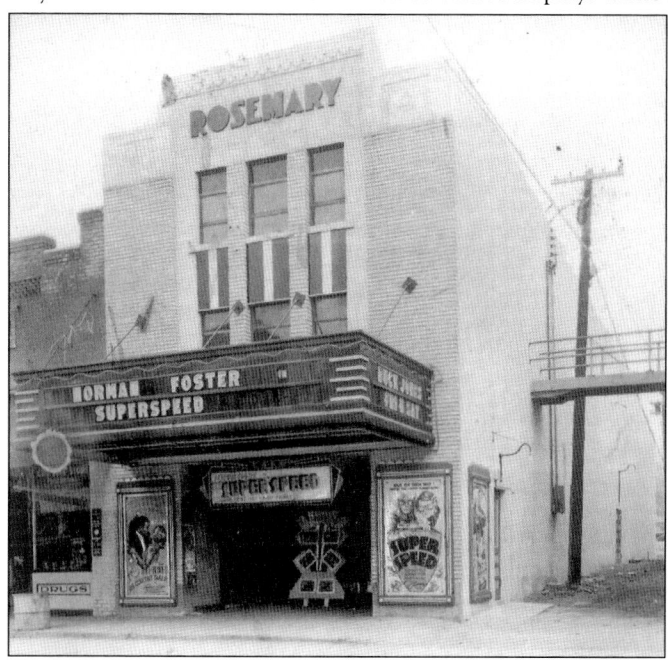

The Rosemary Theater, located on Front Street west of Cotten Alley and east of Washington Street, was named for Rosemary Haven Kirkpatrick. In this c. 1930 image, the theater is advertising *Superspeed*.

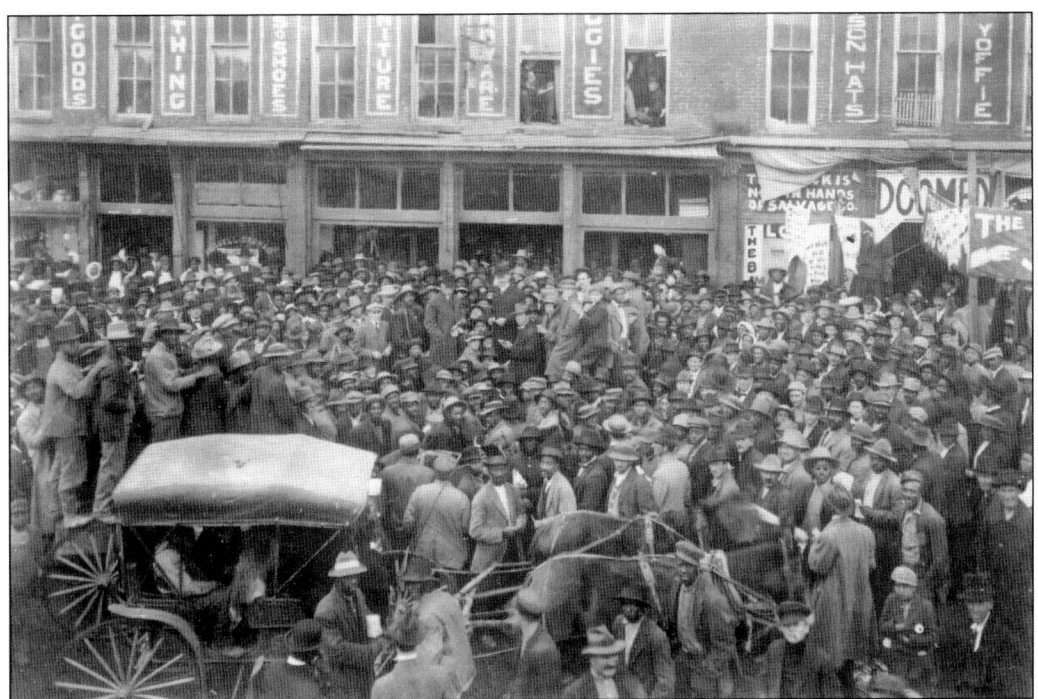

On Christmas Eve 1915, the Fussell-Graham-Alderson Company held a drawing for $500 worth of gold. It appears that most of the county came to the event, as shown in this photograph, with people lining the streets, perching atop wagons, and hanging from windows.

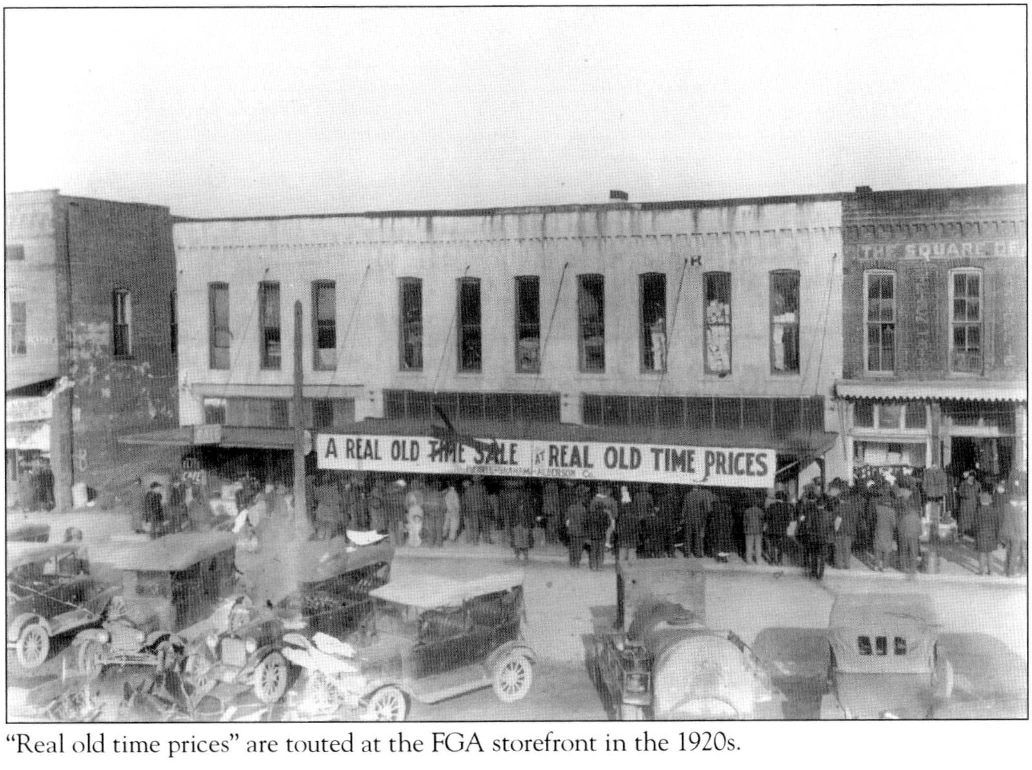

"Real old time prices" are touted at the FGA storefront in the 1920s.

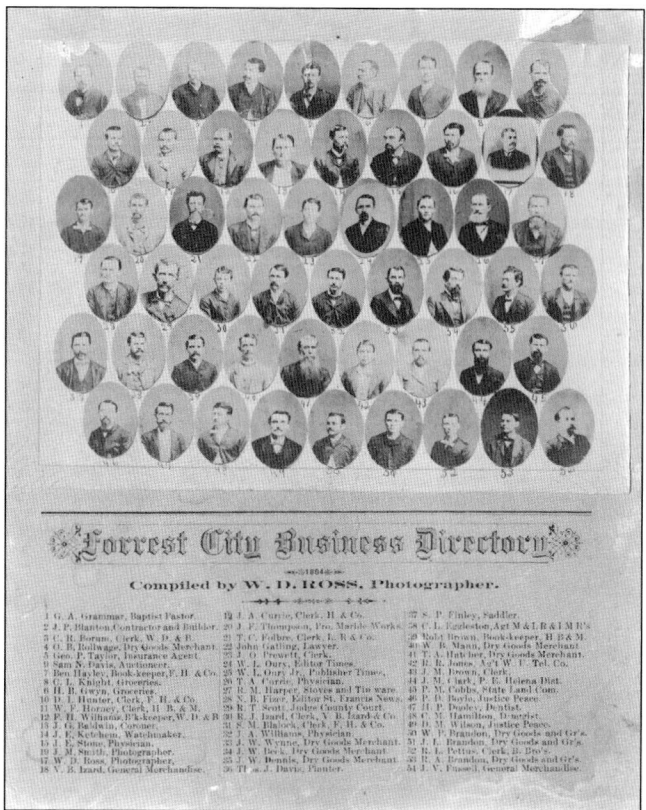

The city was still in its infancy in 1884 when this business directory was compiled. T. C. Folbre, No. 21, would later become a politician. N. B. Fizer, No. 28, edited the *St. Francis News.* J. W. Beck was the namesake of Beck's Spur, located between Palestine and Forrest City. The men here represented doctors, lawyers, photographers, store owners, clerks, politicians, and bookkeepers. These family names are still highly respected in the town.

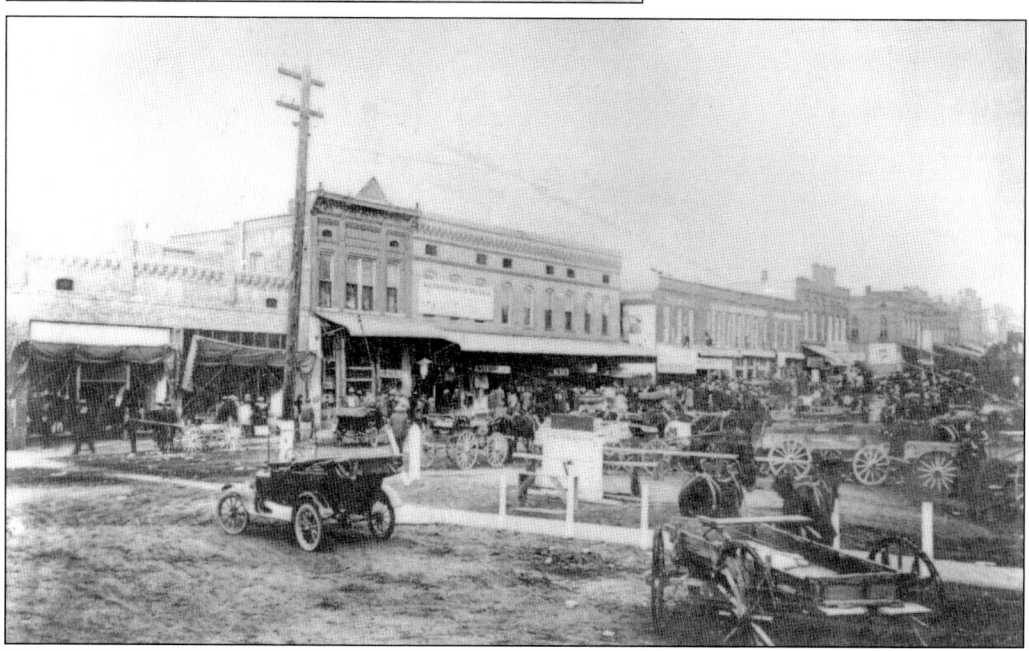

For more than a century, Front Street served as the heart of Forrest City. It is presently in need of some loving restoration, but the strong bones are still there. Any store one desired could be found on Front. Here wagons and a few horseless carriages line the streets.

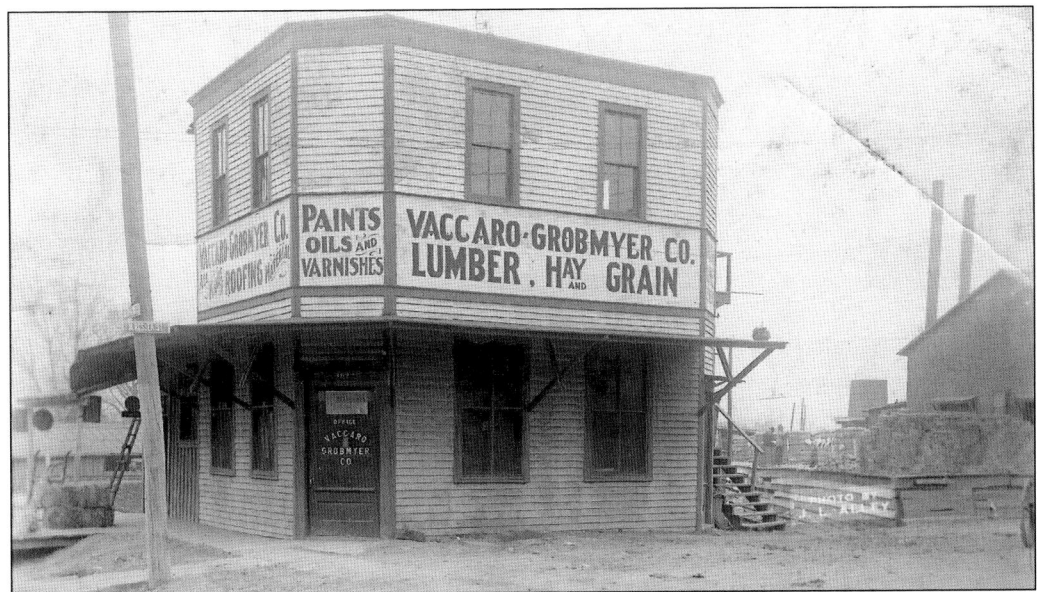

The Vaccaro family has a distinguished history in Forrest City. Since the town's incorporation, the Vaccaros have owned a saloon, a store, a lumber company, and a movie theater, among other businesses. The Vaccaro Lumber Company, seen here in 1910, marked its 100th anniversary in 2007. The original building rested on the corner of Front and Rosser Streets. Today the Vaccaro building sports a spectacular mural of Forrest City by Kathi Martin commemorating the company's centennial.

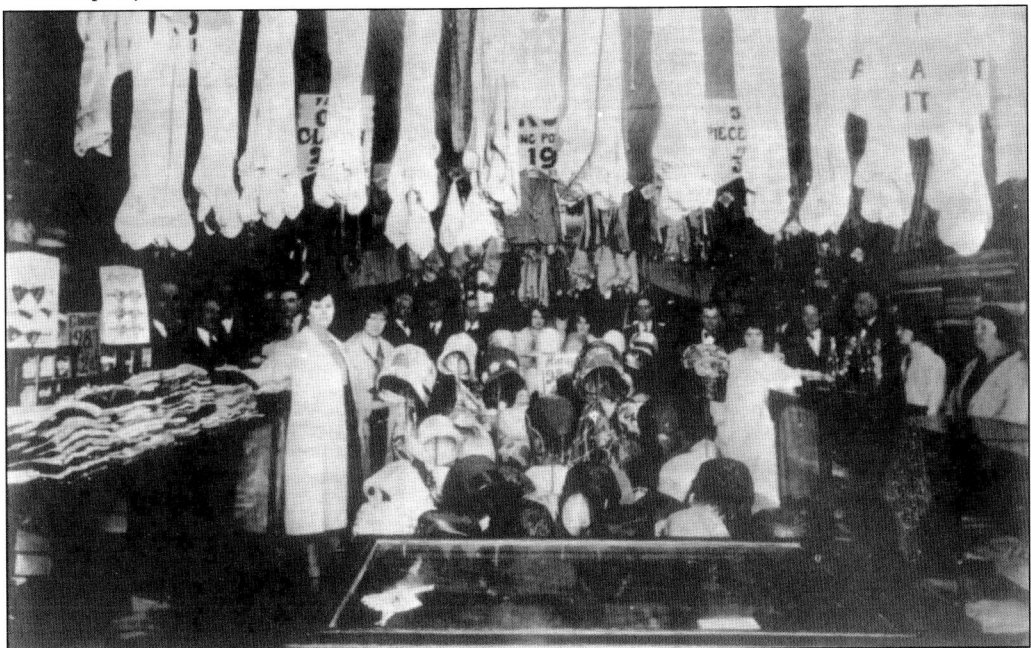

This image was featured in a book titled *Forrest City Centennial* from the 1970s. The fashions are different from those in the other images that have survived, and a wonderful assortment of hats appears in the foreground. The store, called Leavitt's, opened on Front Street on January 22, 1927.

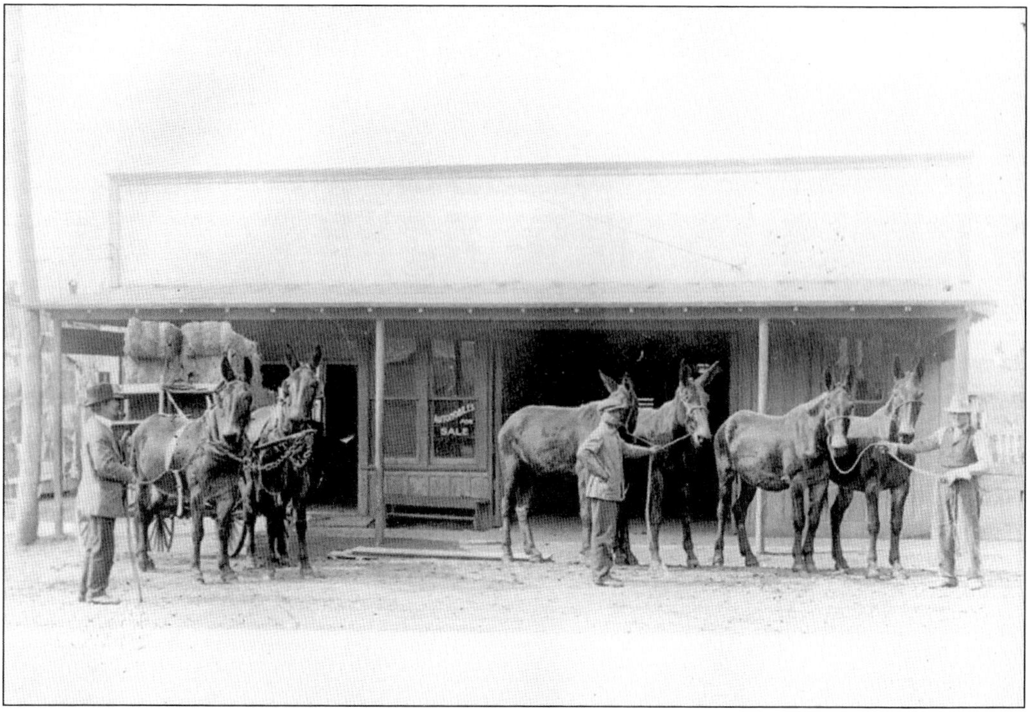

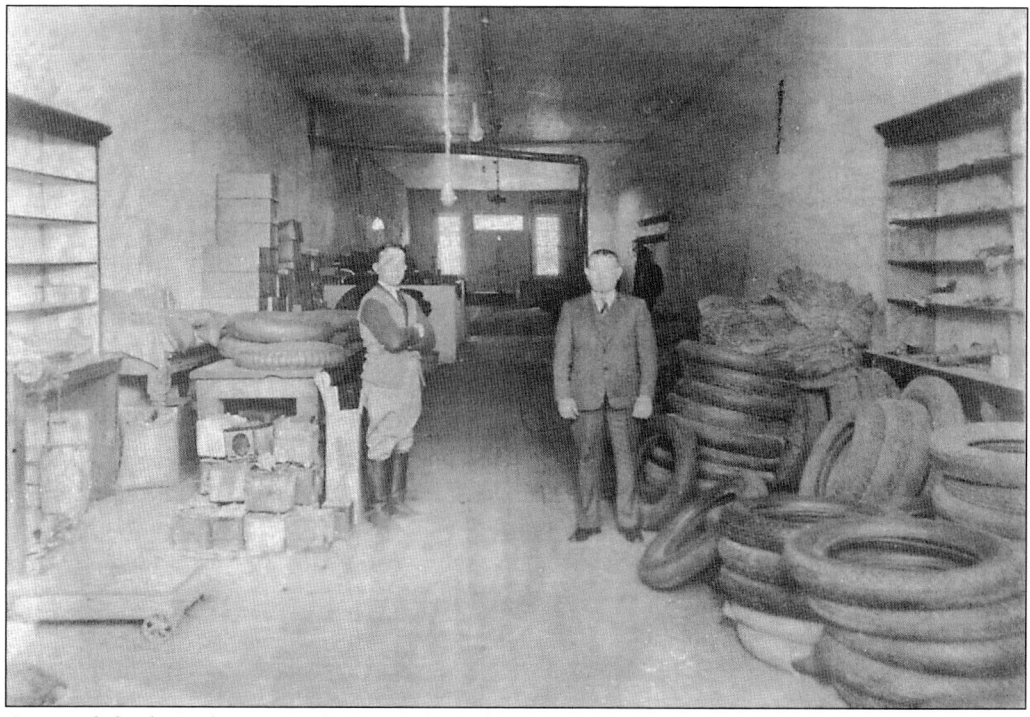

Stables recognized the need to change with the times, though automobiles were still not consistently dependable.

Automobiles brought new industry such as this business, which apparently specialized in tires for the newfangled contraptions.

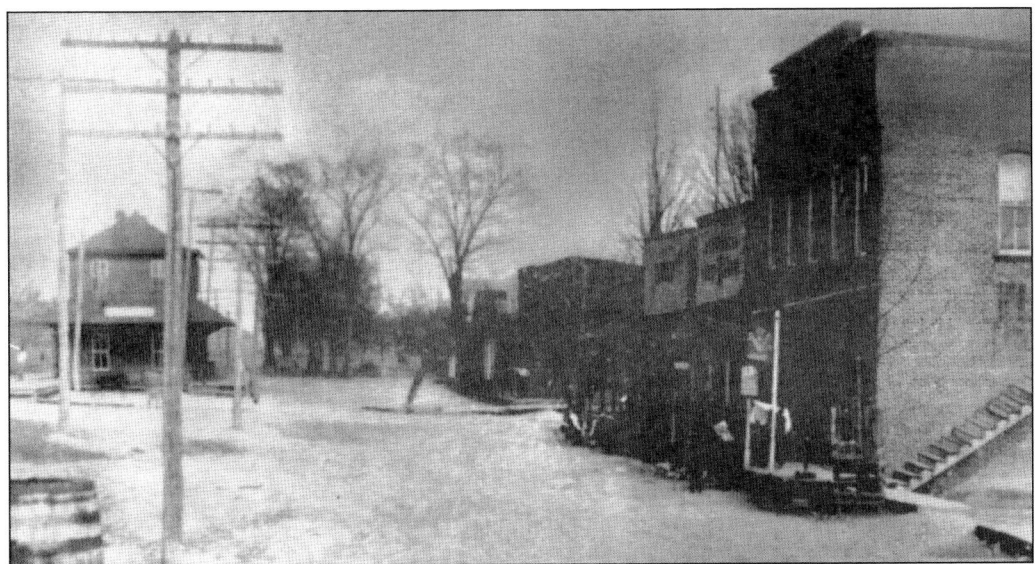

Palestine was a bustling town that grew with the railroad. At one time, a row of stores lined Main Street facing the tracks. These stores included D. K. Burns's, Sulcer's, J. H. Halbert's, and others. Sadly, one store caught fire, and the rest quickly went up in flames. Halbert's and Sulcer's rebuilt, and Donald Burns established a parts store; the difference was that the storefronts then faced to the side. Today Littlefield's occupies the site, and a Parts Plus store is located in the lot.

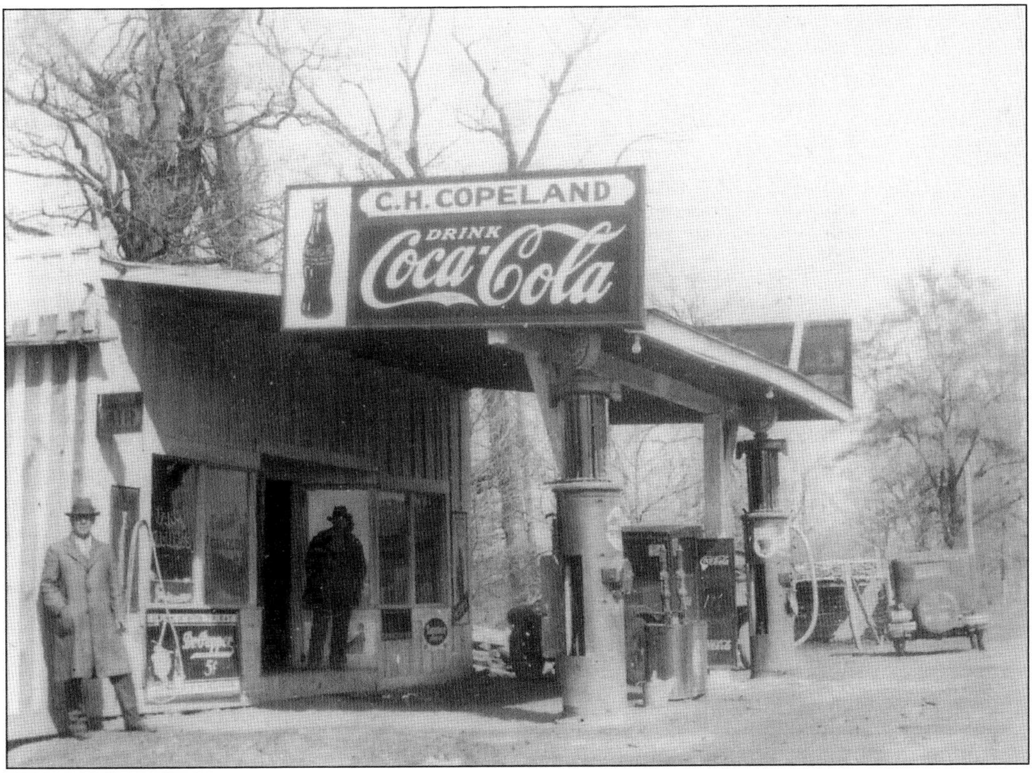

Oh, for the time when gas was under 20¢ per gallon! Look closely at the chalkboard sign, and you just might cry for the good ol' days. These gas pumps were gravity fed.

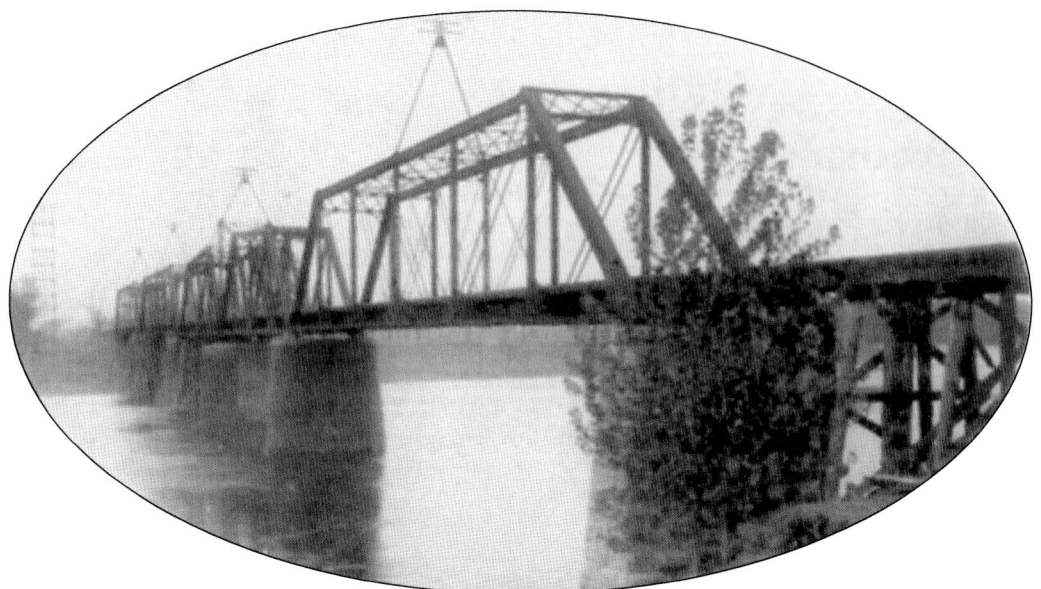

The St. Francis River flows through Madison in St. Francis County. The Choctaw Bridge, pictured in 1905, originally included five trussed spans.

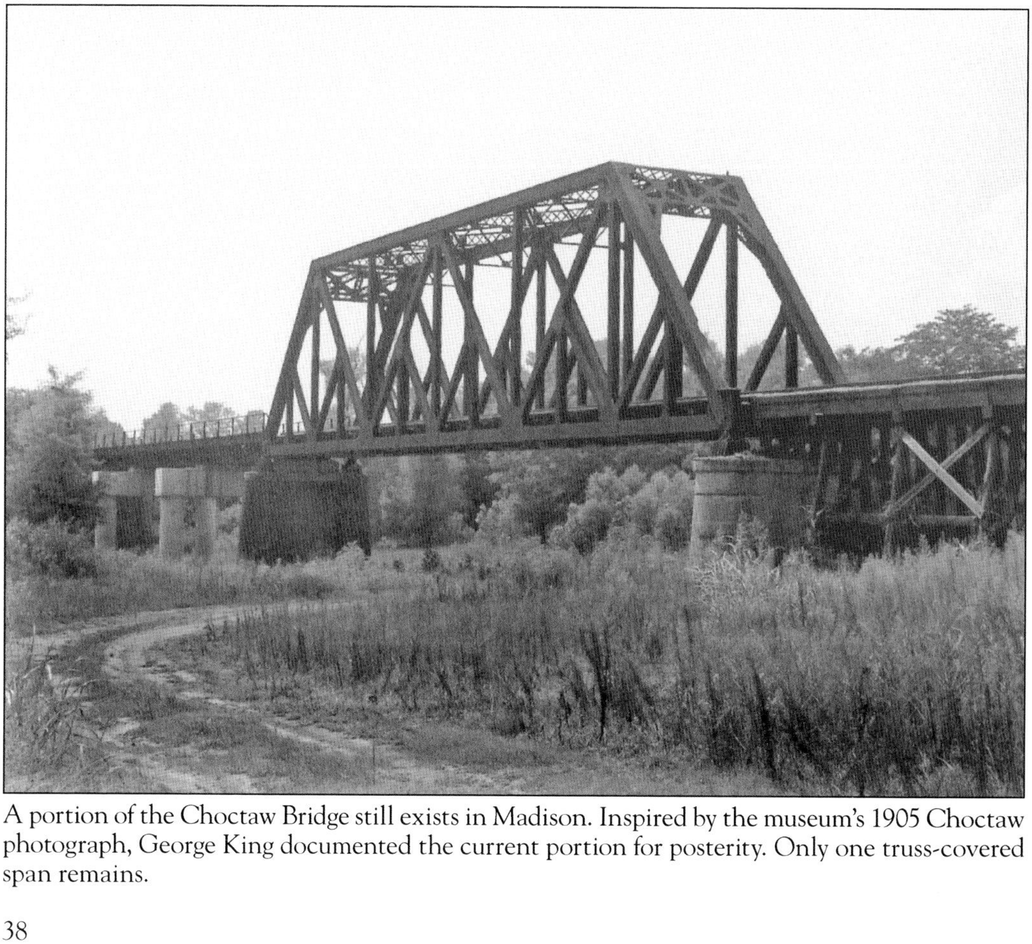

A portion of the Choctaw Bridge still exists in Madison. Inspired by the museum's 1905 Choctaw photograph, George King documented the current portion for posterity. Only one truss-covered span remains.

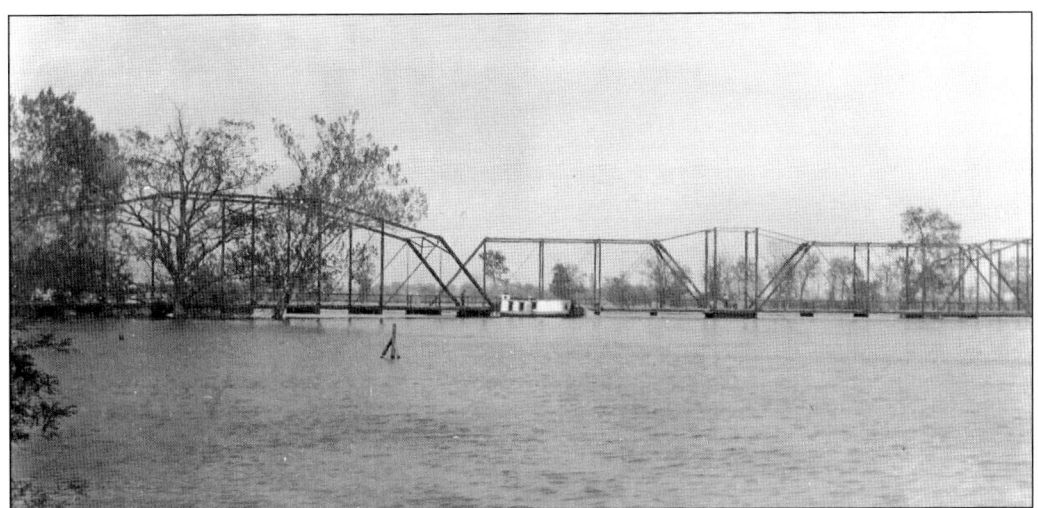

A pair of devastating floods hit St. Francis County—one in 1927 and another in 1937. It is not clear which flood is depicted in this photograph. The waters are so high they reach to the top of the railroad tracks in some places. In the distance, a portion of the Choctaw Bridge is visible.

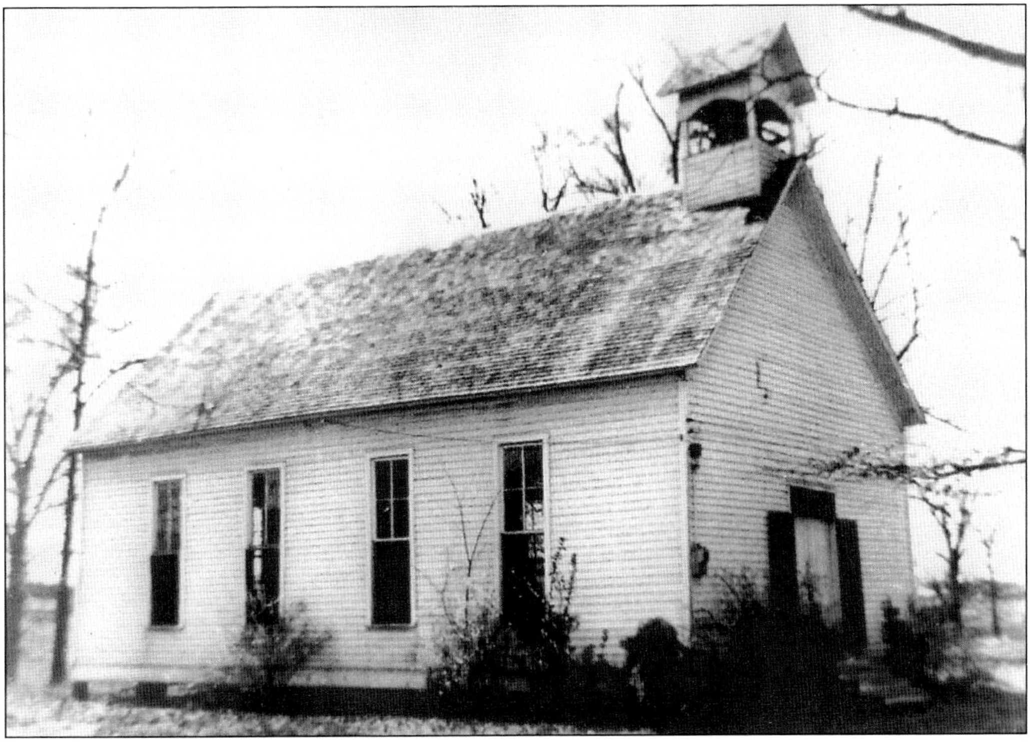

The Palestine Cumberland Church is one of county's oldest active congregations. The original building housed a union church, meaning one week was for the Methodist service and the next was for Cumberland Presbyterian. The structure was located approximately 1.5 miles south of present-day Highway 70. Later the congregation elected to construct a building across from the Burns Gin close to Wood Street. The second, wood-frame building was replaced in the 1950s by a new church with a stone facade. Its beautiful chimes have summoned citizens to worship for decades. It is one of many blessed churches in the county.

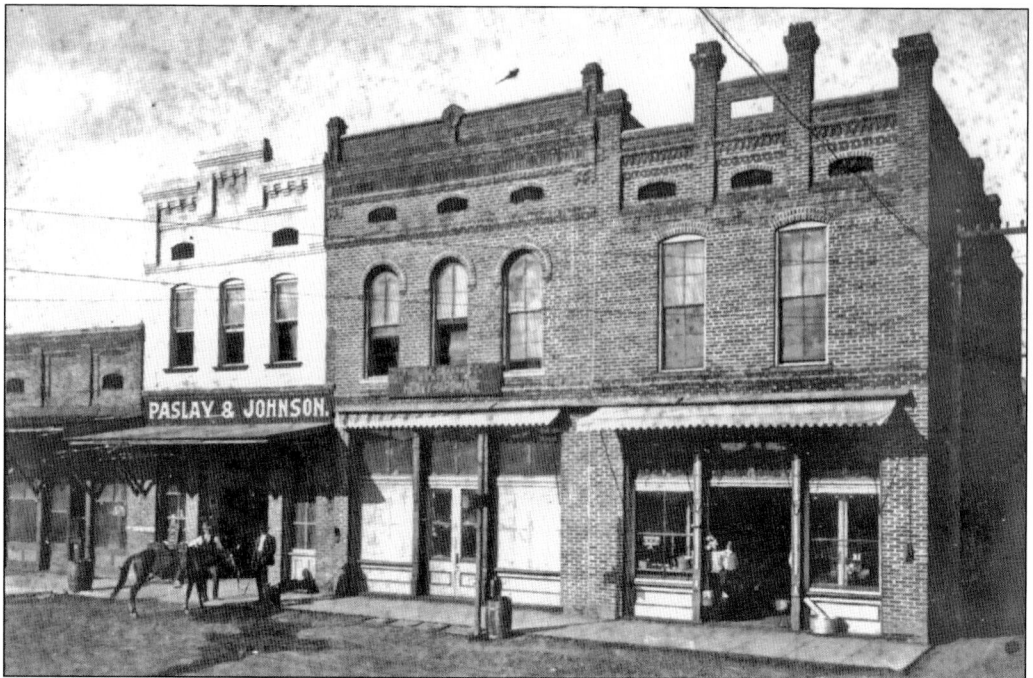

Horses are hitched up outside the Paslay and Johnson store. At the time, all businesses and residences in Forrest City were required by law to have hitching posts. The Rush-Gates House still sports its original hitching post. The authors have not been successful in officially documenting the store's location and years of operation.

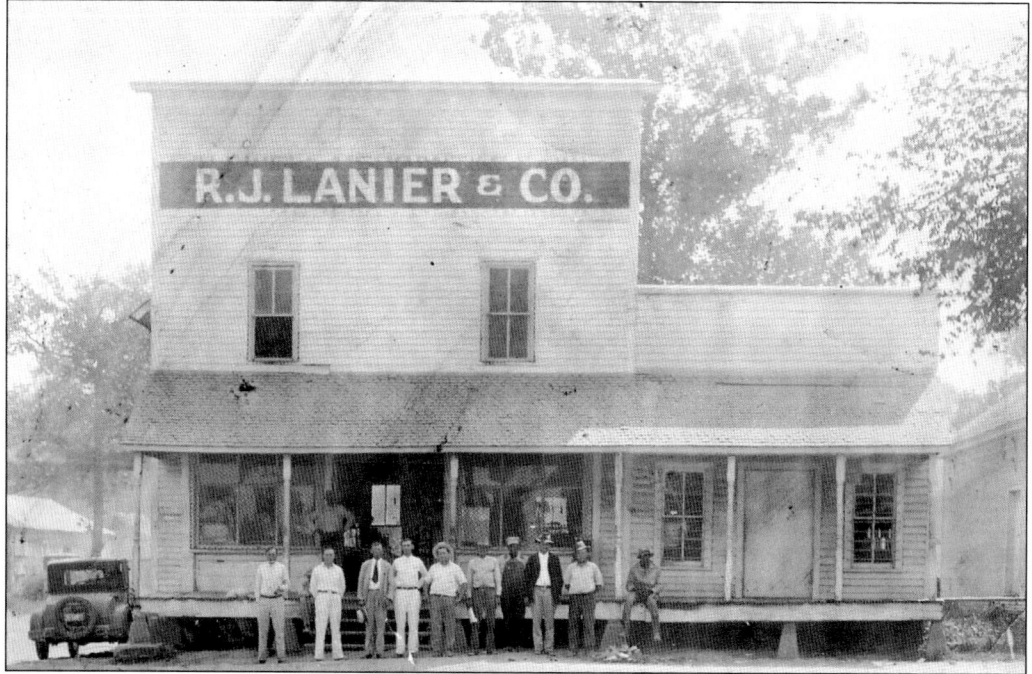

The R. J. Lanier and Company store likely operated in the eastern portion of the county. A photograph was also taken in later years, when the store appeared to be a post office.

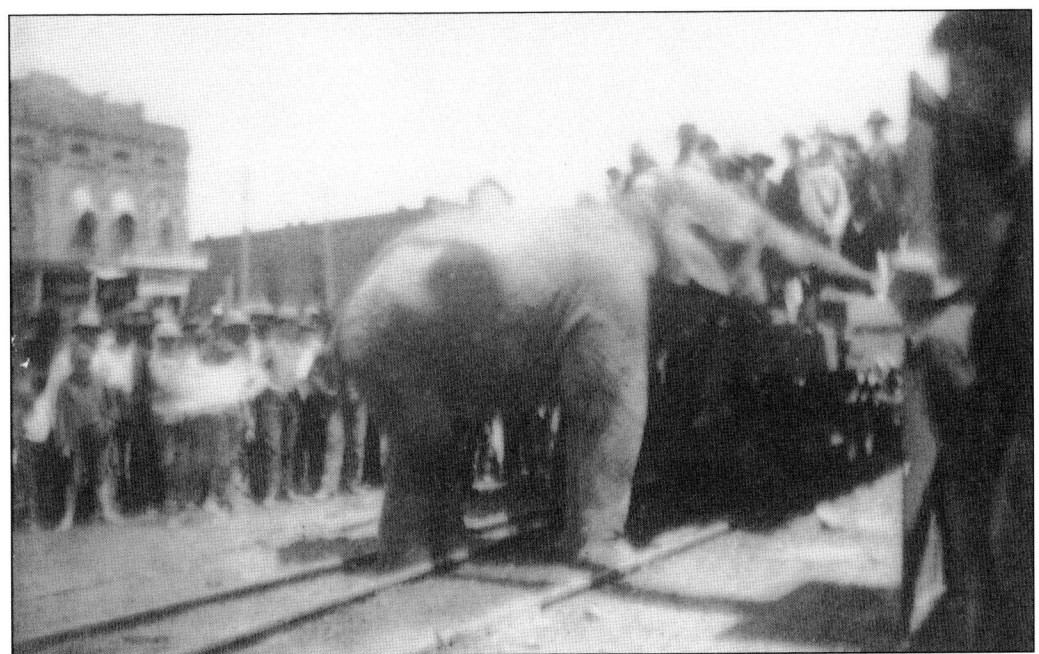

What this photograph lacks in clarity it more than makes up for in character. The authors' favorite image, this fuzzy memory recalls a time when the circus coming into town was a monumental event. The elephant appears to be walking along the tracks by Front Street, especially poignant because much of the road now lies in disrepair. The town is currently trying to secure a Main Street America grant to restore some of the grandeur that existed when this view was taken. Front Street was where everything happened; the elephant would have cruised in front of the Marion Hotel, the Rush-Gates House, and the courthouse.

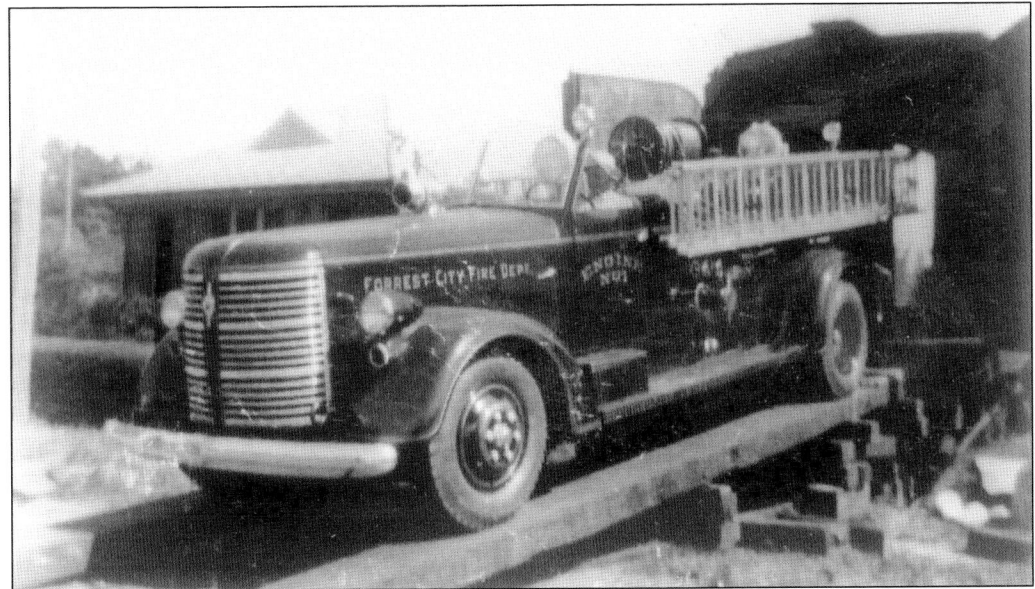

Here a 1946 American LaFrance fire apparatus is unloaded from a rail car in Widener. It was Forrest City's first fire truck after World War II. Production had ceased during the war, with all available trucks going to the war effort.

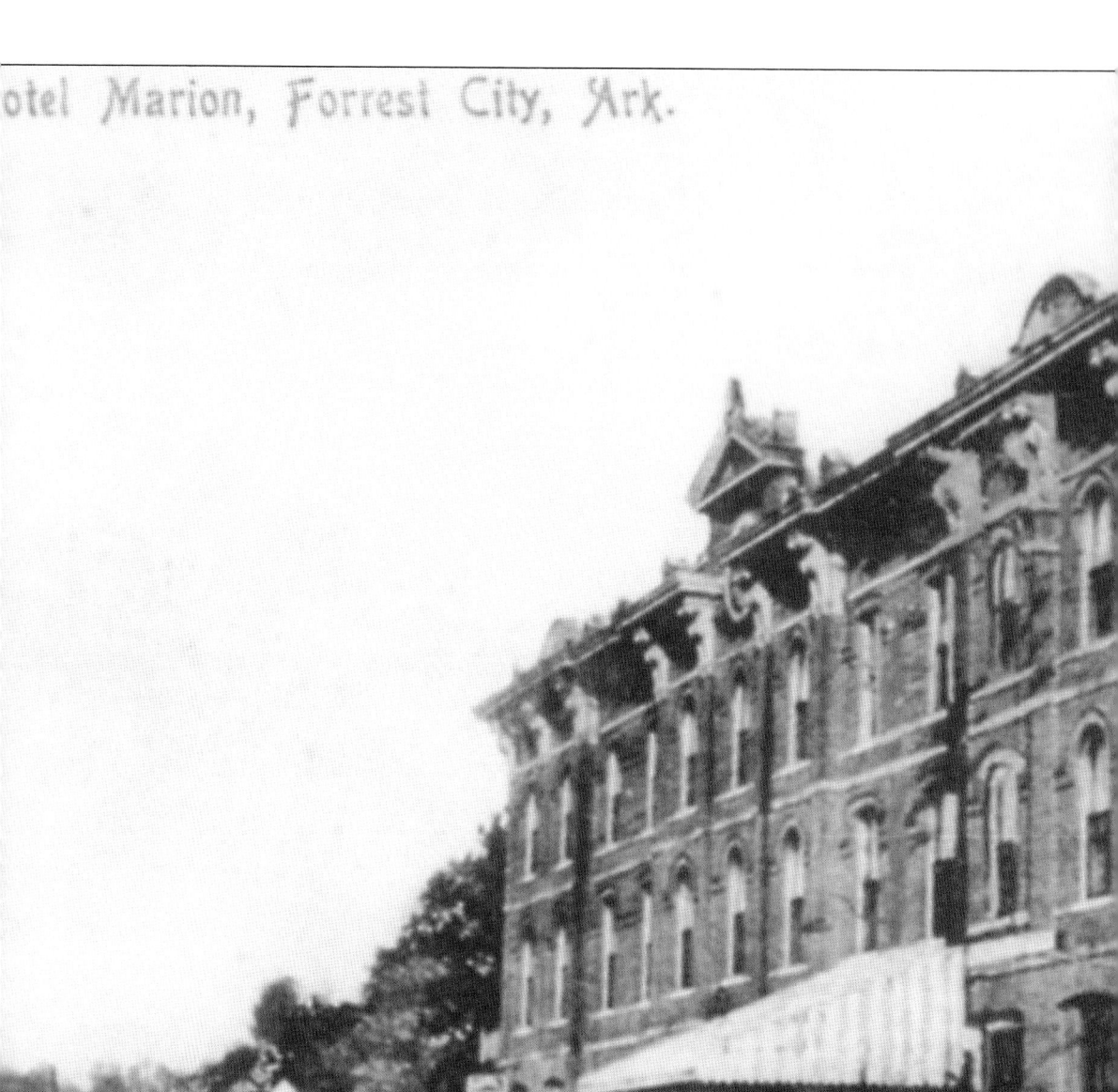

At the start of the 20th century, the Marion Hotel was the grandest hotel in eastern Arkansas. Though the establishment underwent several name changes, most still remember it as the Marion. Pauline Goddard served as the manager for quite some time. Records tell of "bear steaks, a delicacy," as standard fare at the hotel. Standing adjacent to the rail depot on Front Street, the Marion was the lodging of choice for many travelers on the north-south and east-west rail lines. It was built

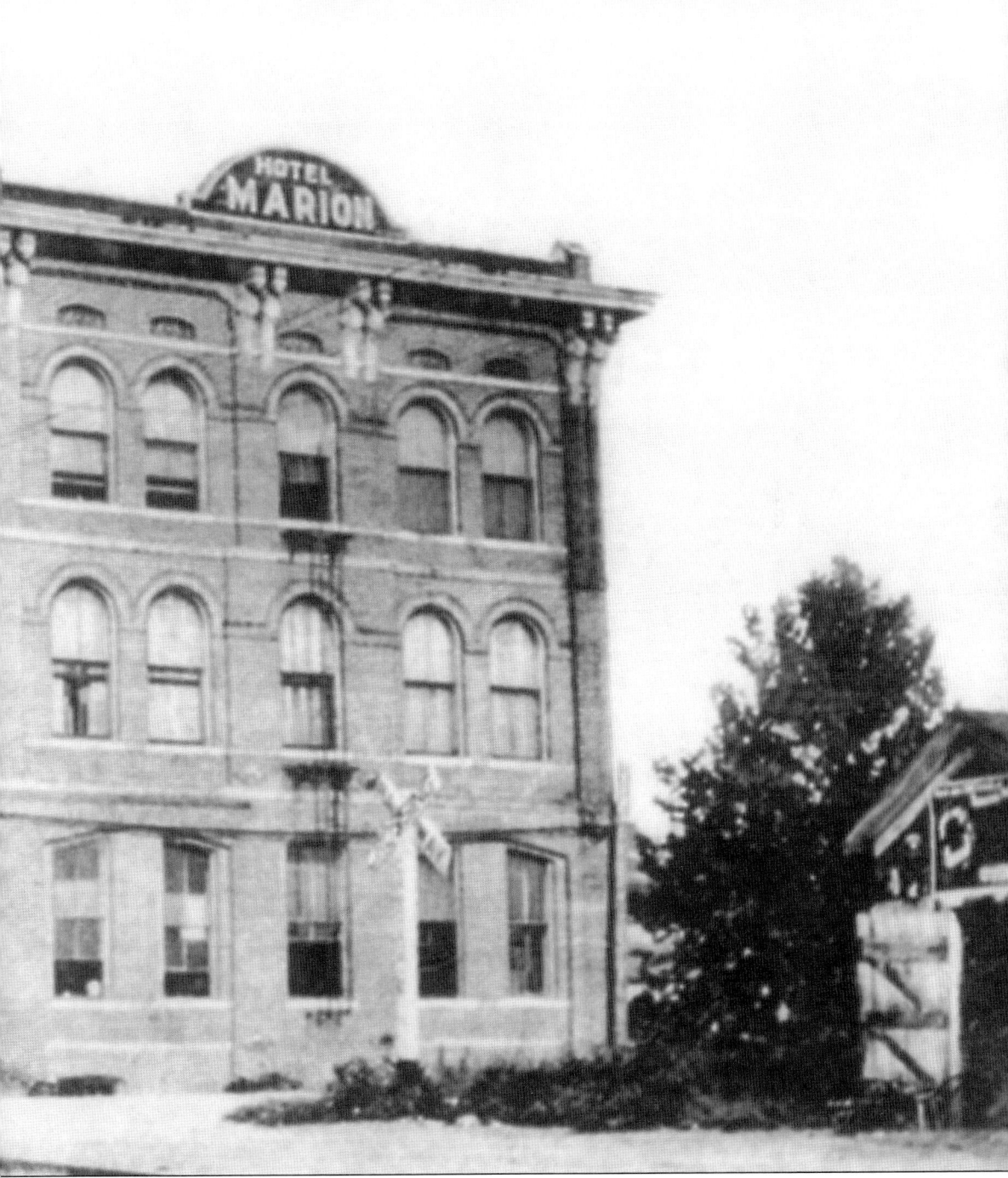

on the same lot now occupied by National Carpet One. The authors have dated the building into the mid to late 1940s and perhaps to the early 1950s. An informal survey of residents found that the hotel was razed around 1950. In the 1897 book *Goodspeed*, the Marion was referenced as the greatest hotel west of the Mississippi. It is rumored that presidents stayed there.

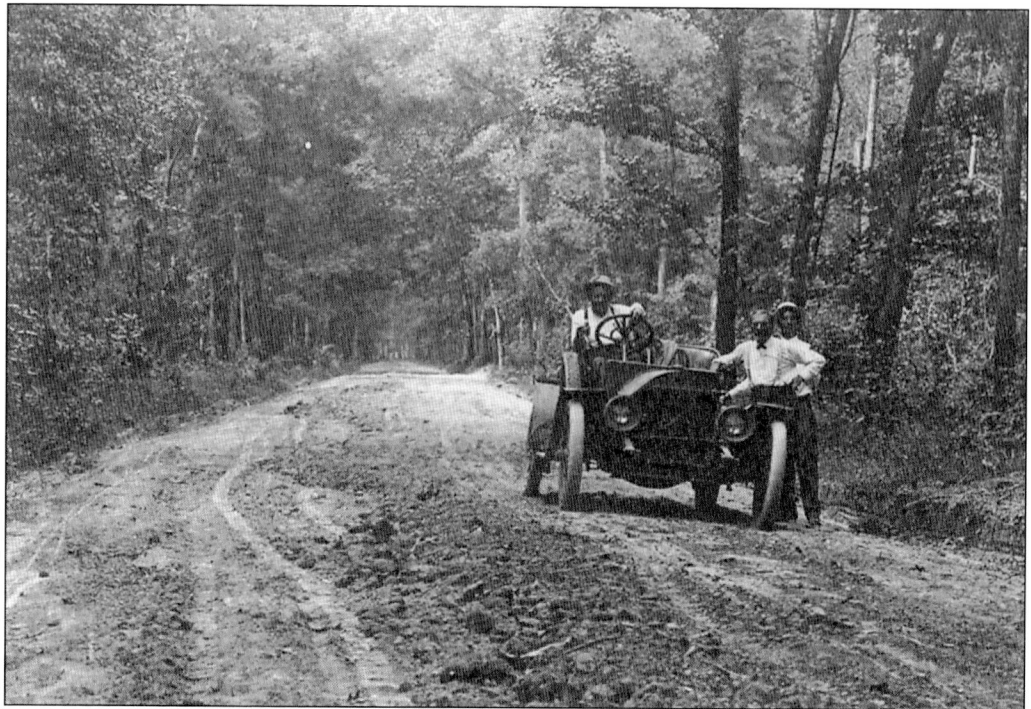

This photograph is labeled "1913 survey." Note the dense forest in the background. At this time, there would still have been many logging operations and swampy areas to be negotiated. The collection of Harry Schellhous, the original surveyor of the county, was donated to the St. Francis County Museum by his family. It is not known if he is one of these men.

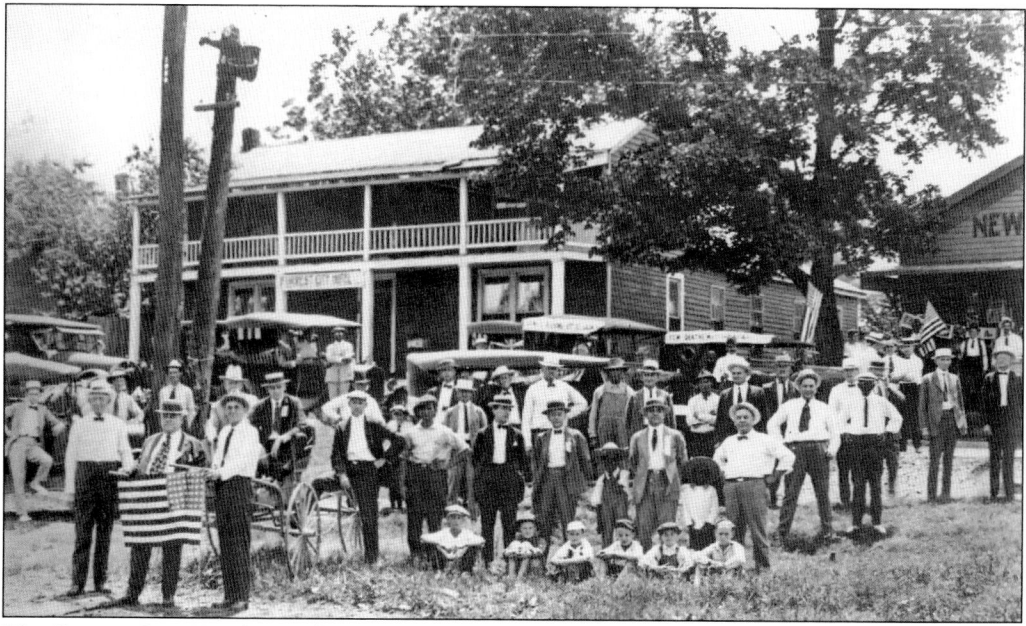

The Forrest City Hotel was also a well-known place of rest. On this day, however, it was a site of excitement and activity, presumably a political rally. The man holding the flag is perched between the poles of a buggy.

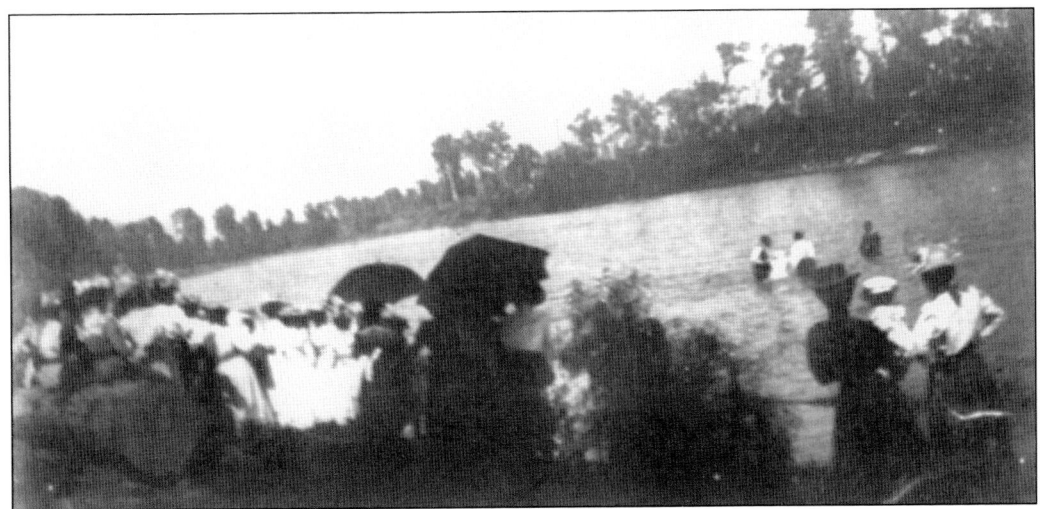

Titled "Negro Baptizing in the St. Francis River," this photograph was first published in the 1905 *Forrest City Times* art souvenir. St. Francis County is located in the heart of the Bible Belt, and church life has played a huge part of the culture here for centuries. Next to church, the most important thing in most African American families was the matriarch. The grandmother often still serves as the central figure in Southern families.

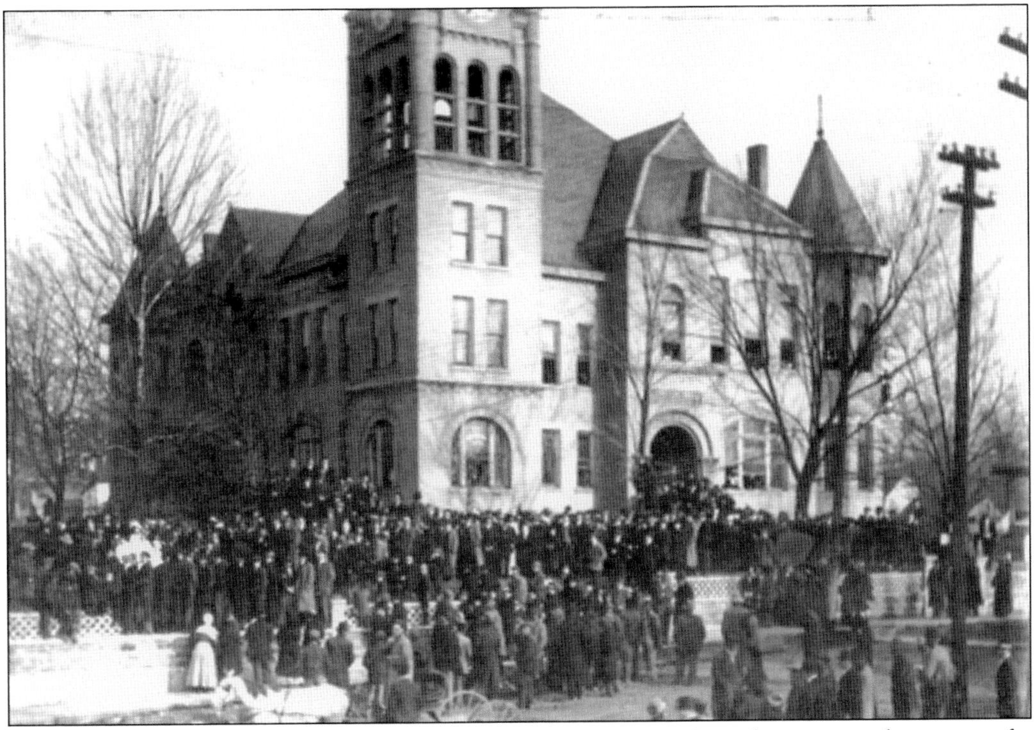

Shortly after the close of the 19th century, the St. Francis Courthouse was the scene of a great revival. The *Forrest City Times* proclaimed the event as "the answer to a wife's prayer." There was much celebration as a number of citizens professed their faith at the courthouse worship service.

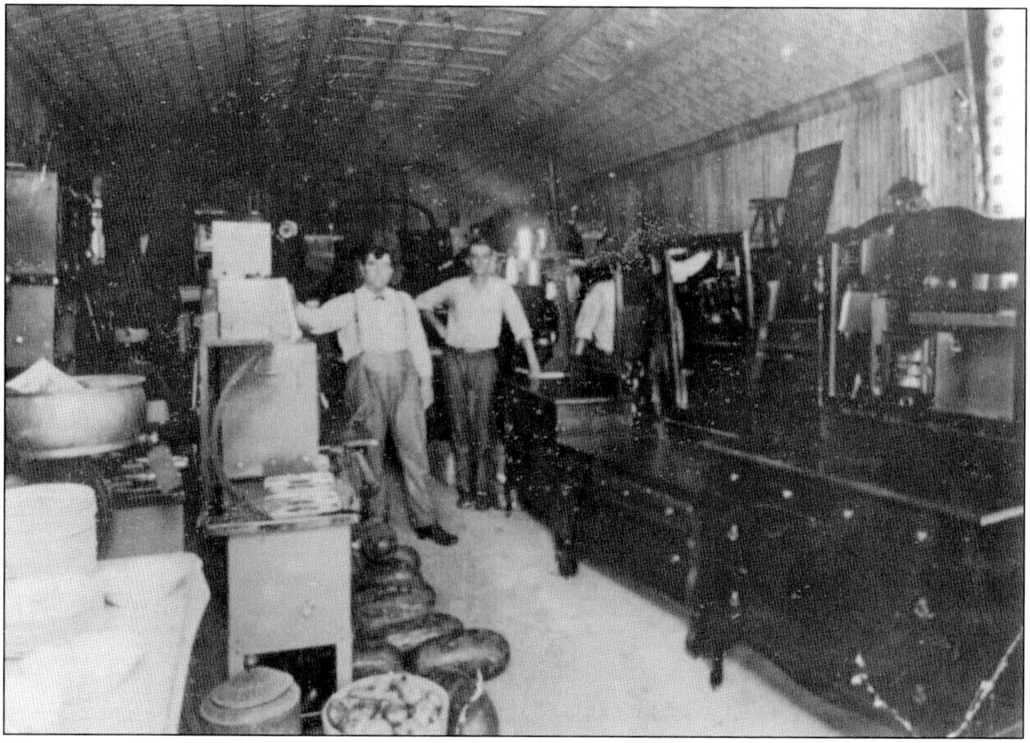

This store sold washtubs, bedroom dressers, watermelons, and everything in between.

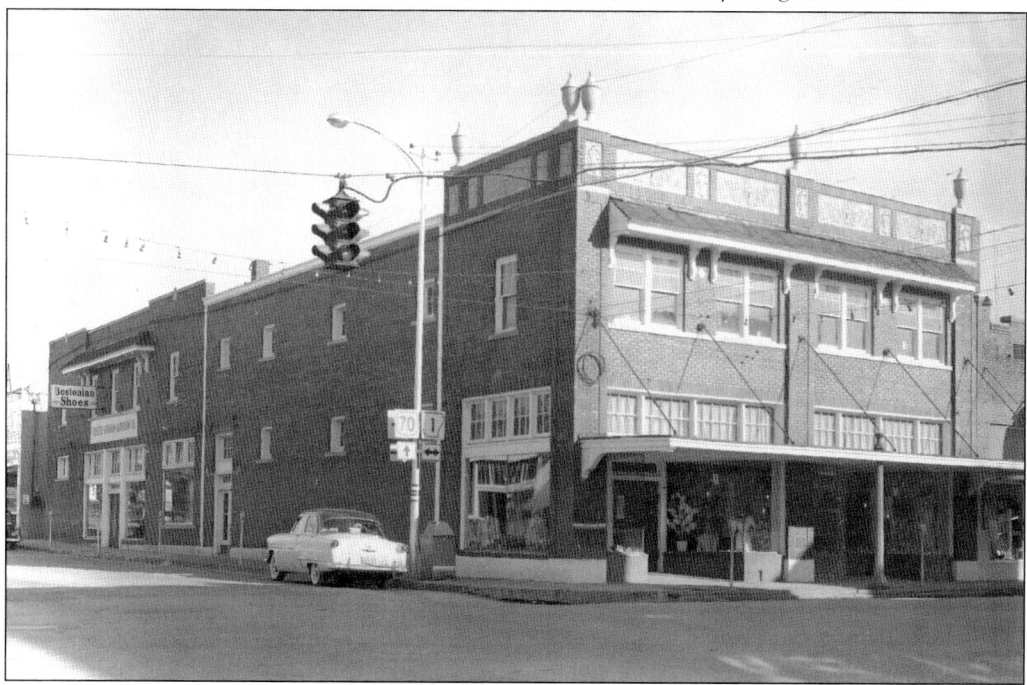

The corner of Highway 70 and Highway 1 (Washington Street) is probably the most traveled in Forrest City. The building stands today, with minor modifications, and houses a few apartments and financial offices. The streetlight has been replaced by a modern stoplight.

This sheet music was discovered at the St. Francis County Museum in 2006. When descendant Minnie Handy looked at a copy, she was extremely happy; the family had believed the piece was written after W. C. Handy moved north.

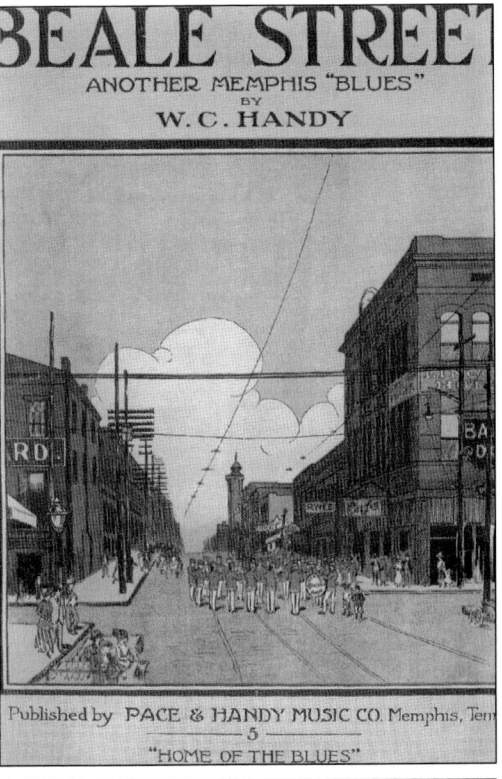

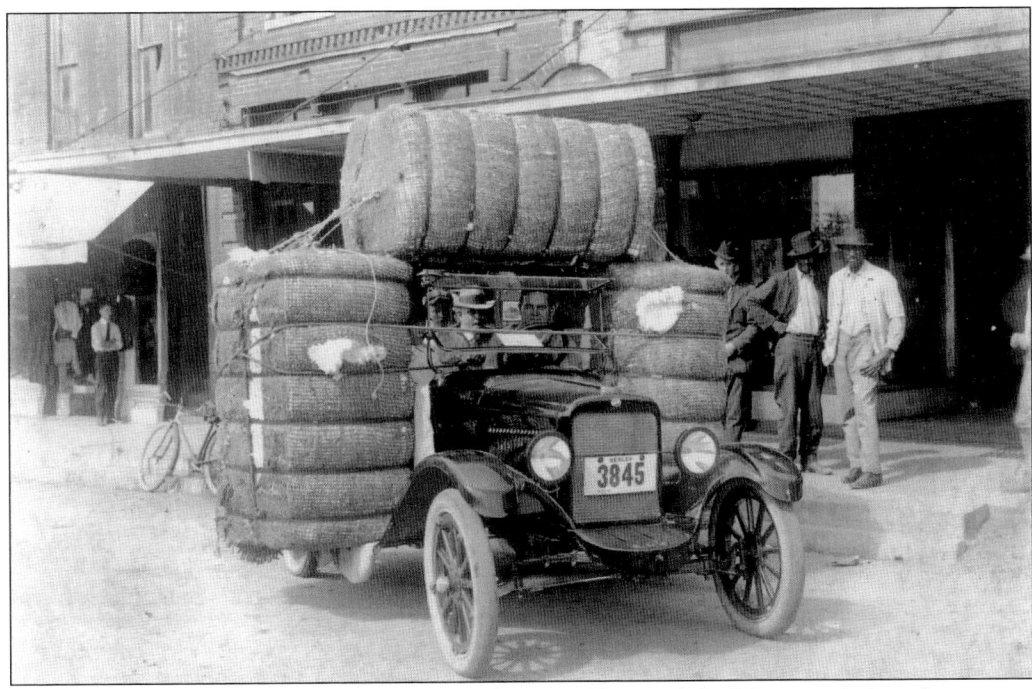

N. B. Rice, a former mayor of Forrest City, drives a Chevy while delivering bales of cotton to Cotton Alley on Front Street in 1936. The gentleman in back wearing a white hat is believed to be Dr. J. O. Rush, in part because of the tags on the car.

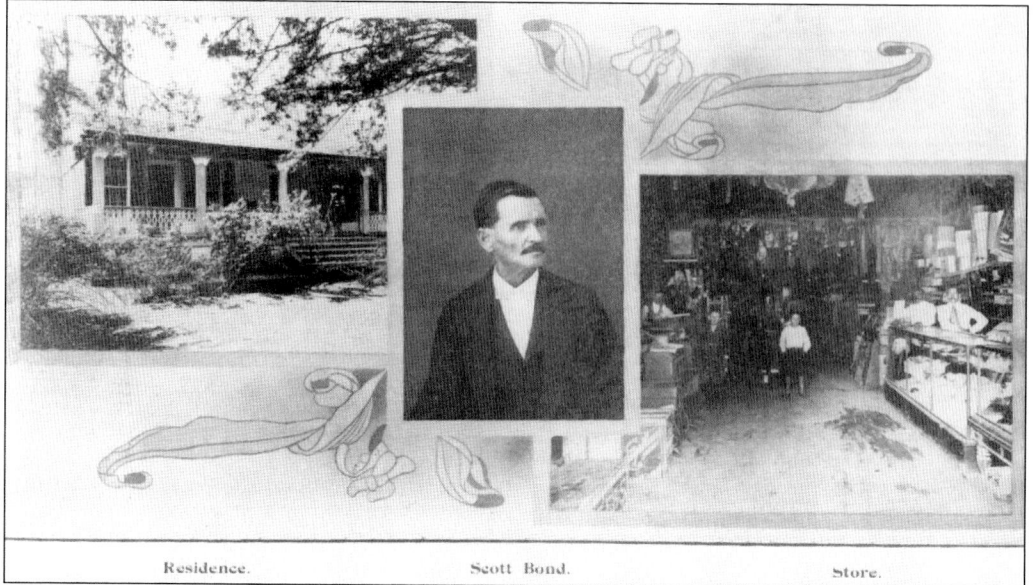

Scott Bond was the first African American millionaire in Arkansas. Born in Madison County, Mississippi, in March 1852, he was the son of a slave and her owner. Incredibly ingenious and shrewd, Bond began as a farmer and worked his way up to landowner. He invented a special plow and then made his fortune selling gravel to the railroad. His home in Madison is pictured, along with one of his businesses. Bond was later gored to death by one of his prized bulls.

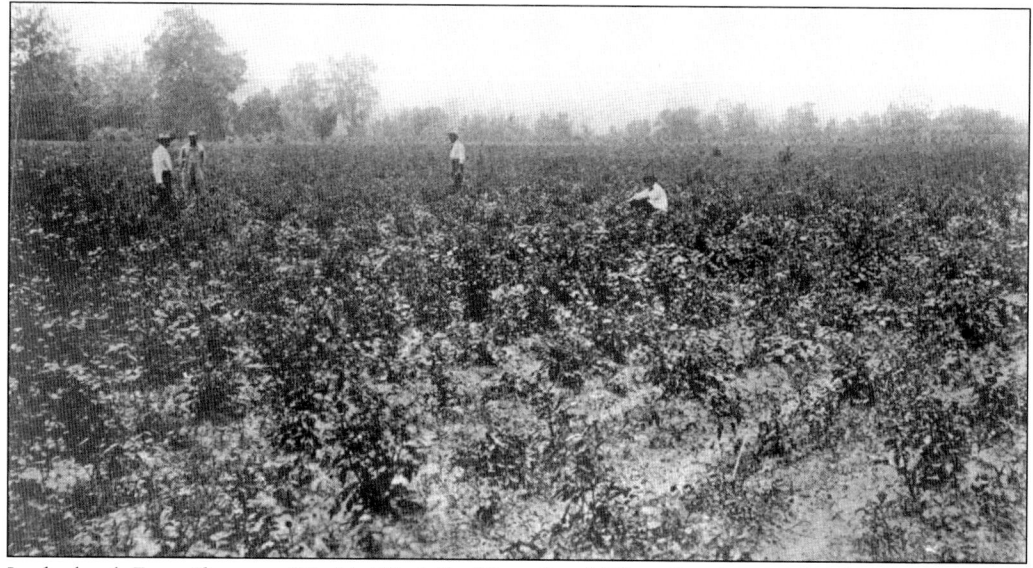

In the book *From Slavery to Wealth: The Life of Scott Bond*, Theo Bond wrote that he included many images of his father, Scott Bond, at home in his fields. Here he appears in the distance wearing a flat-brimmed white hat. Scott Bond and his descendants are buried in the cemetery at Madison, now a nationally registered landmark. Starting with little or no credit, Scott sharecropped and built his farm to 2,200 acres. This would have been unheard of for any tenant farmer, much less a mulatto with nothing but the clothes on his back. Upon his marriage to Magnolia Nash at 22 years of age, Scott literally did not have a pot to cook in. Magnolia used the kettle for brewing and then cooking.

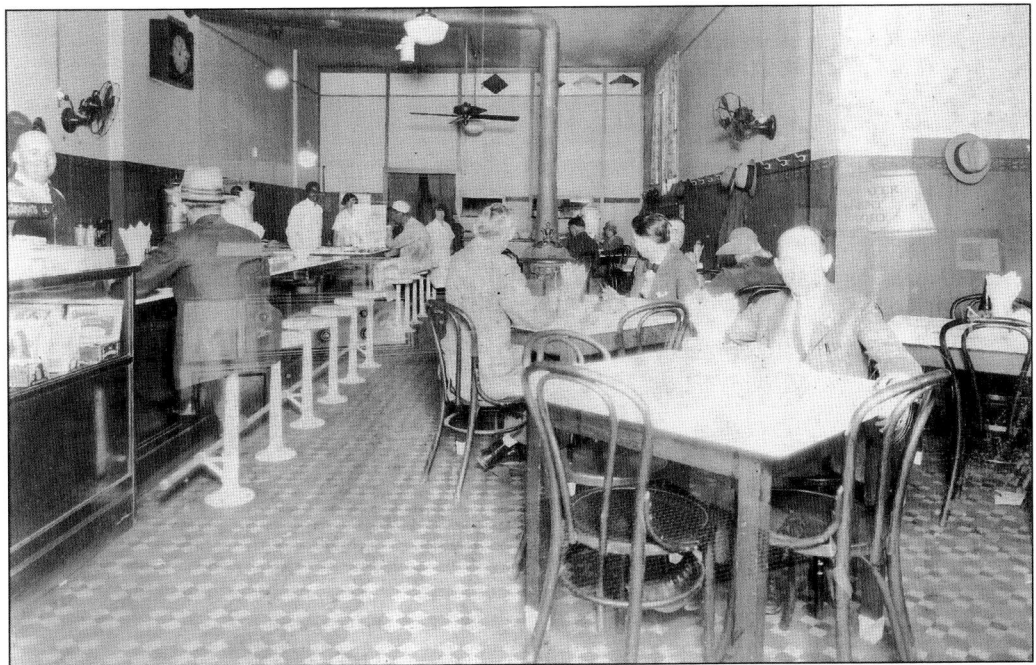

This eating establishment is believed to be Watkins, located in the outdoor garden east of present-day Mallard's Restaurant. Oscar's, owned by Judy Sweet, was the former inhabitant of the building.

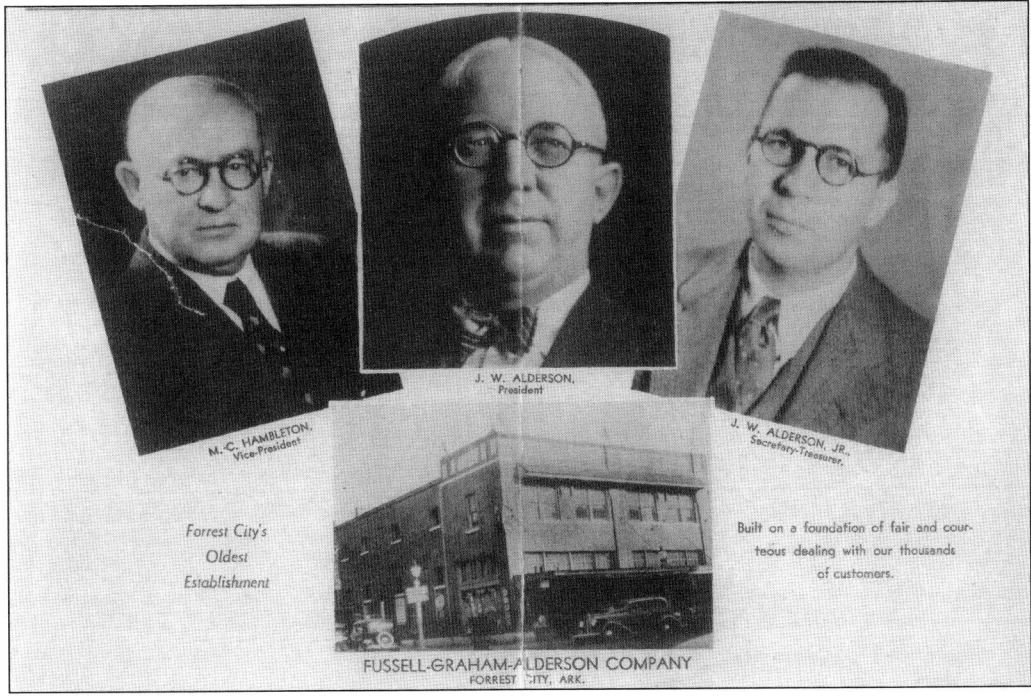

From left to right, M. C. Hambleton, vice president; J. W. Alderson, president; and J. W. Alderson Jr. are shown in a flyer advertising the Fussell-Graham-Alderson Company, the oldest establishment in Forrest City.

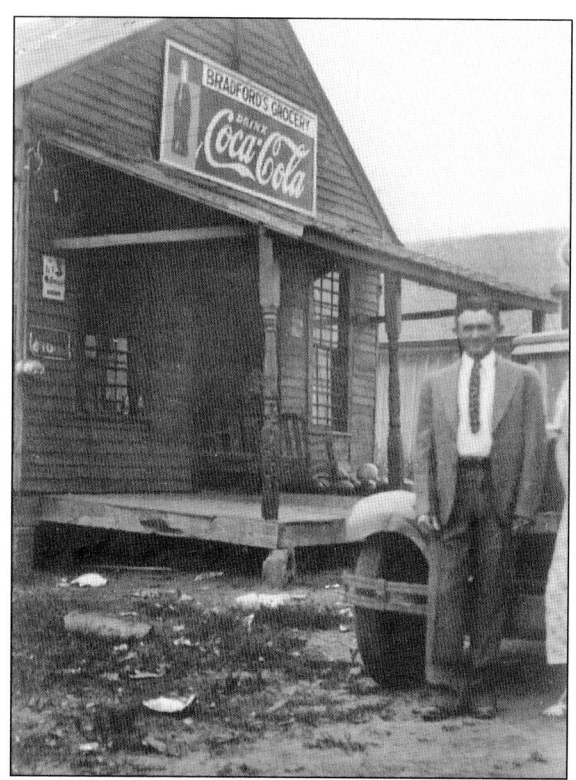

Stores like this dotted the county until the last decade or so. The county is extremely wide and narrow, so stores like Bradford's Grocery (pictured) and Dodson's Corner were the main suppliers for many rural families. As travel improved, major chains like Kroger, Harvest Foods, and Wal-Mart have edged out the little corner stores.

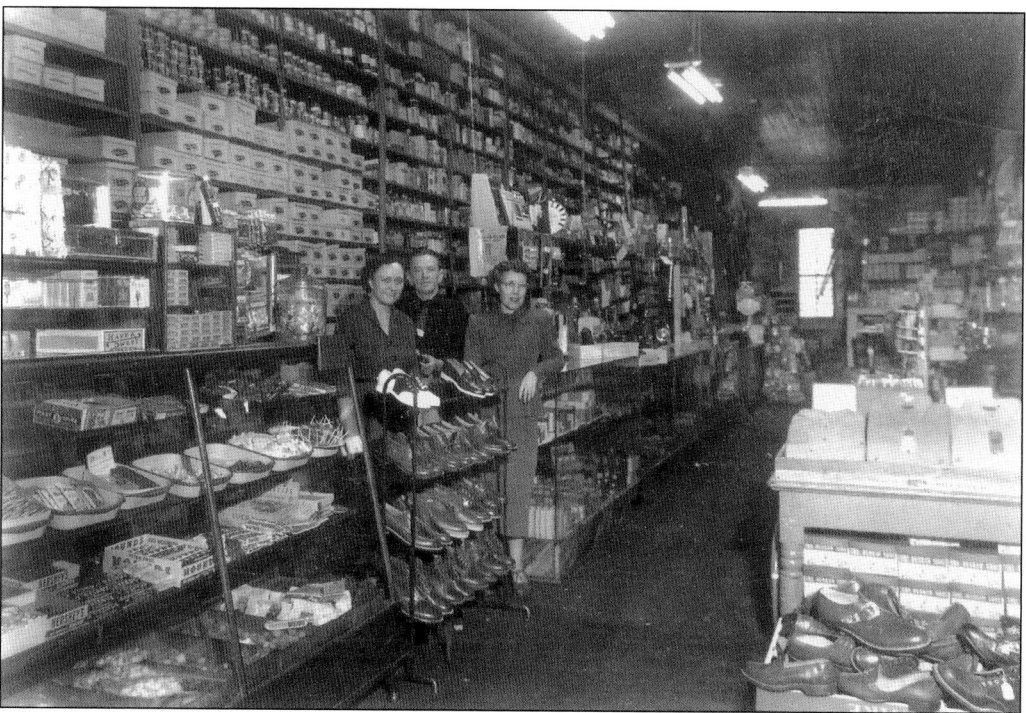

From left to right, Clemie Lee, Bert Sulcer, and Earnestine Burns stand in Sulcer's, located on Main Street in Palestine. Today Littlefield's Grocery is the only store still operating along Main.

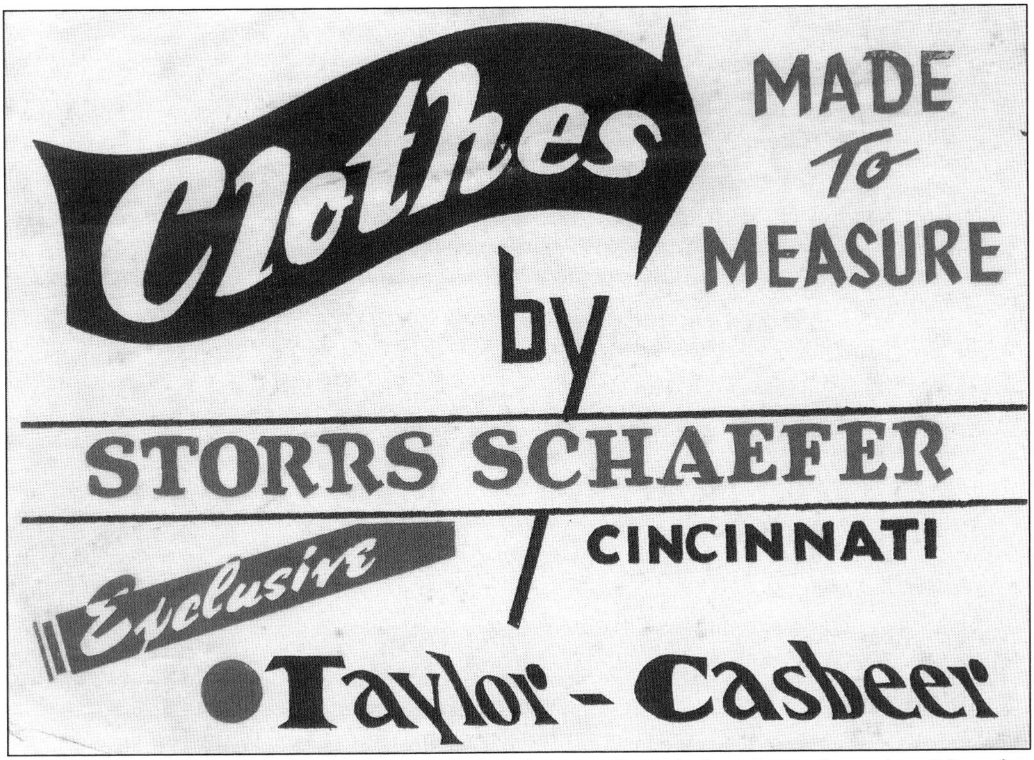

For more than half a century, major designer labels not ordinarily found any closer than Memphis or Little Rock could be had at Taylor Casbeer. It is indeed a bittersweet time, as the Forrest City clothing store has closed its doors as of March 2008.

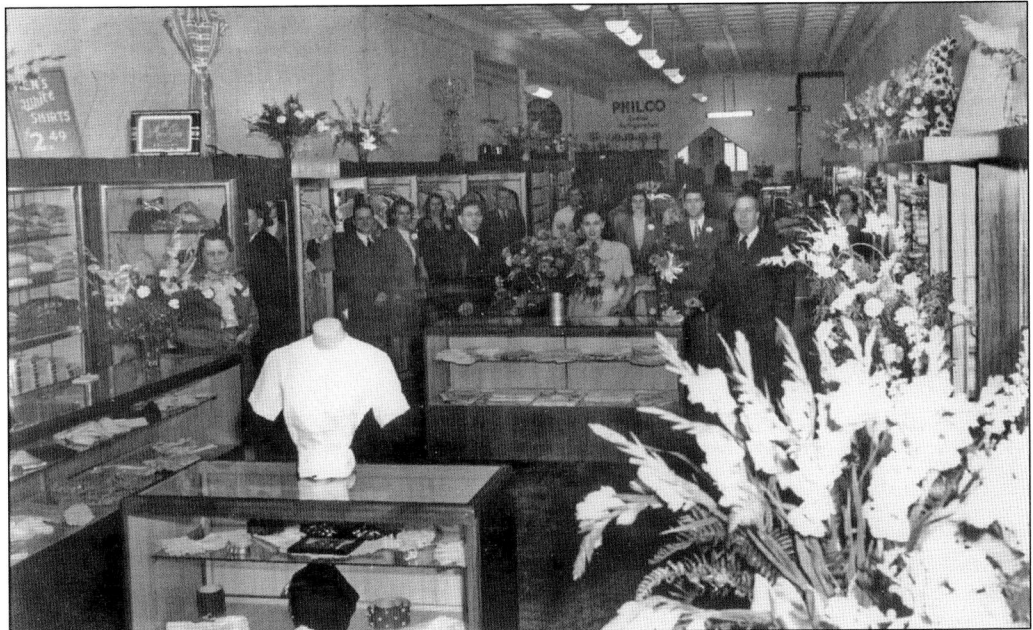

Fresh gladiolas are a lovely welcome into this store, which is believed to be the original Taylor Casbeer building.

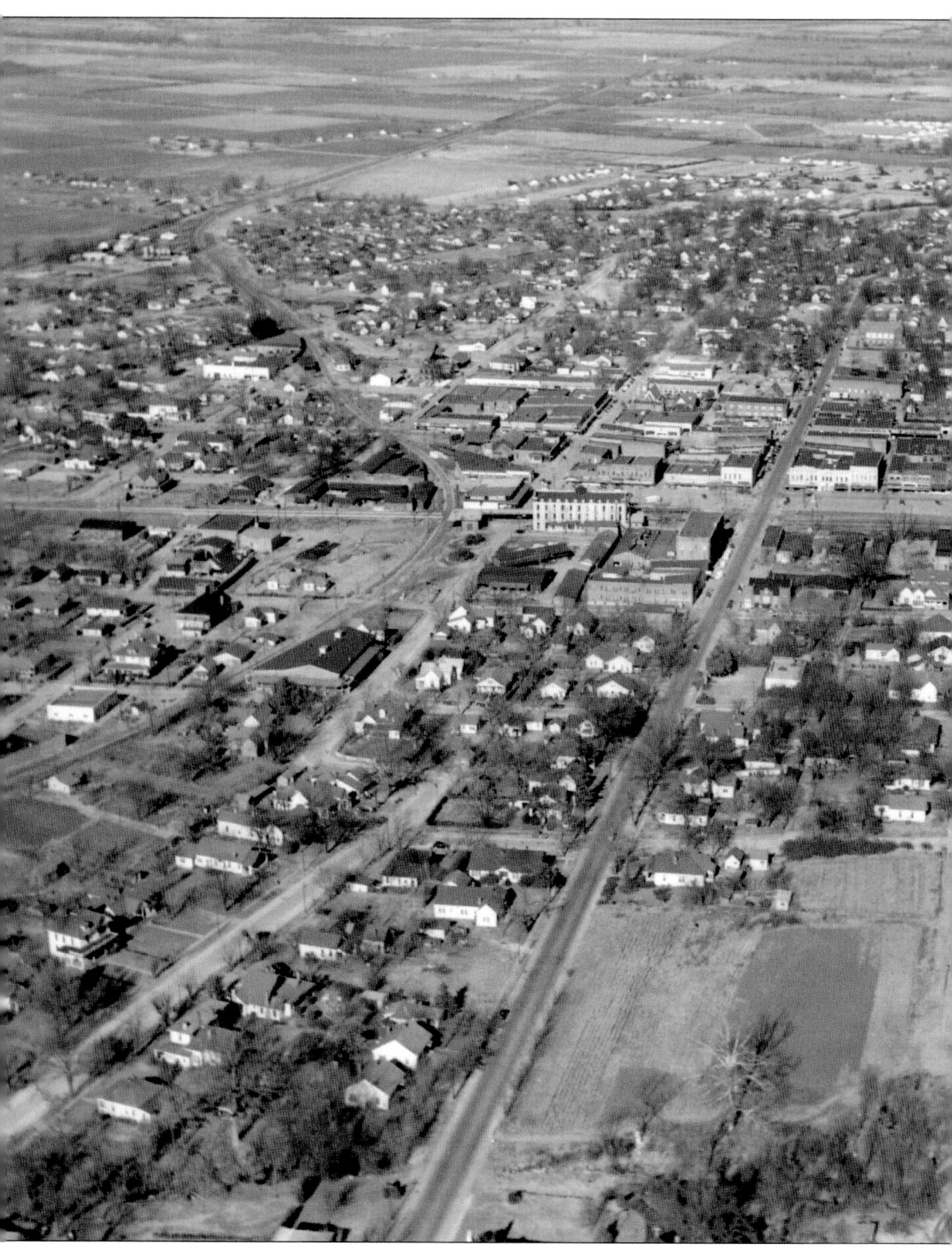

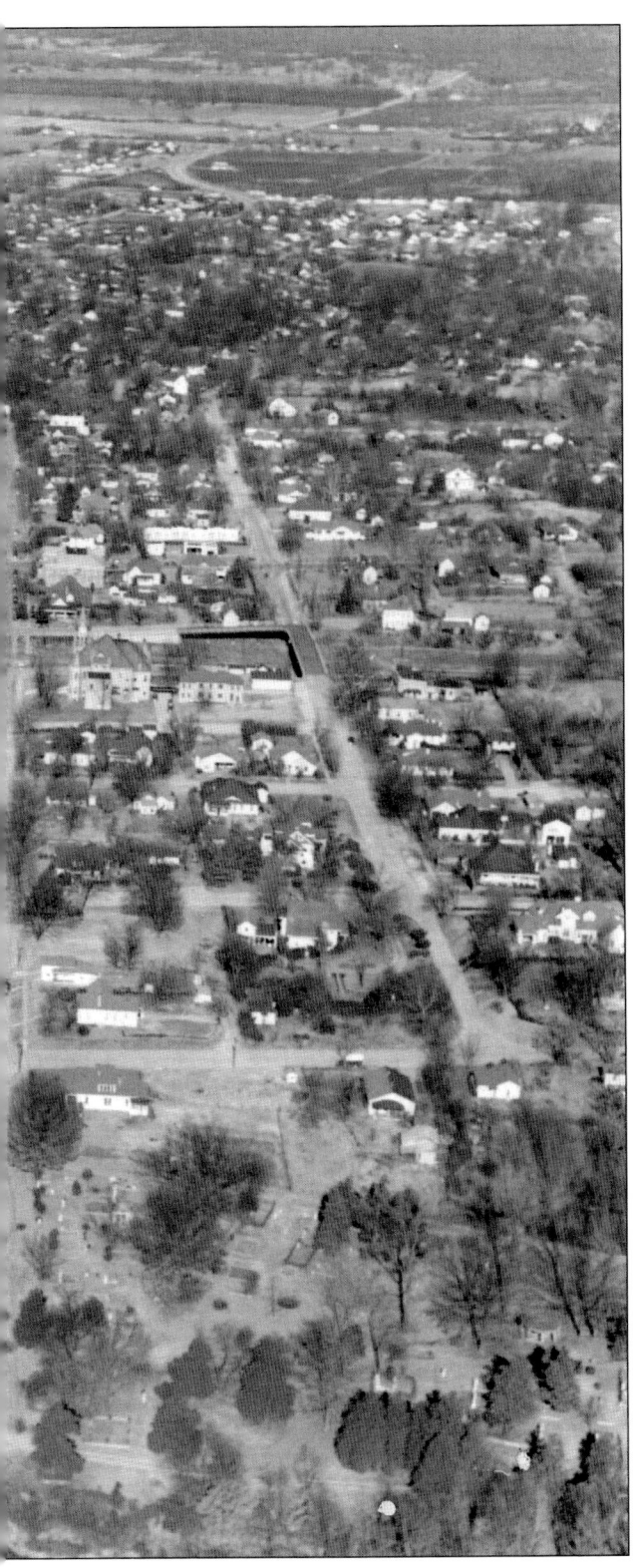

This skyline offers a wonderful trip back to the middle of the 20th century. The Marion Hotel is still visible near the center, an element that helps date the image to prior to the mid-1950s. Front Street is clearly pictured, along with many businesses that are no longer there. The interstate, not even imagined yet, was later placed where the top of the view cuts off. Highway 70, the Broadway of America, was in heavy use at this time. The town was in its heyday.

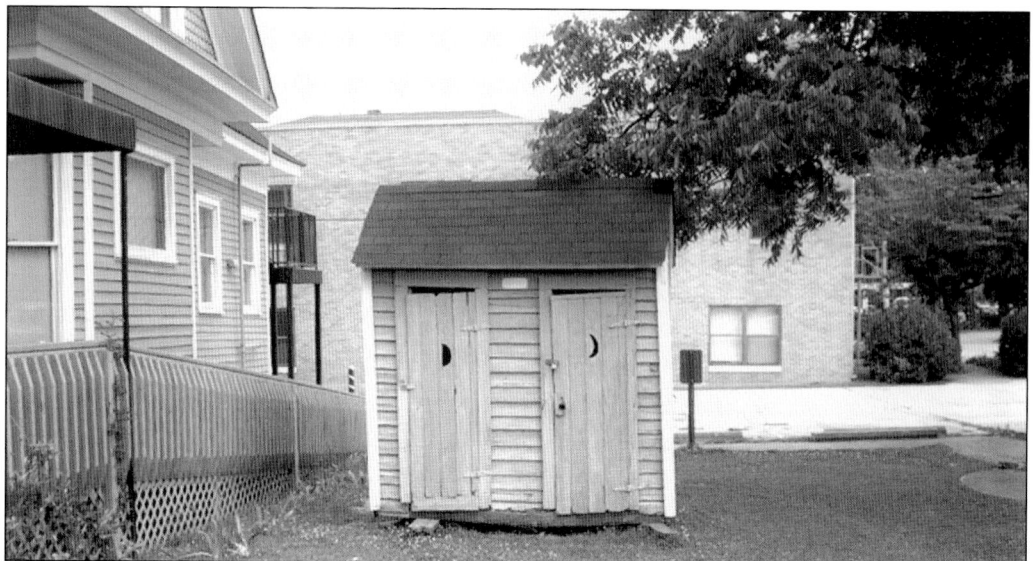

This outhouse is a landmark in its own right. It was built with two stalls but not because it was meant separately for males and females. Like everything else in the South at the time, the outhouse conformed to Jim Crow laws. Dr. J. O. Rush's office and home were designed with running water, but patients were not allowed to use the inside restrooms; Cora Rush directed all patients outside. The office had separate entrances for black and white, with the outhouse serving as a testament to the way things were. Although not a wonderful memory, the outhouse teaches children about the Jim Crow laws of yesterday in the hopes that they will never be repeated.

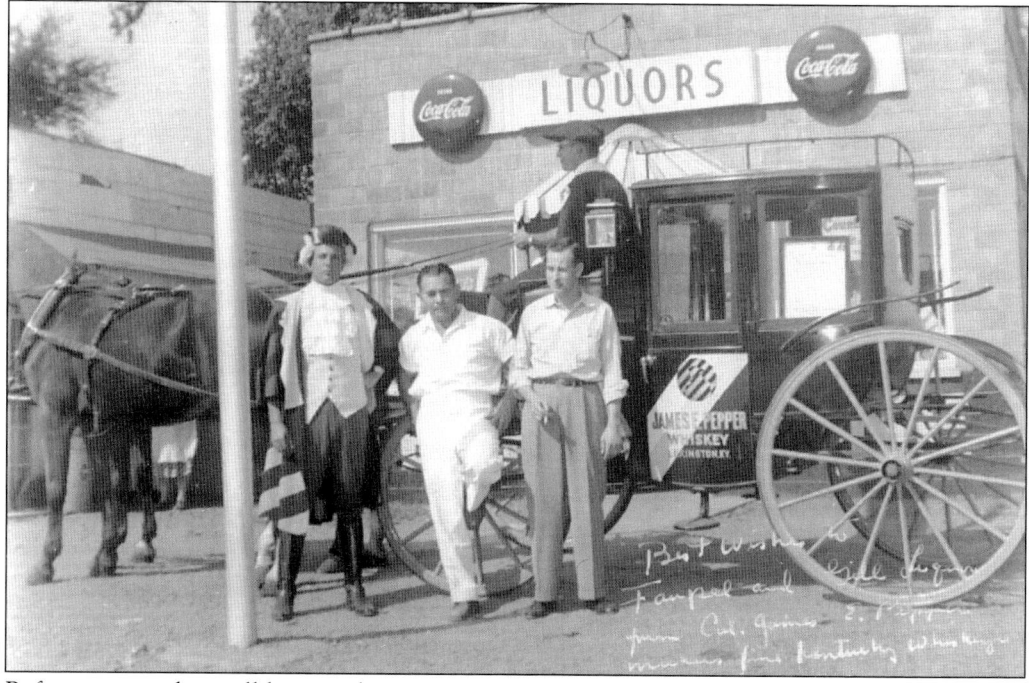

Before starting his well-known diner, Warren Faupel (right) operated a liquor store with his partner, Hazel "Gil" Gill (center), in downtown Forrest City. The third man is an unidentified whiskey sales rep.

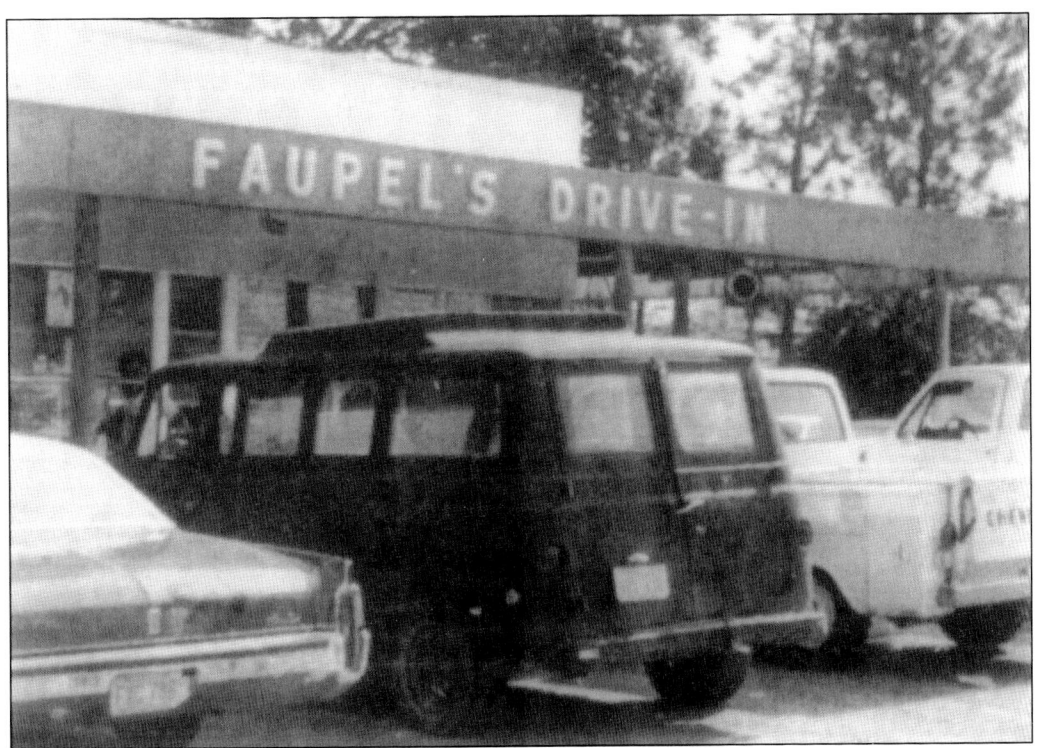

After a successful partnership with Gil, Warren Faupel added a dairy bar to his business enterprise. Located on the west end of Highway 70 in Forrest City, it reportedly served some of the best food around. Faupel maintains a relationship with his decades' worth of customers as a greeter at Wal-Mart when his health allows. He is a wonderful asset to this community.

WARREN FAUPEL HAMBURGER RECIPE

For tasty hamburgers, use three pounds regular ground beef, five slices finely ground stale white bread and five ounces or more of cold water. Salt and pepper to taste. More water may be needed to get a slack mixture.

Mix thoroughly and press into desired size patties. (Four or five to the pound.) Experience will help to get the desired mixture. It should be fairly slack. It helps to place in the freezer (wrapped) and chill until patty is stiff-nearly frozen. This will help prevent sticking when frying. Fry in a cast iron skillet at about the same temperature you fry hot cakes. Also may be grilled.

Readers of all ages will recall with fondness the famous Faupel burger and dairy bar. From the middle of the 20th century to the early 1980s, Warren Faupel dished up his own special brand of cooking that just cannot be replicated. For those who want to try his hamburgers, Faupel has graciously allowed his recipe to be printed here.

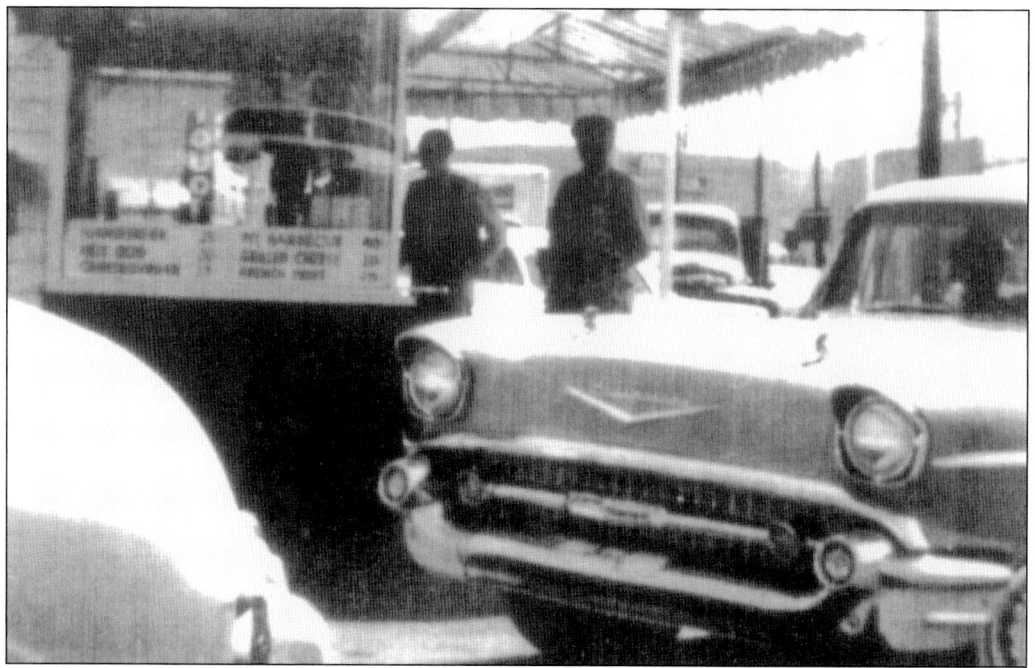

Faupel's Diner is pictured here in the 1950s, when grilled cheese sandwiches cost 10¢.

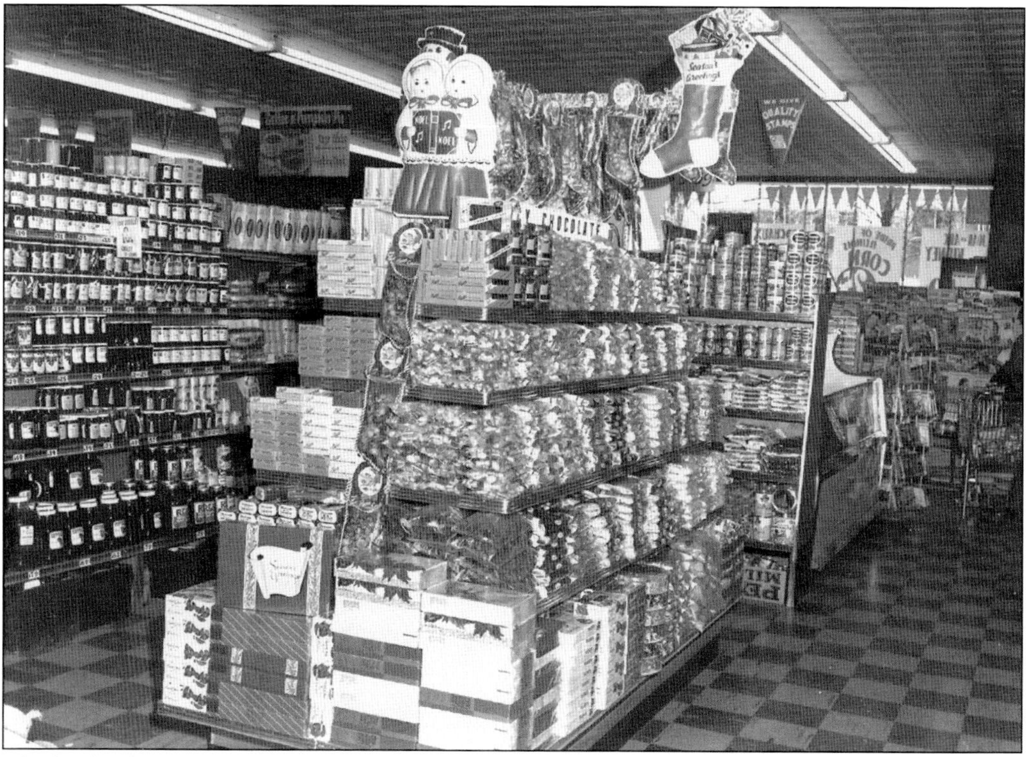

The back of this photograph is labeled with the name of the store, "Big Star." The decorations and special items for sale are reminiscent of Christmases past. The overflowing shelves represent the prosperity of the time.

The Hamilton Moses steam generating plant is located on Highway 70 between Palestine and Beck Spur and is now run by Entergy. It was in its first few years of operation during the time of this photograph. Brand new, the plant cost $15,000.

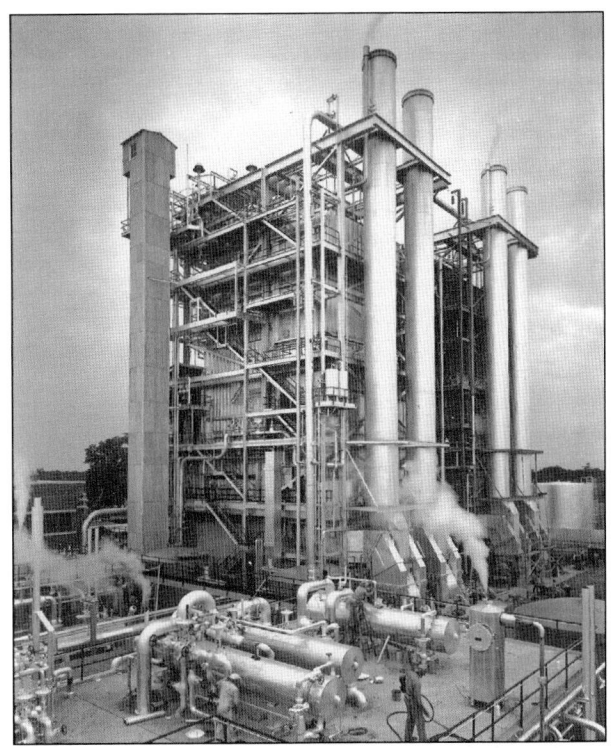

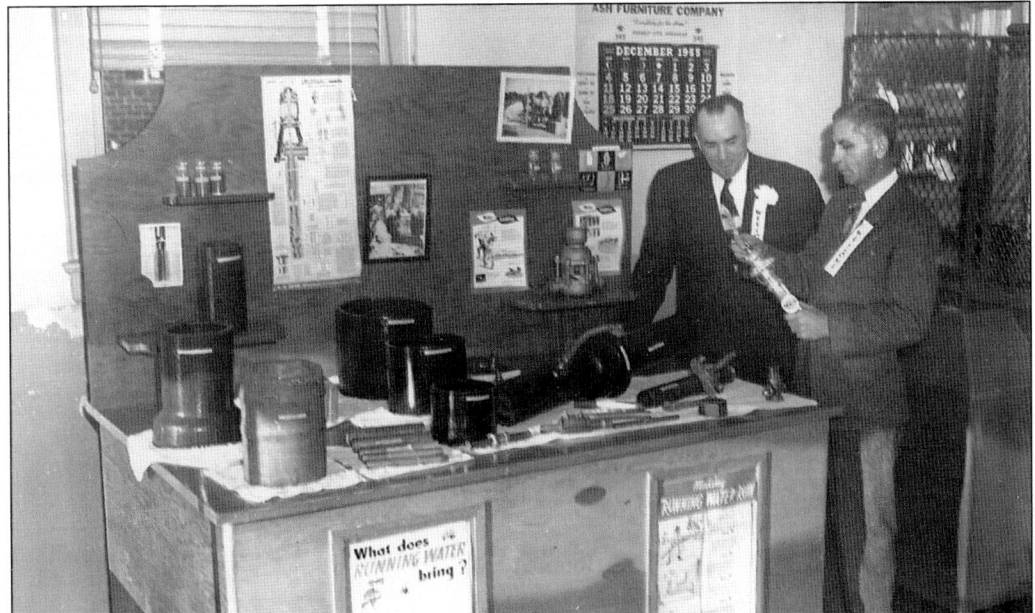

Nall Brantley (right) and an unidentified friend look at a booth touting the benefits of running water. In the 1800s, people flocked to the different springs in the county for their natural healing benefits. The waters at Stuart Springs were said to soothe teething babies. Improvements in water plants increased the capacity for farmers to irrigate and allowed homemakers more ease in cooking and cleaning. Much like today, change was not always readily accepted. Some still needed to be convinced that running water was a good thing.

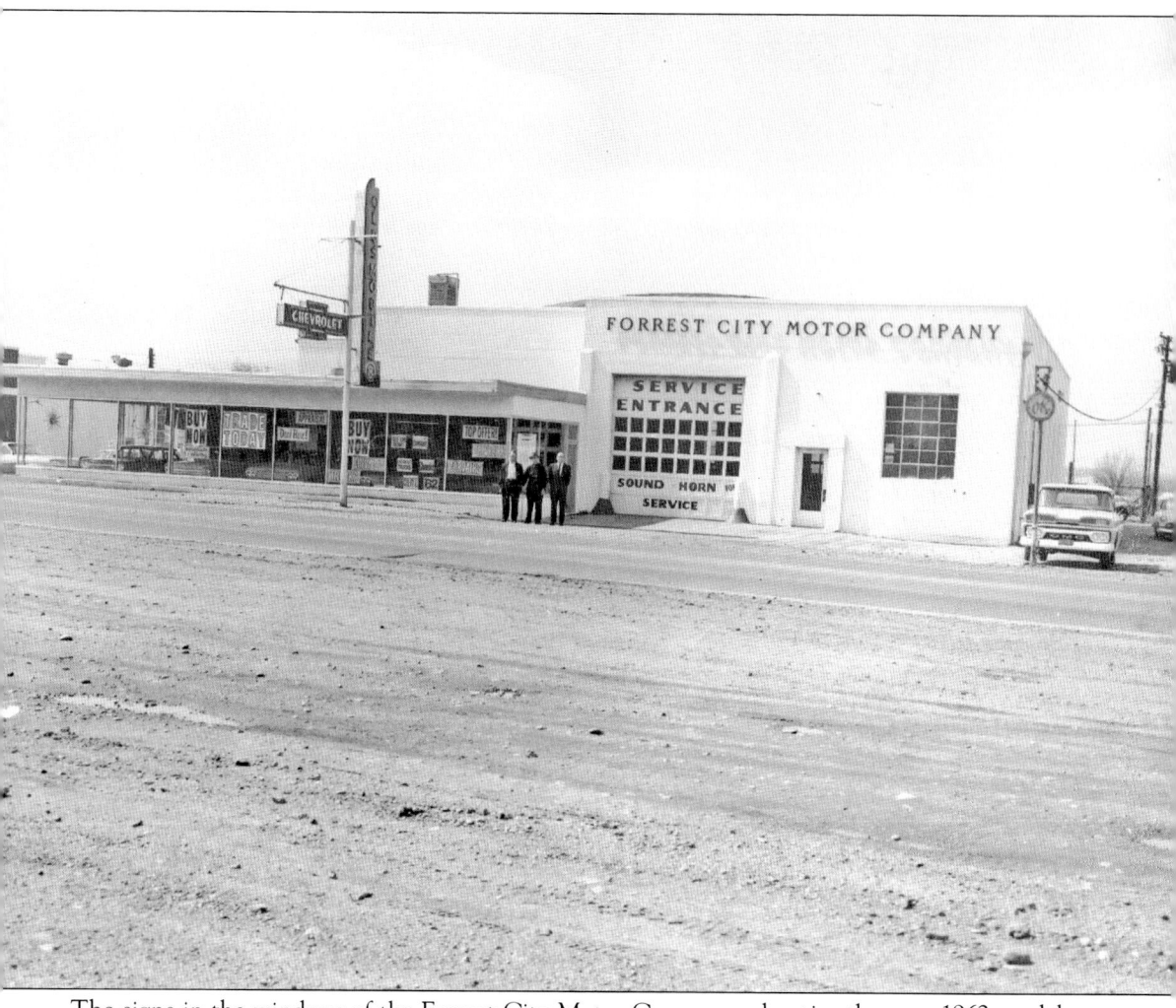
The signs in the windows of the Forrest City Motor Company advertise the new 1962 models. The Eldridge family owned the dealership.

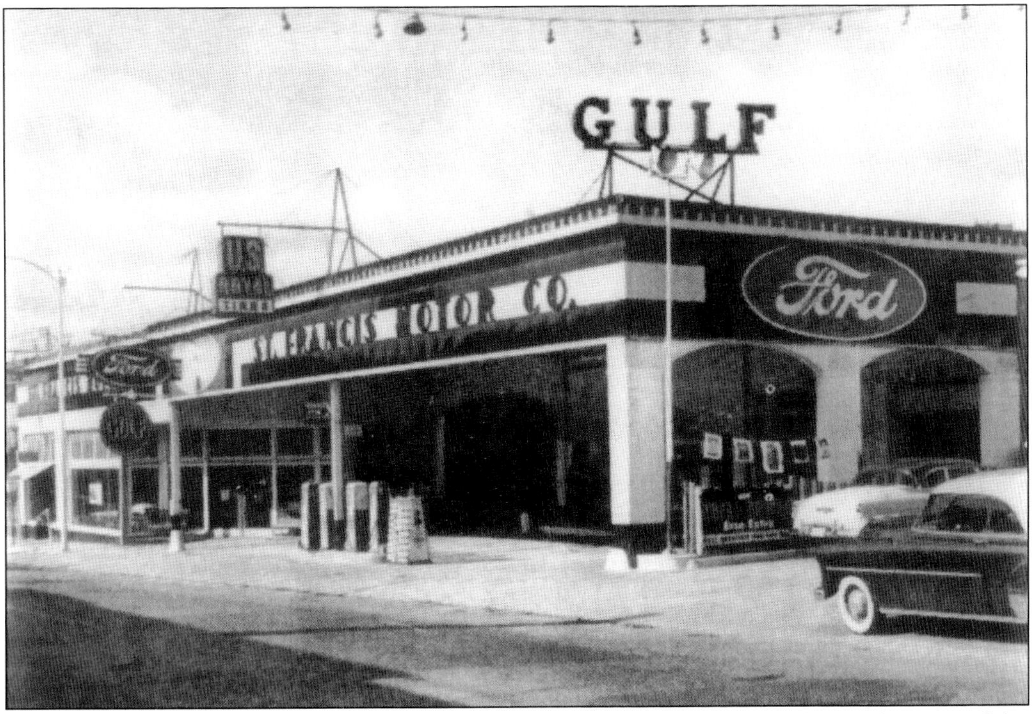

The St. Francis Motor Company was located next to Bishop Esso. It was the predecessor of the Machen Ford dealership.

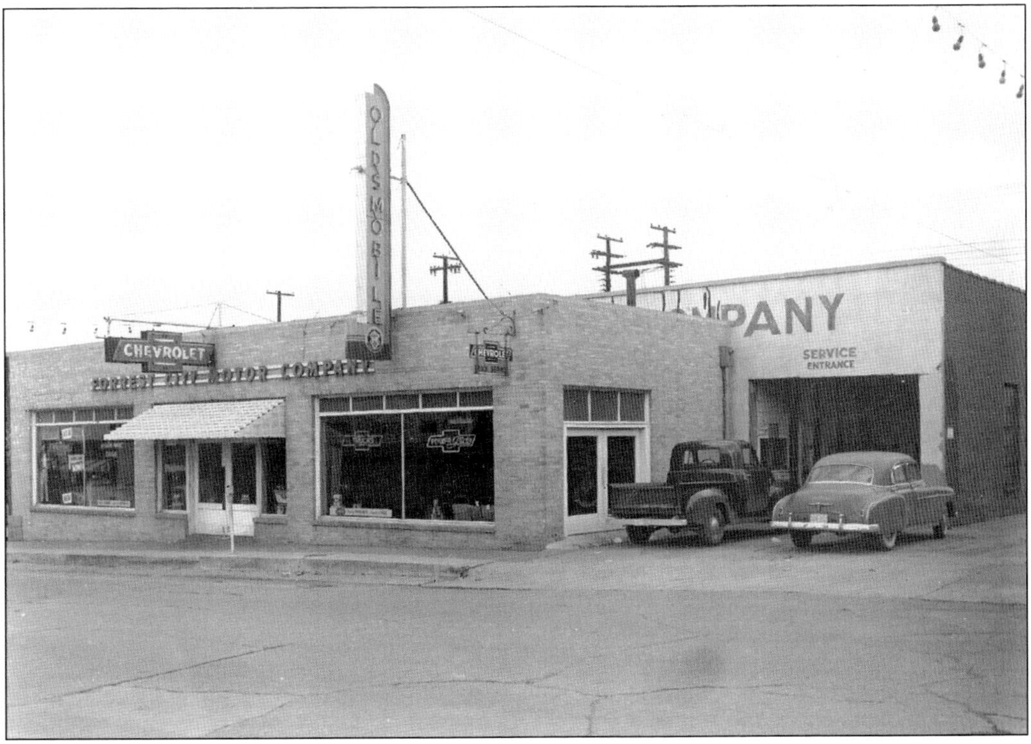

This photograph of Eldridge Chevrolet features a 1952 car.

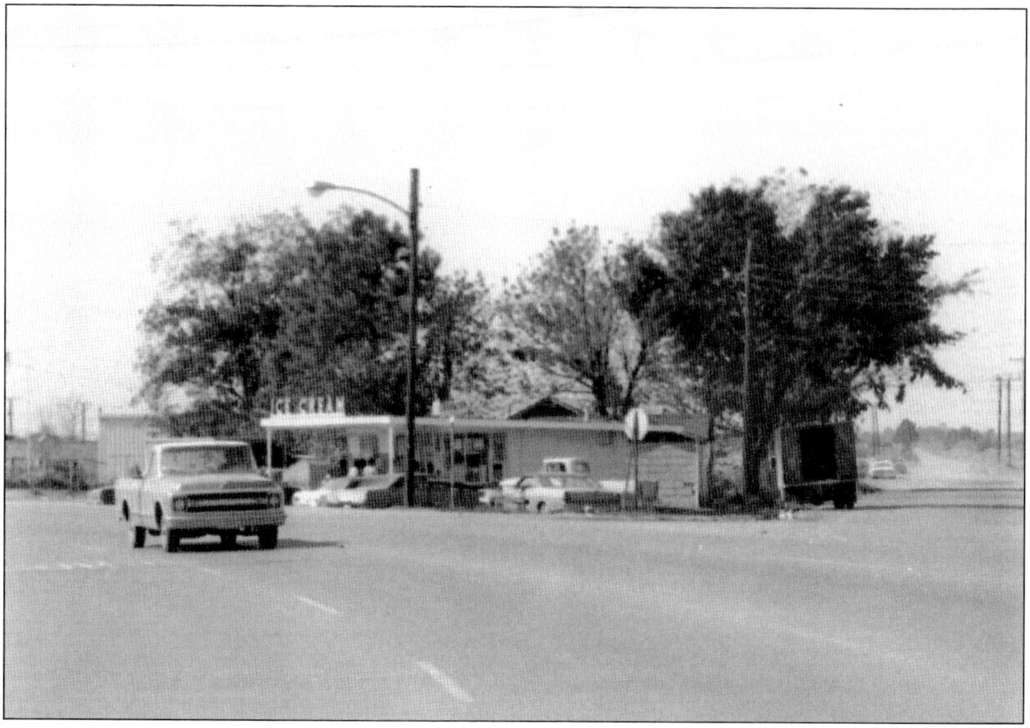

Joe Berry's Dairy Bar was located in the curve on Highway 70 near present-day Turner Road. Across the road was the Pepsi-Cola bottling plant.

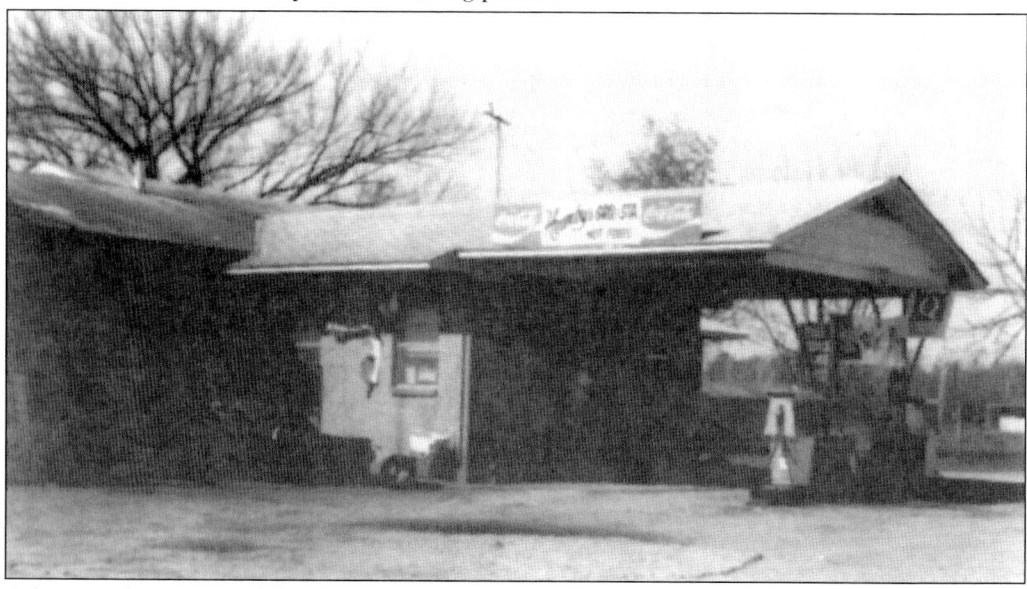

A business has occupied this location at the corner of Highway 261 and Highway 70 for almost a century. This incarnation was Hamby's. Since the high school stood just across the street, many students walked there at lunch to have Janell Hamby's famous "Hamby-burger." After closing the store and realizing retirement was a little too boring, David and Janell Hamby are now in the contracting business. Jan-Cour Construction specializes in commercial building and improvements all across the state.

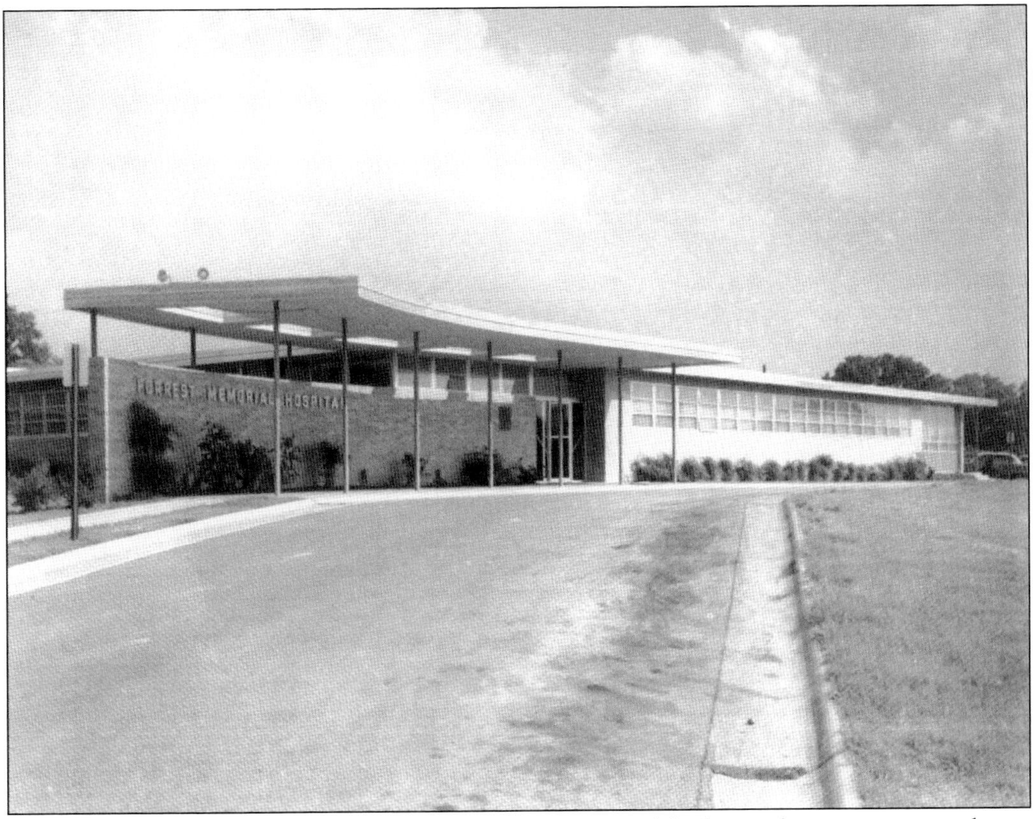

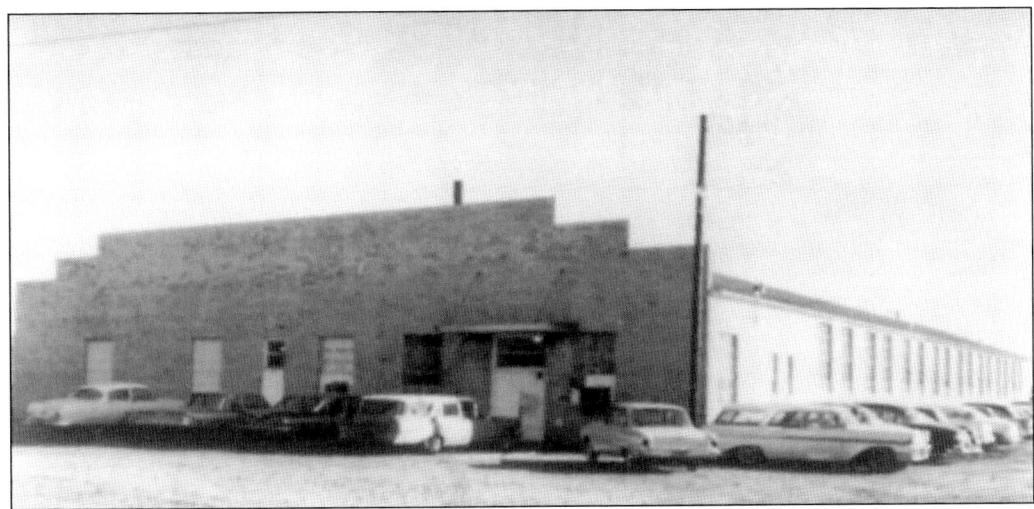

The original Forrest Memorial Hospital was a county-owned facility and is now a nursing home on the corner of Lindauer and Kittle Streets. The current hospital, Forrest City Medical Center, is located on Holiday Drive, right next to the interstate. It is undergoing an emergency room renovation and addition.

Rel-toc ("Cotler" spelled backwards) was a pants factory owned by Lerner-Sloane. The building still stands but has been inoperable as a factory for some time. Cotler kept a twin-engine Beechcraft aircraft at Dodson Field.

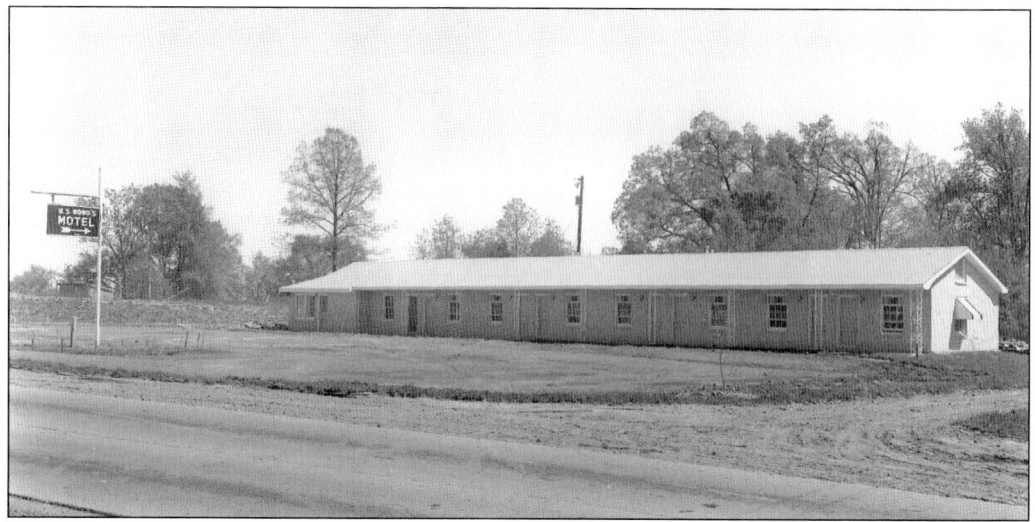

Scott Bond's son Ulysses continued in his father's enterprising spirit with the Bond Motel. Located in Madison, it was known as "one of the most famous hotels for colored in the U.S.," with all the modern amenities.

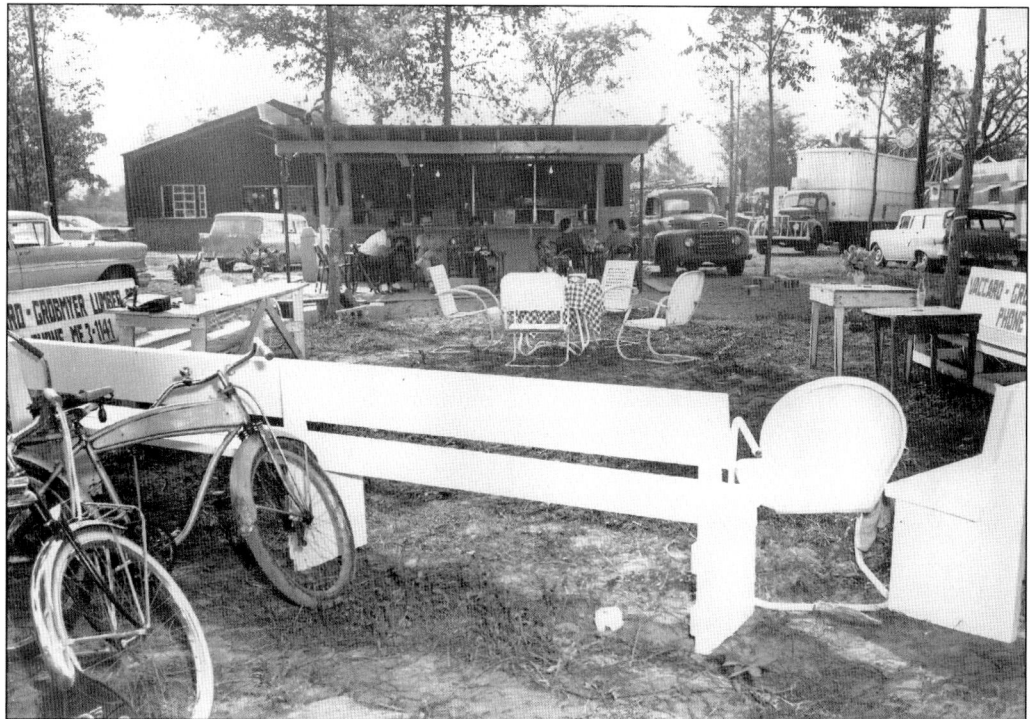

The St. Francis County Fair has been held every year for more than a century. The original fairgrounds included a racetrack. Children come looking for the midway, but parents come for the Kountry Kitchen. It began as a small building with a covered porch but was later expanded to an eating area with seating for at least 100. This photograph shows regular fair workers and board members, including Thomas Dodson (second from left), Elizabeth Burns (right, seated at table), and Mary Taylor (inside screened kitchen). The exhibit hall in the background has changed little. Money is currently being raised for a renovation to the Kountry Kitchen.

Three
AGRICULTURE

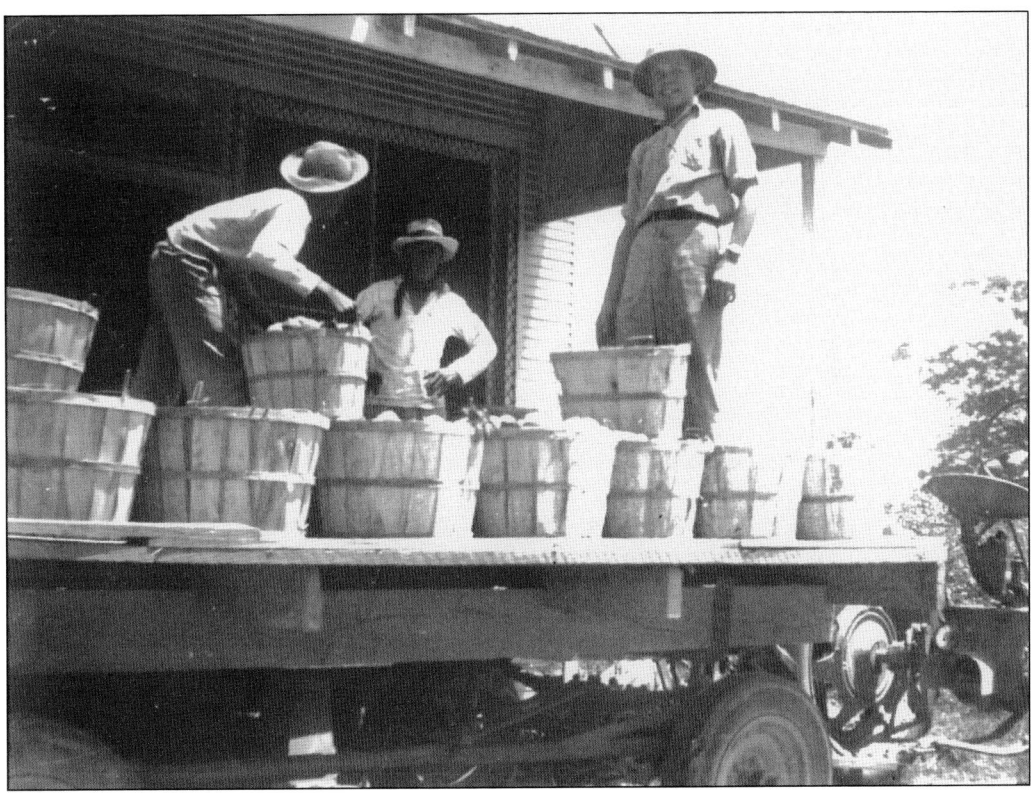

The Lindsey farm is shown during a peach harvest in the 1940s. Peaches have been as much a part of eastern Arkansas culture as apple pies have been to America. It is obviously summertime when the Worleys, Jarretts, and others open up the familiar peach stores. The one thing most missed by those who leave Forrest City is the sweet peach, which cannot be rivaled elsewhere. Today an annual peach pie cook-off is held at the St. Francis County Museum.

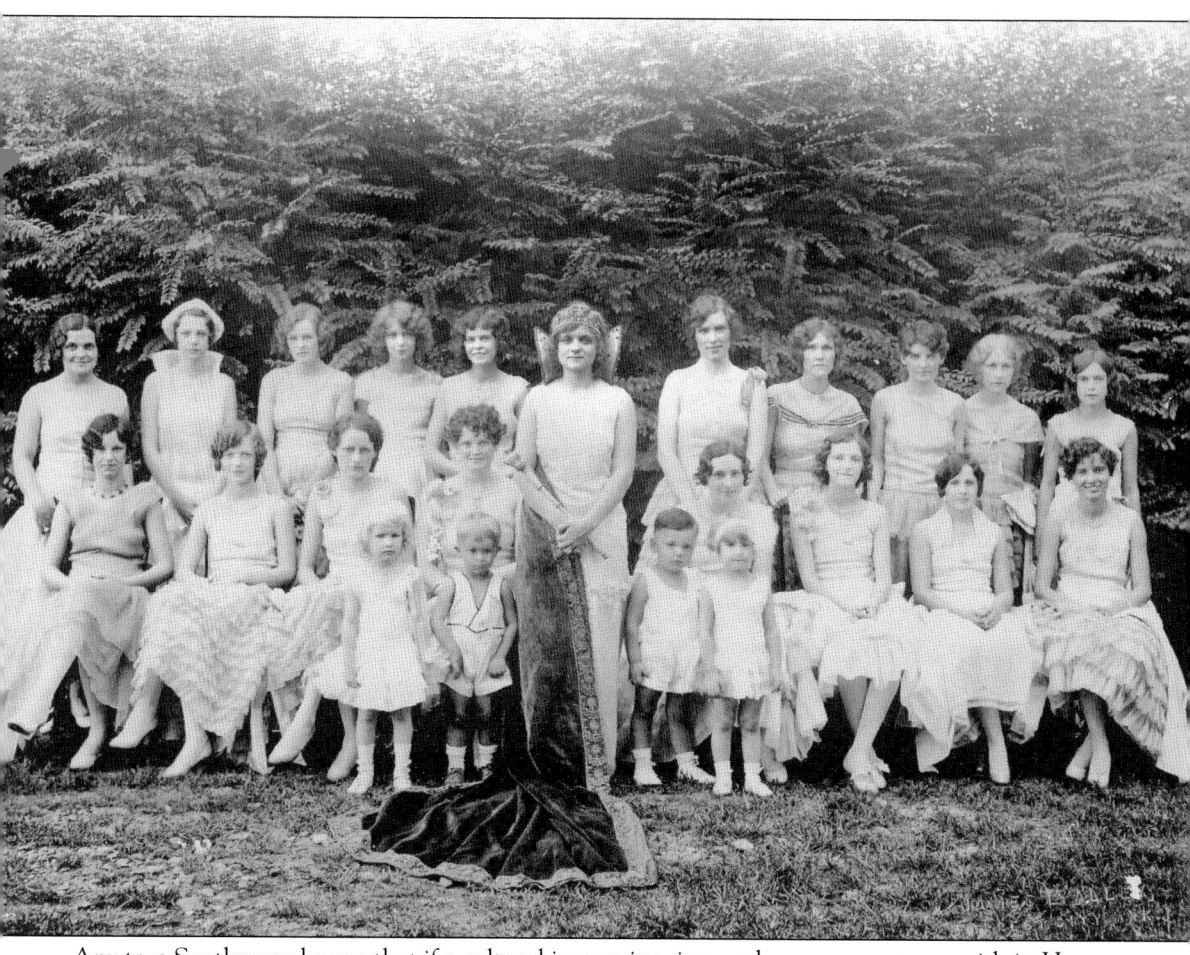
Any true Southerner knows that if a cultural icon exists, it must have a queen to go with it. Here Southern belles line up to compete for the title of Peach Queen in the 1930s.

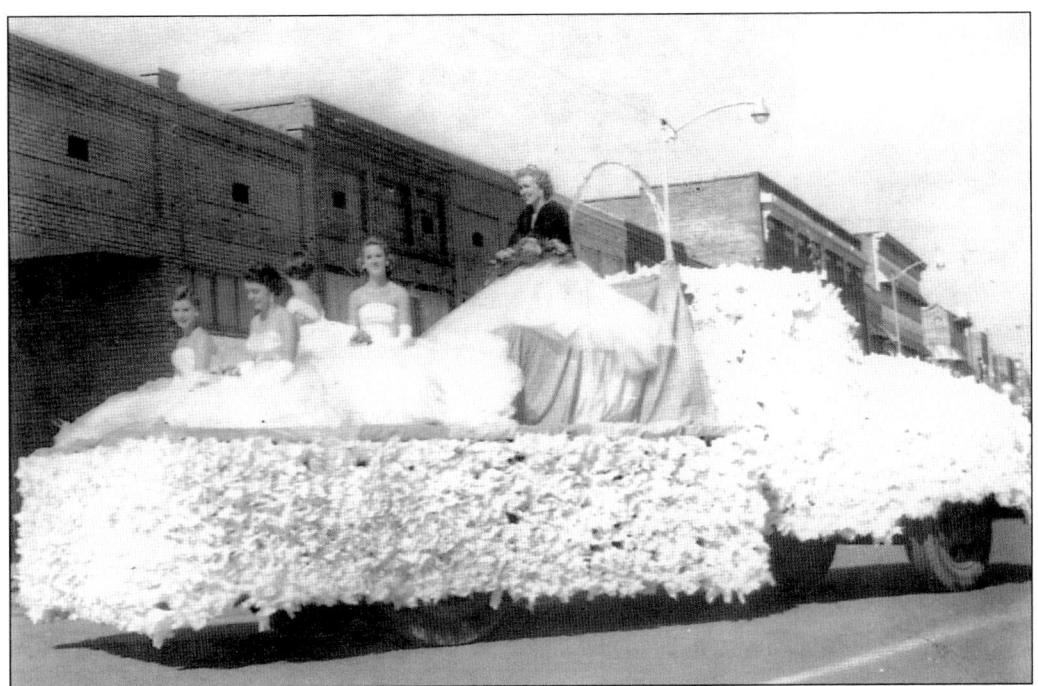
Any queen worth her scepter knows that royal duties include reining supreme on a float. This float is ruled by Tina McDaniel during the annual Peach Parade.

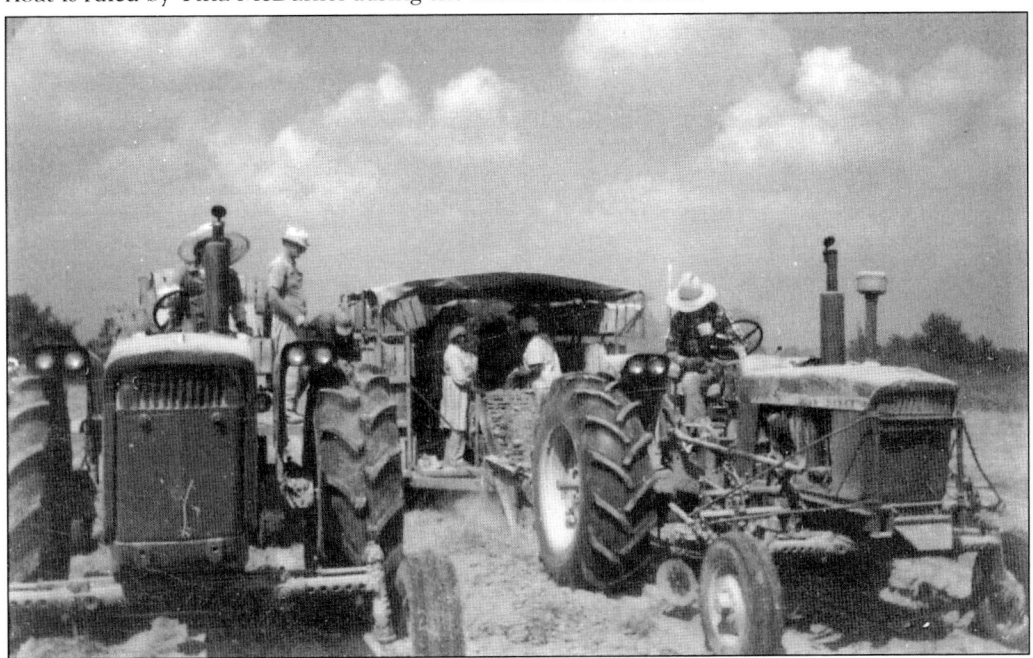
Sweet potatoes may not have a queen to go with them, but they nonetheless have been a mainstay of St. Francis County culture. The Dodsons have been known for decades for their sweet potato crop. Annie, her children Elizabeth, Newton, and Thomas, and their children worked the fragile potato beds and sold the harvest from truck beds and roadside stops. Thomas's son Tommy continues the tradition. If it can be made from sweet potatoes, the Dodson family knows the recipe.

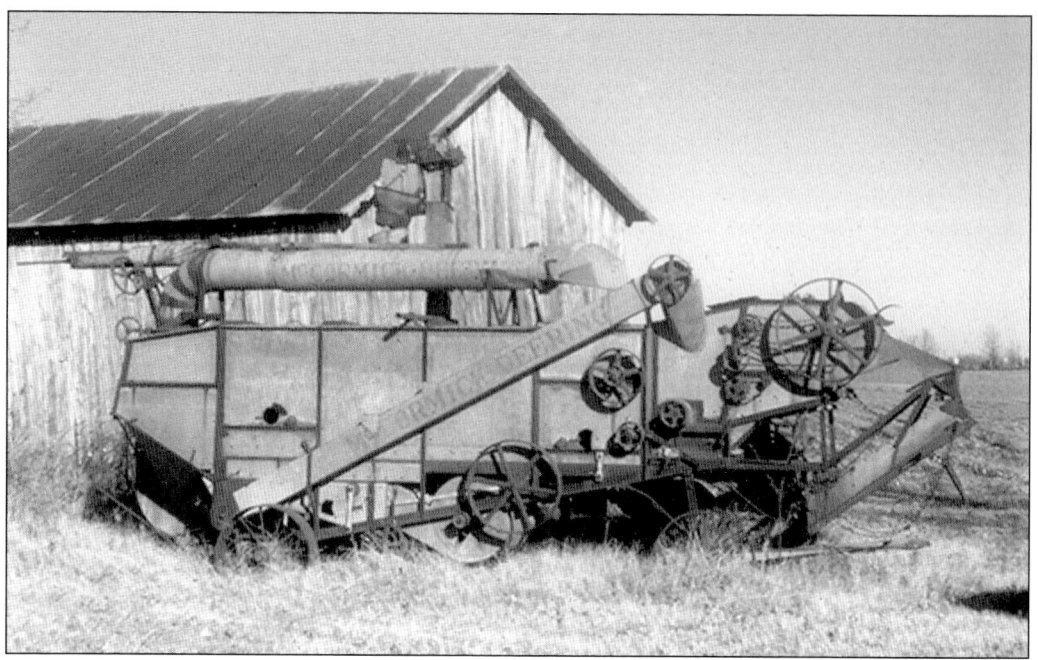

The thresher was set up in an inactive place in the field. The rice was shocked in the old-fashioned way and brought to the thresher, which separated the grain from the rest of the plant. The Abe Burns farm in Palestine used this thresher for its first rice crop. The next year, the Burns brothers bought a self-propelled combine to expand rice production. Rice performs very well in the flatlands of the county.

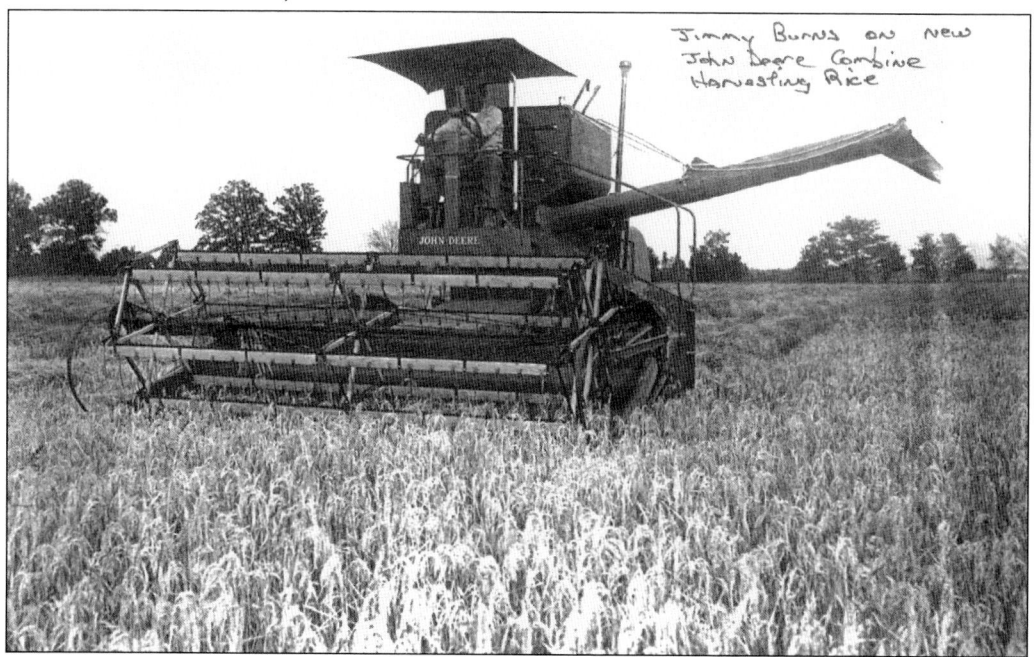

Jimmy Burns sits on the first self-propelled combine owned by his family. While the stationary thresher required a full crew, one person could harvest an entire crop on this new, self-propelled combine.

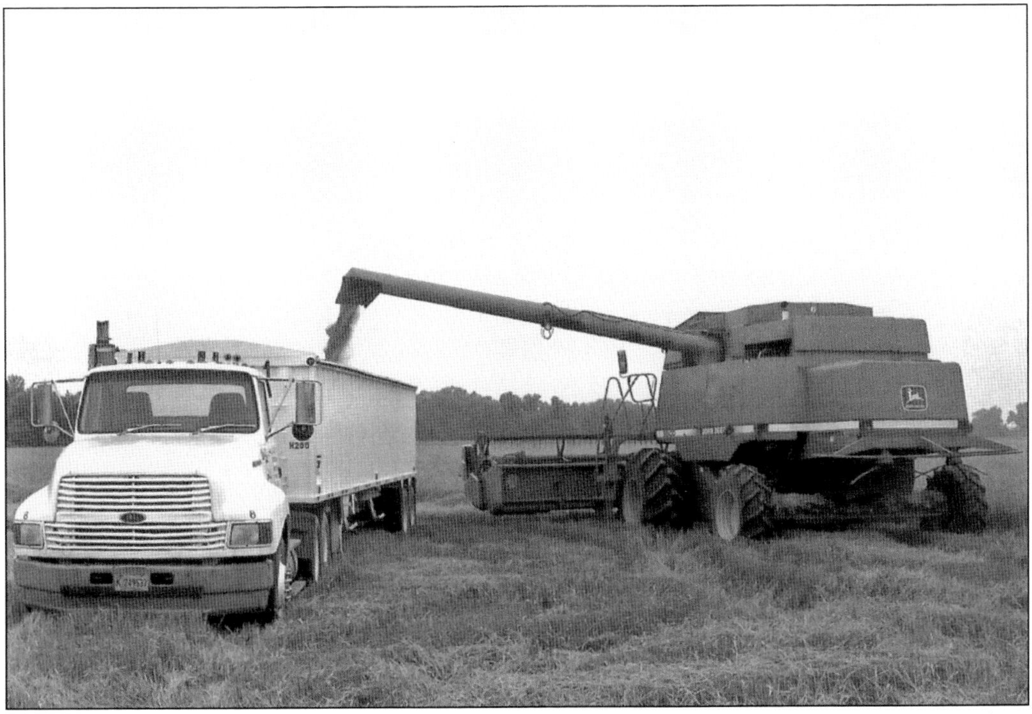

Wheat in this area is generally used to make cookies. "Lite bread" is generally known as white sandwich bread and rolls, while "heavy bread" refers to corn bread.

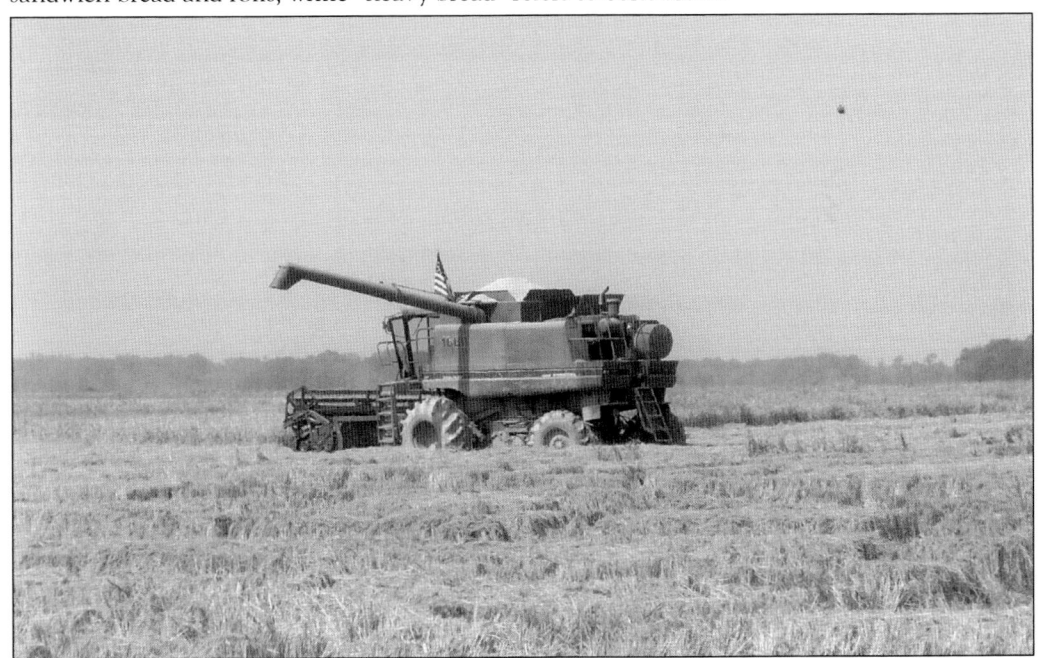

Chad McLain's combine, bearing a patriotic tribute, comes to a rest in Wheatley. Two-way communication, cell phones, and GPS devices, as well as laser surveying systems, save tremendous amounts of labor and time in the field. Fields that would have taken three or four men a day to survey can now be completed in an hour by one man with a laser surveying rig.

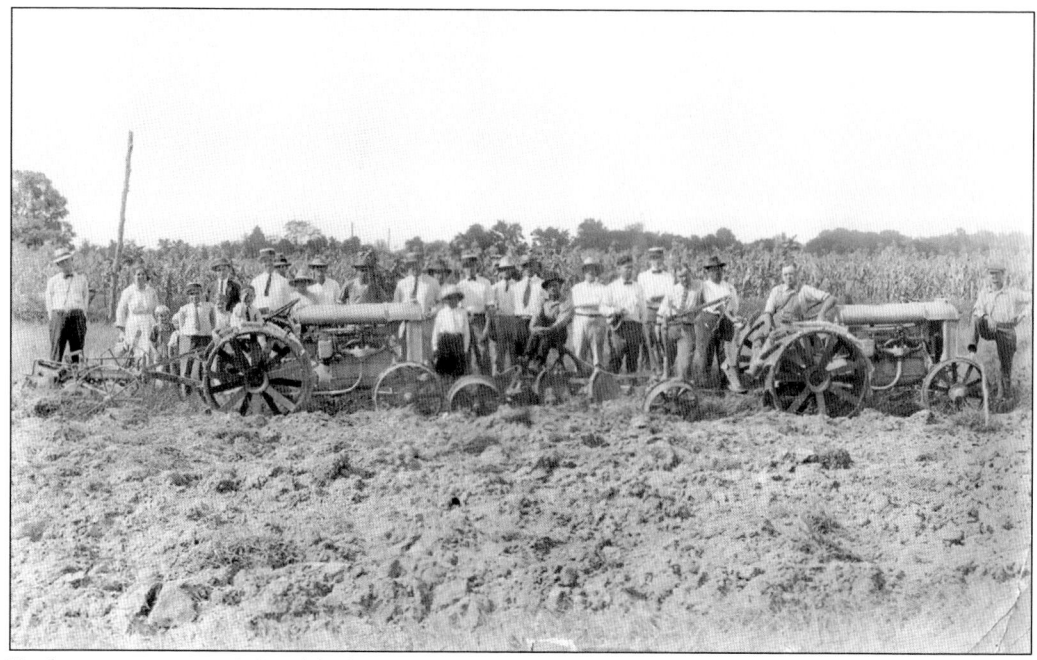

Fordson tractors are exhibited for farmers and their families. Dealers often held on-site demonstrations to market their equipment. Farmers were sometimes wary of modern equipment and often preferred their tried-and-true horses and mules. Demonstrations like this gradually won over those who were hesitant to change.

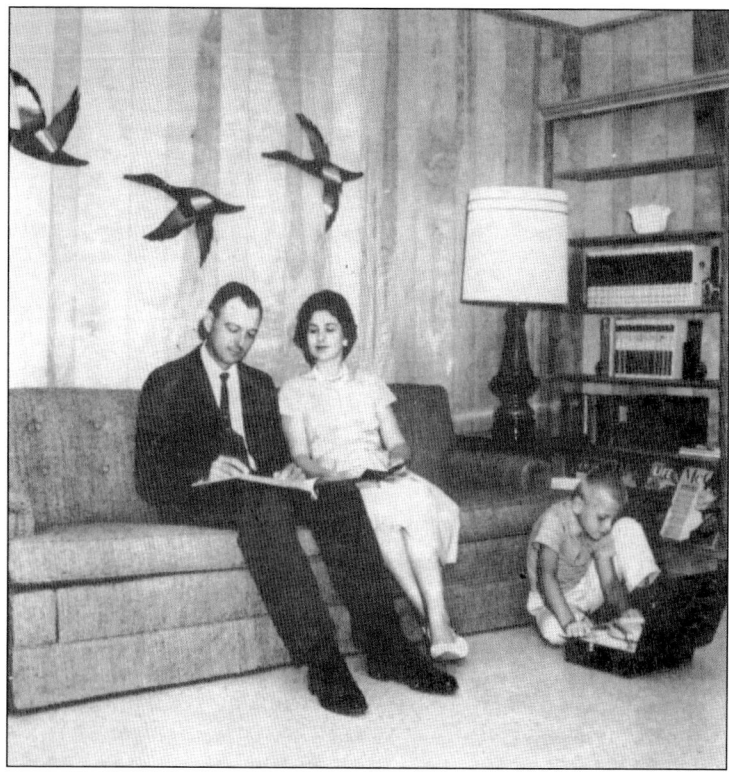

From left to right, Gene, Mildred, and Terry McGraw are pictured in their home for being Farm Family of the Year. Agriculture is the backbone of eastern Arkansas, and a different family is honored each year for continuing that culture. Other winners throughout the years have included the Brent Howton, Ron Hall, and Henry Dale Jayroe families.

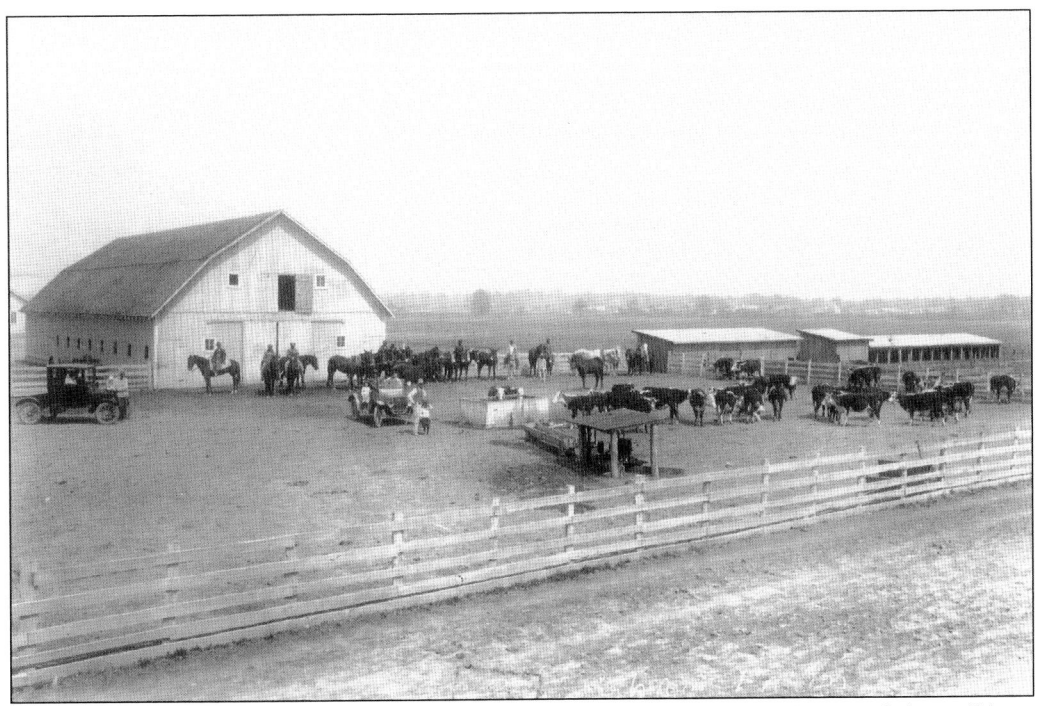

This large barn and farmyard represent another change. The size of the barn and the well-kept fences, along with the presence of more than one vehicle, give us a glimpse into the kind of profit the farmer made.

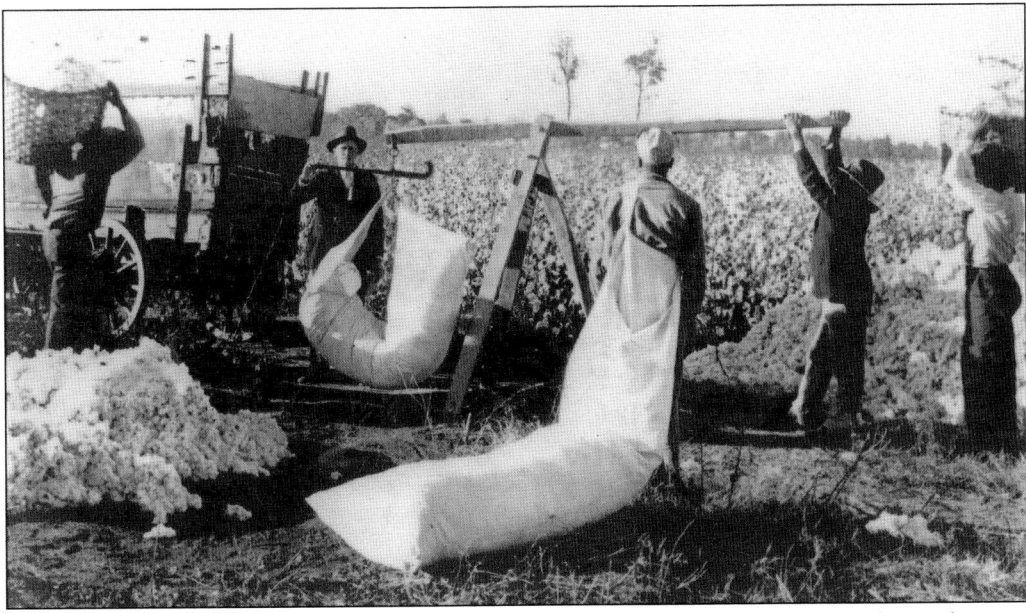

Cotton was king for most of the South's history. It still is, but a few things have changed. Many over the age of 50 vividly remember picking and chopping cotton, and even waiting to return to school until the harvest was finished in the fall. Babies were carried on the tails of the cotton sacks being dragged through the fields, and toddlers were given feed sacks to fill with cotton as soon as they were old enough to walk. Here a harvest is occurring in the 1930s.

PBW-1

PINK BOLLWORM QUARANTINE STALK DESTRUCTION

COTTON STALKS THRUOUT THE STATE MUST BE DESTROYED BY APRIL 15

The owners of the land on which the cotton is grown, the operators, and the tenants are jointly and severally responsible for compliance with stalk destruction.

Deadline for Stalk Destruction. All cotton fields must be treated in a manner that will bury or destroy all cotton bolls and locks by April 15.

Suggested Methods for Destroying Stalks

Method 1. By cutting, shredding or discing down all stalks followed by flat breaking, or by bedding in such a manner that all bolls and locks will be deeply buried.

Method 2. Heavy Grazing: All bolls and locks must be consumed by livestock. (The cotton field should be fenced away from any other acreage which might furnish grazing, and there should be at least one cow per acre.)

Method 3. Mechanical Stripper Harvesting: A thorough job of stripping must be done and all green-boll dumps must be deeply buried or otherwise thoroughly destroyed.

Any of these methods should be effective in destroying or burying all bolls and locks. However, if because of careless handling, nature of the soil, weather conditions, or for any other reason the bolls and locks are not satisfactorily buried or destroyed, additional means must be used until all bolls and locks are buried or destroyed, and this must be completed by April 15. Plant Board will inspect fields, either as soon as possible after being notified of completion, or soon after.

Seed Cotton Storage. All seed cotton storage areas including handling and harvesting equipment must be cleaned of all bolls and locks and these bolls and locks must be treated in a manner that will either bury or destroy them. All carry-over seed cotton must be fumigated under the supervision of the Plant Board or U.S.D.A.

Should any fields, storage areas, handling or harvesting equipment be found not in compliance by the April 15 deadline, the Chief Inspector may cause the destruction of all bolls and locks of cotton, the expense thereof to be charged against the owner, custodian, or occupant, as provided by law. In addition the Plant Board will each year list any owners, operators, or tenants who have failed to meet the stalk destruction or other requirements thru reasons other than extreme hardship, and at the beginning of the ginning season will send such list to all gins. Ginners are prohibited from ginning cotton for persons whose names appear on said lists, until said persons present to the ginner a written release from the Plant Board or USDA to be given only after adequate assurance has been given by said persons to the Board that the Board's regulations will thereafter be complied with. Ginning for said persons without release is grounds for cancellation of gin's dealer-carrier permit by USDA or Plant Board.

PURPOSE OF THE STALK DESTRUCTION REGULATIONS

The pink bollworm overwinters in cottonseeds, both seeds saved for planting or feeding, and seeds in bolls and locks left in the field after picking. If pink bollworms are present in a field, many or even all worms will be destroyed by burying the stalks—including all bolls and locks that are lying on the ground—and the deeper the better. Growers are urged to pick fields out just as soon and clean as possible, and destroy the stalks immediately thereafter. Do not put off destroying the stalks until just before the April 15 deadline. Early stalk destruction not only gives a better kill of pink bollworms, but will also aid in other insect control.

Copies of this notice can be had from your County Agent.

IMPORTANT: All gins in the state will close February 5. IT IS UNLAWFUL TO HOLD UNTREATED SEED COTTON AFTER FEBRUARY 5, EITHER ON FARMS OR AT GINS.

OKRA — Commercial plantings of okra is placed in the same category as cotton with regard to stalk destruction and plowing under the residue.

State Plant Board in Cooperation with U. S. Department of Agriculture

One Delta town has a statue dedicated to the boll weevil, but the authors thought older residents might enjoy a different kind of reminder of the problems that came with cotton. This notification described the steps that had to be taken after the harvest to eradicate the pink bollworm. The notice was posted at gins, which had to get rid of all their trash before a certain inspection date. Farmers also had to cut stalks to keep the insects from over-wintering in the gin trash and stalks, which provided an excellent habitat for the devastating creatures.

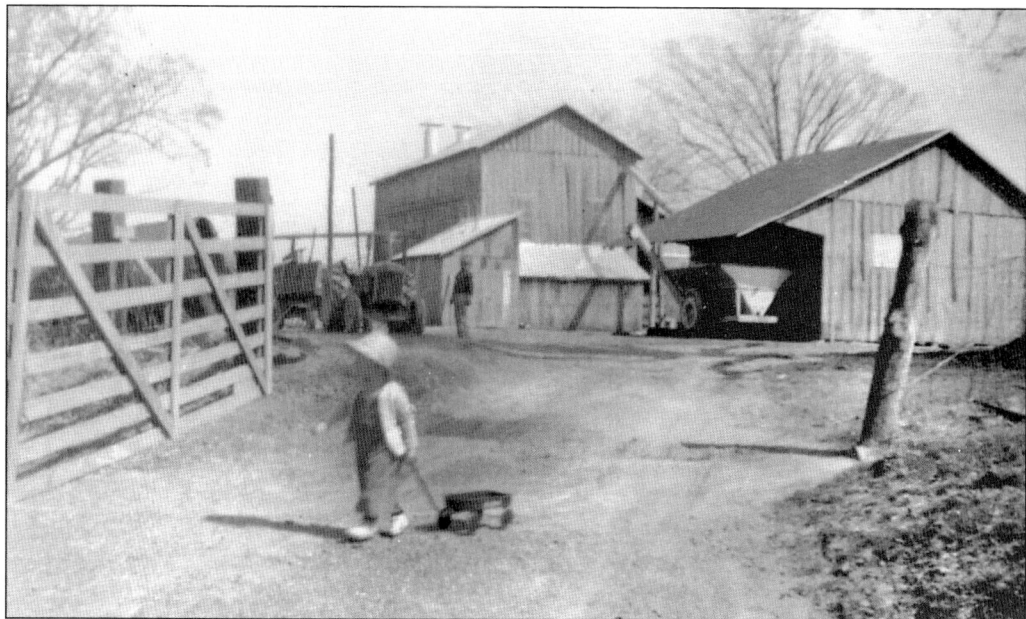

Farm life was definitely a family affair. Children grew up learning to operate equipment, chop cotton, and read the signs of a crop. Here a young David Burns plays with his little red wagon in front of the gin. The Burns Gin was a landmark for years, as it stood next to the Bankhead Highway (Highway 70) before the road was rerouted. It was replaced with a metal building, and the gin is now mostly used for farm storage.

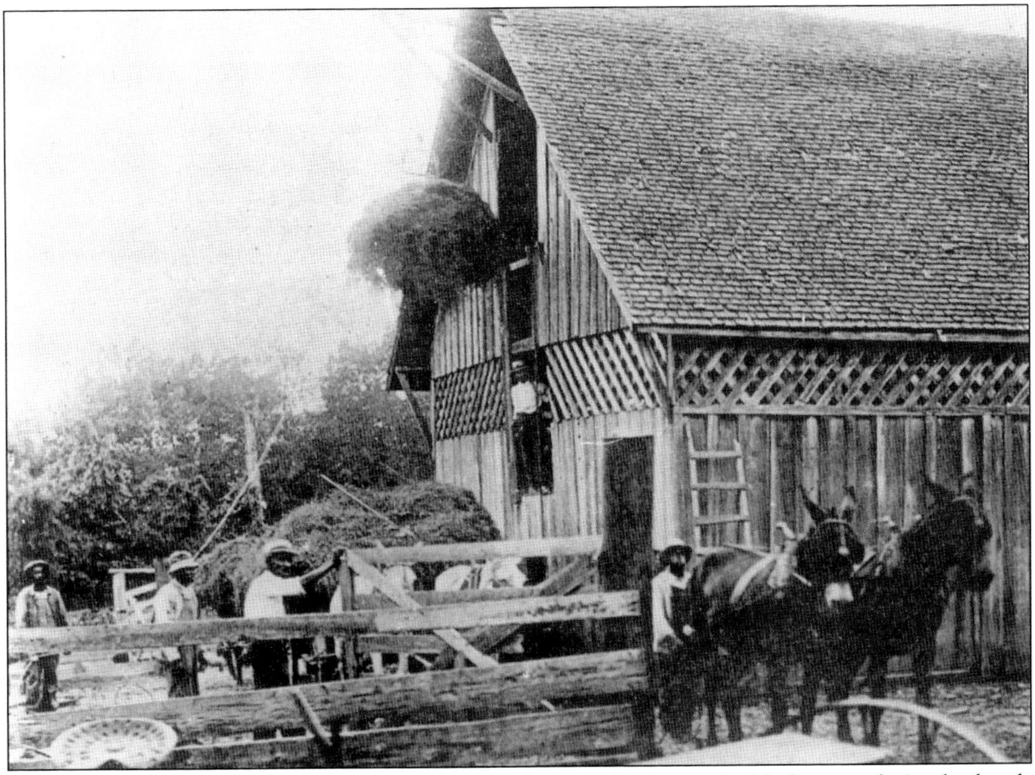

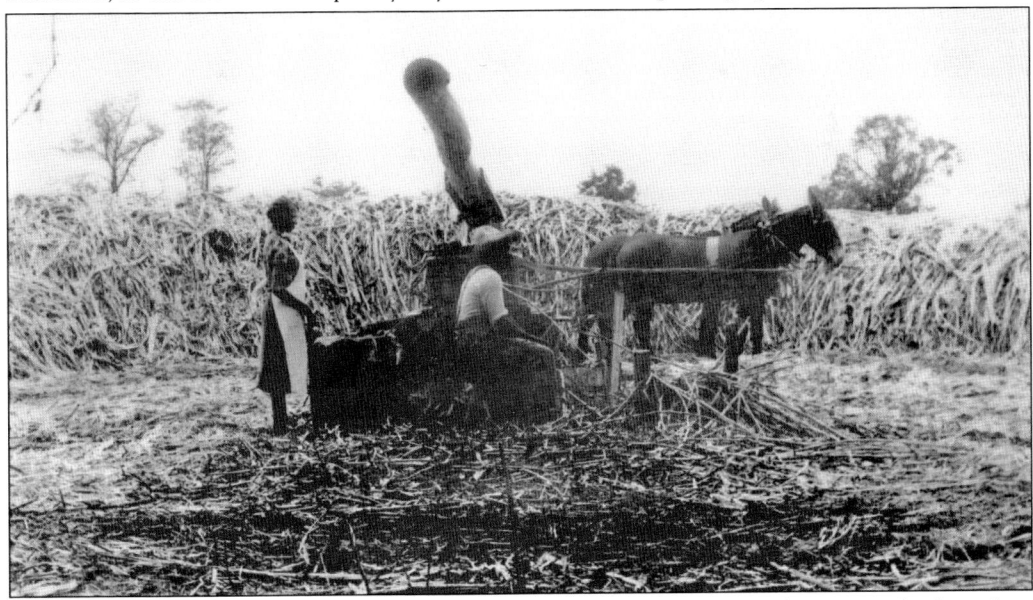

As the swamps and forests were cleared, livestock were able to profitably be raised. As the herds increased, so did the need for quality hay. These farmers are putting up hay for the winter.

Sorghum is made into molasses by crushing the cane and collecting the juice, which is then cooked off. It was a staple in everyone's pantry in the early 20th century. The extended part of the pole, seen in the middle of the photograph, is a counterweight used to offset the pulling of the mules.

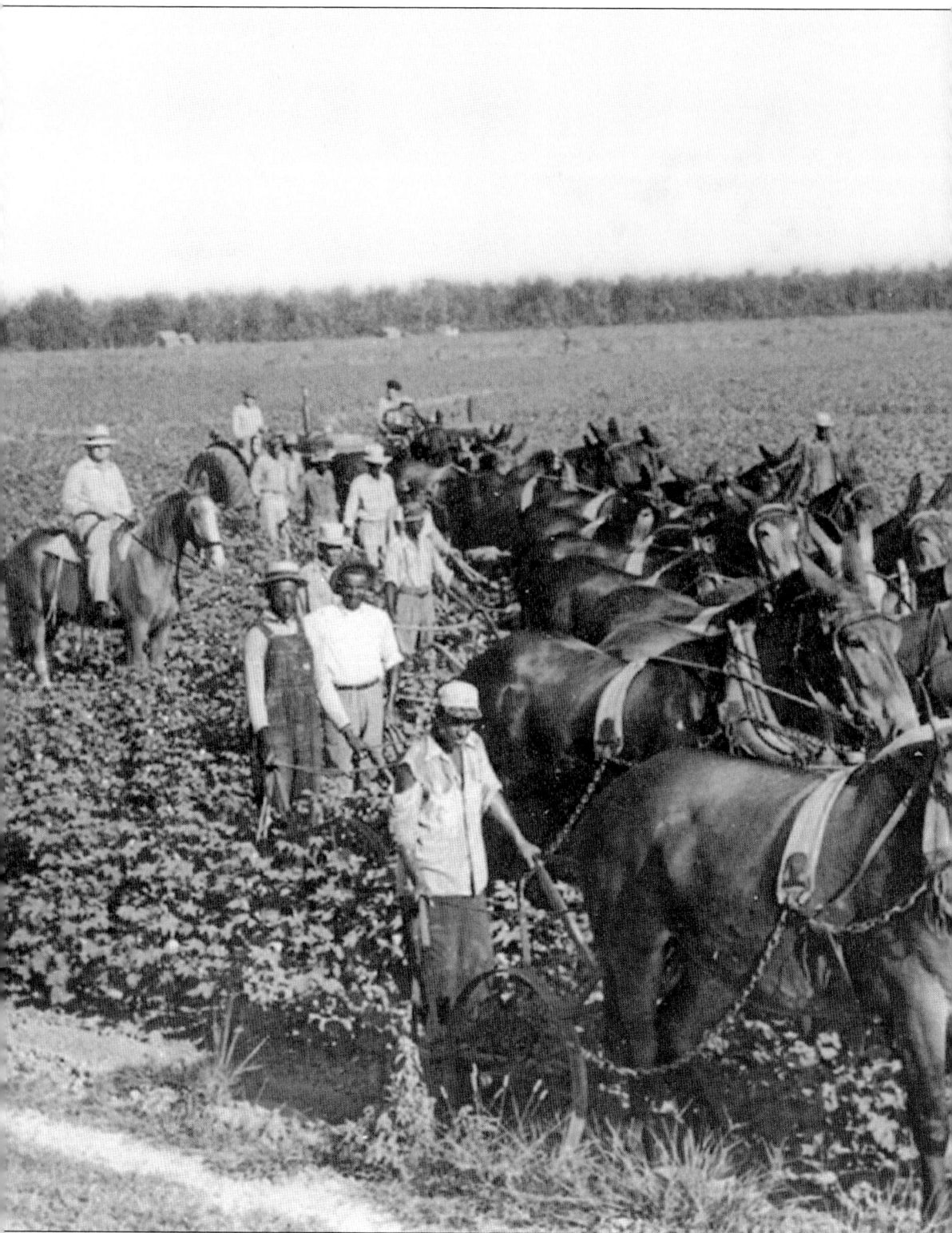

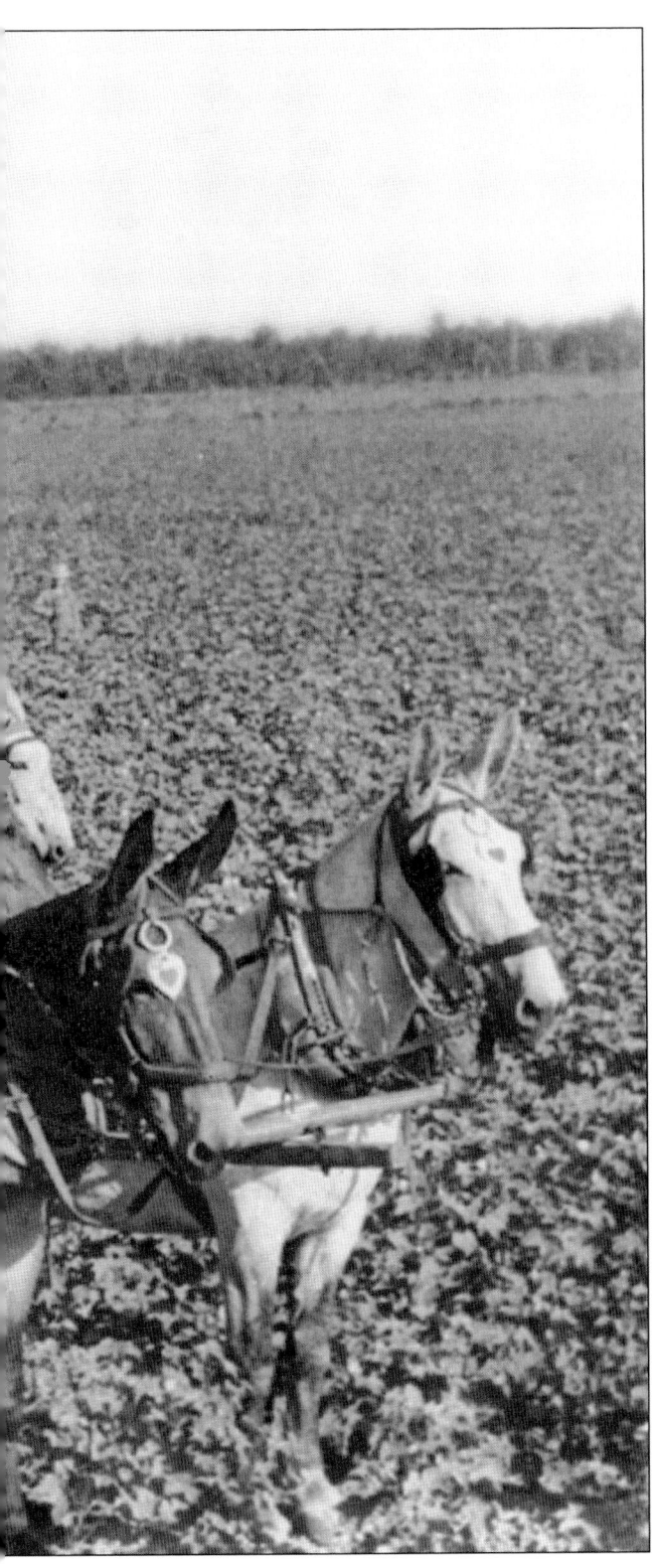

This photograph represents a blending of older and more modern methods. Farm folks call this last plowing for weeds "laying the cotton by." The man sitting on the horse is normally called a rider—either the plantation owner or supervisor. In recent years, chemicals, ever-increasing machine size, and emerging technologies have gradually replaced most of the farm workers and all of the horses. Genetically engineered seed has changed the face of current cotton farming.

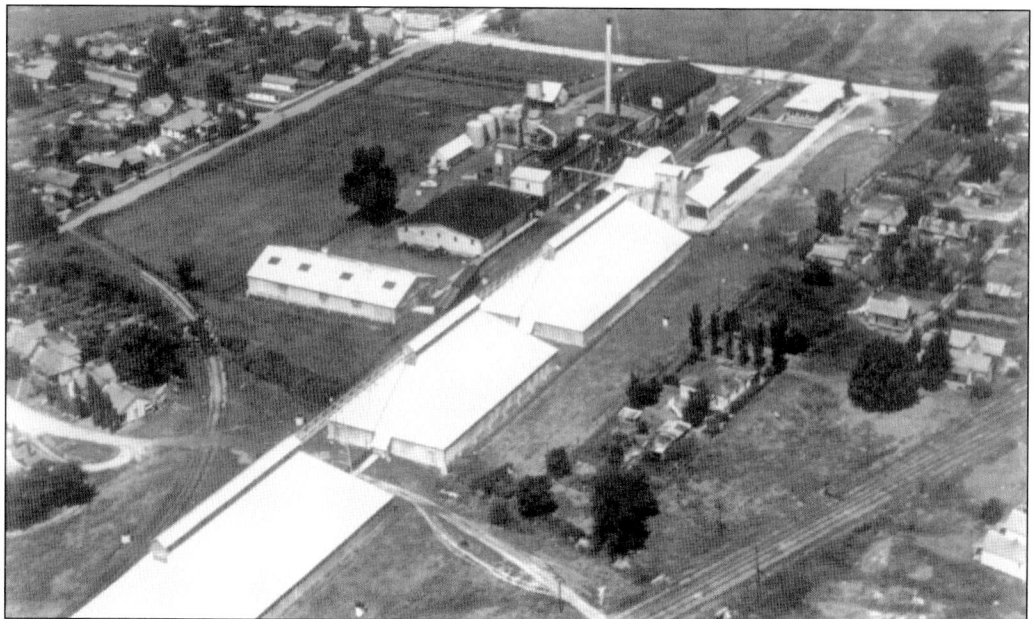

The cotton oil mill at Forrest City, pictured several decades ago, is still in operation today. Here the cotton seed is pressed, expelling oil.

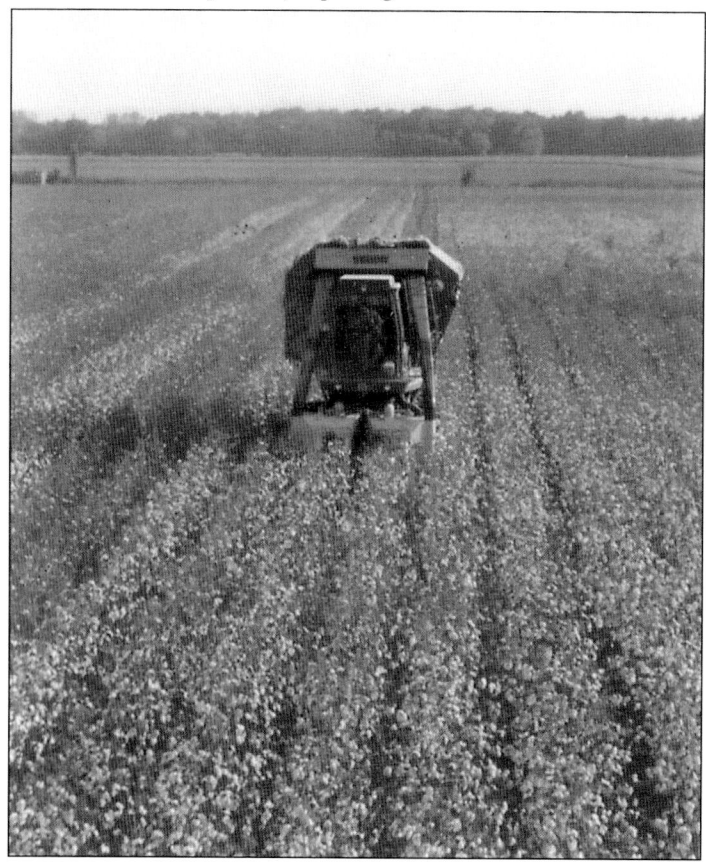

The Whittenton farm in the Yocona (pronounced "yock'nee") community is still one of the largest cotton producers in Arkansas. This series of aerial photographs was taken during picking time around 1993.

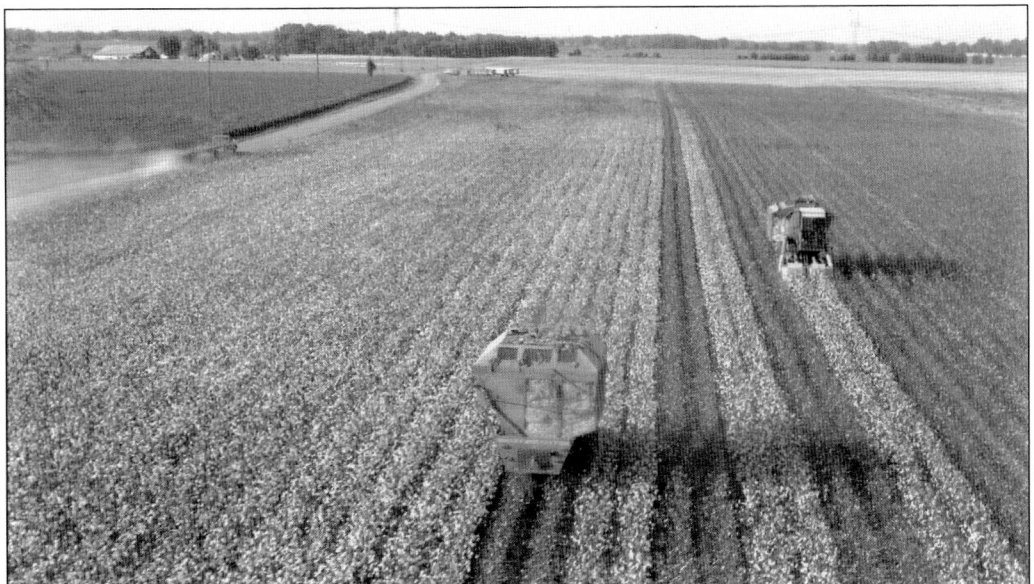

Picking cotton is no small job, with the pickers at work from dawn to dusk and often longer. These two laborers operate in tandem to get the harvest in.

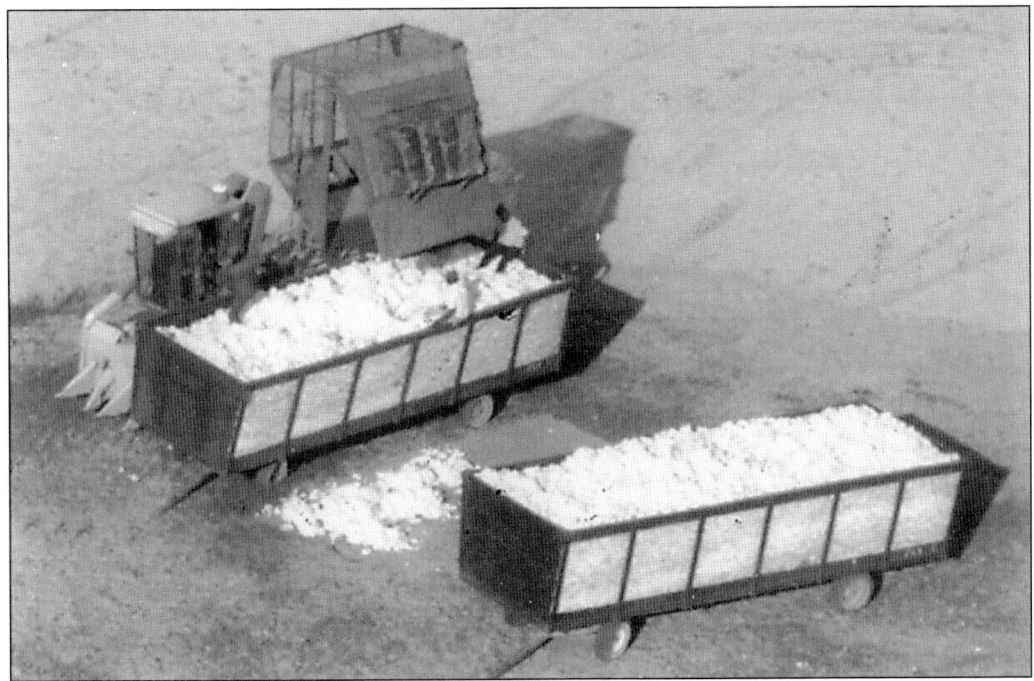

This overhead view demonstrates the next phase of the harvest: transferring from picker to cotton trailer. Notice the man, or tromper, in the trailer. His job was to "tromp" the cotton down to enable more compression in each trailer. In the next few years, there will be a revolutionary change in the way cotton is ginned. Last season, with much secrecy, a new picker was tested in eastern Arkansas that will produce tight, round bales in the cotton field through much the same process as hay baling. These new bales are automatically wrapped, allowing for much less waste. Currently, the bales lose cotton every time they are moved.

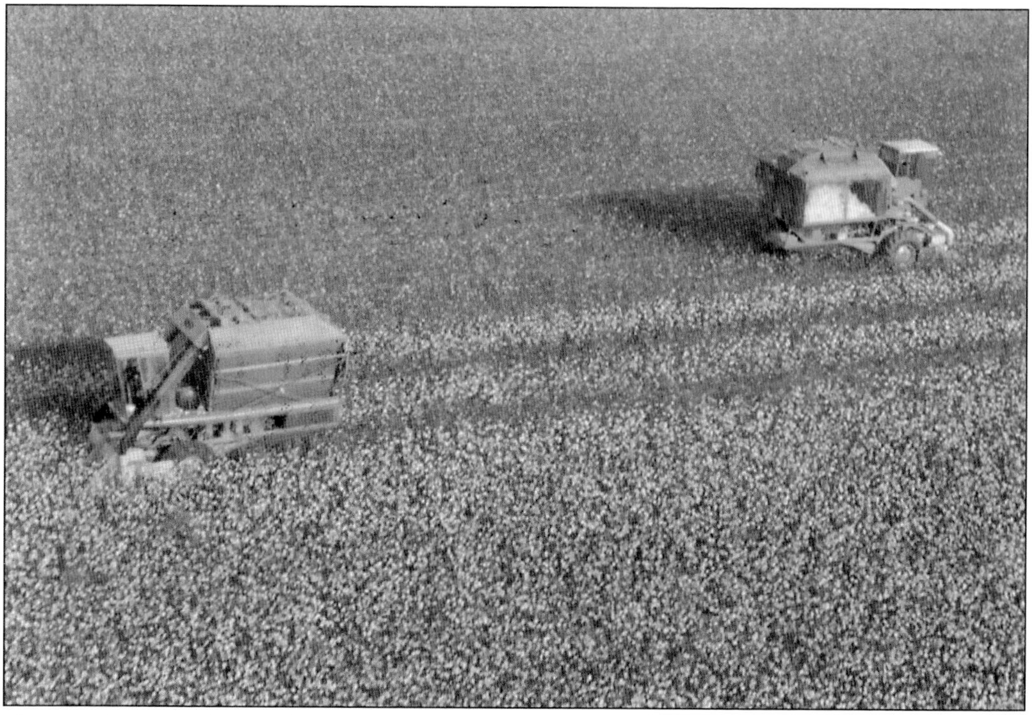

Cotton pickers work together to stack up the rows on the Whittenton farm about 1993. The cotton is piling up in the picker on the right side.

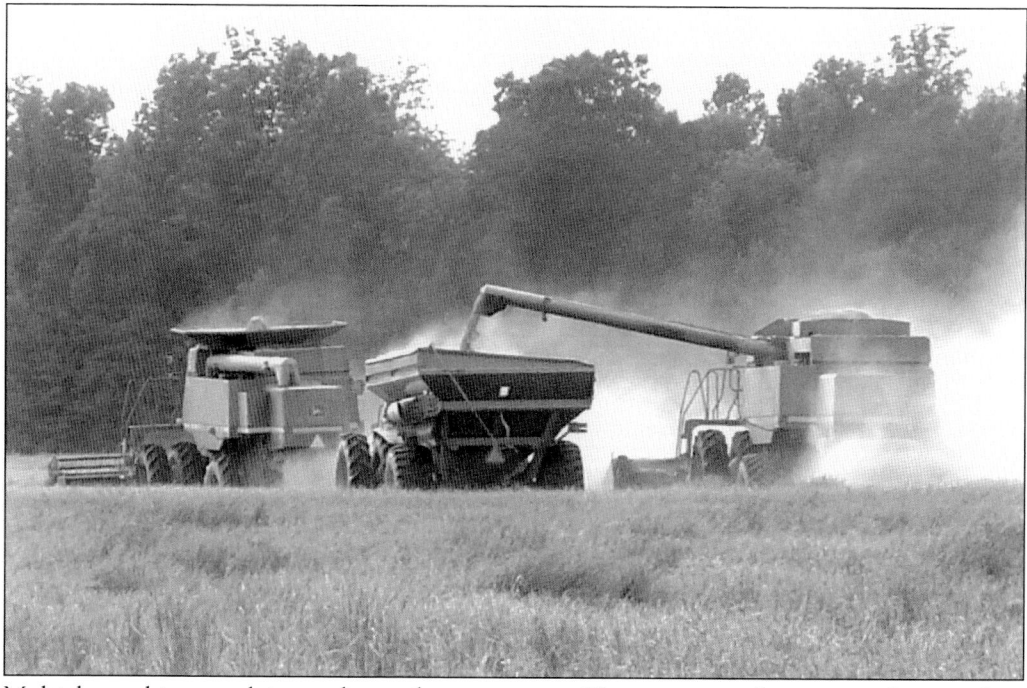

Multiple machines work in tandem to harvest a crop. The processes of cutting with more than one machine and carrying grain to storage require carefully choreographed dances. This would not be possible without the technological advances of the last decade or two.

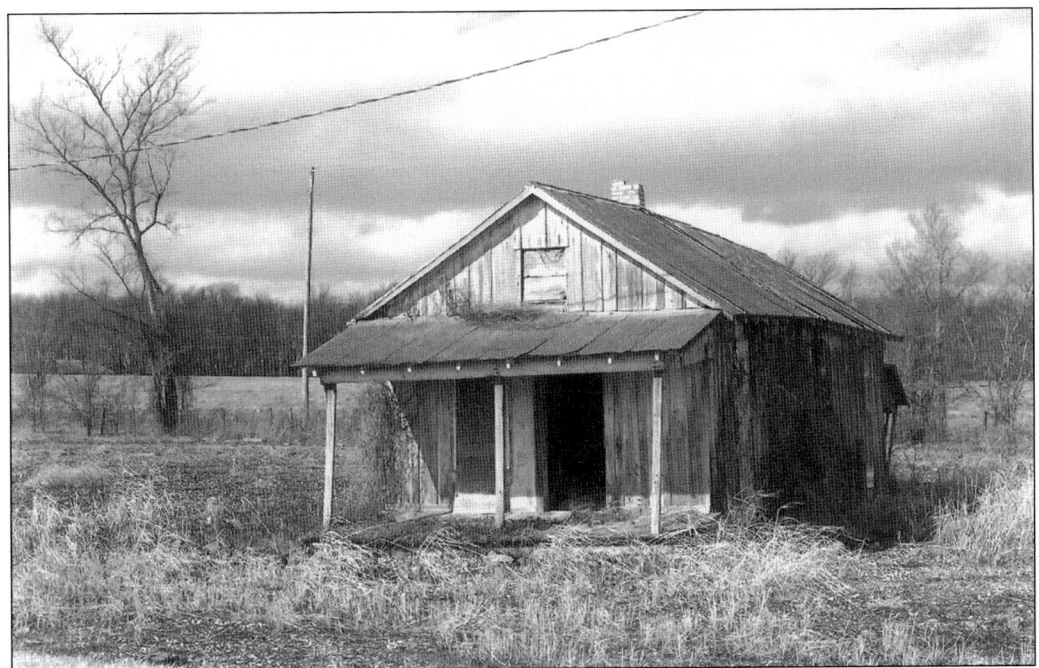

On the way from Forrest City to Hughes, in the east side of the county, is a cluster of old tenant farmhouses. Some are in good shape, while others are in need of restoration. These homes remind one of the hardships faced by tenant farmers on a daily basis. Today many are only standing because they serve as billboards advertising hunting tours and guides.

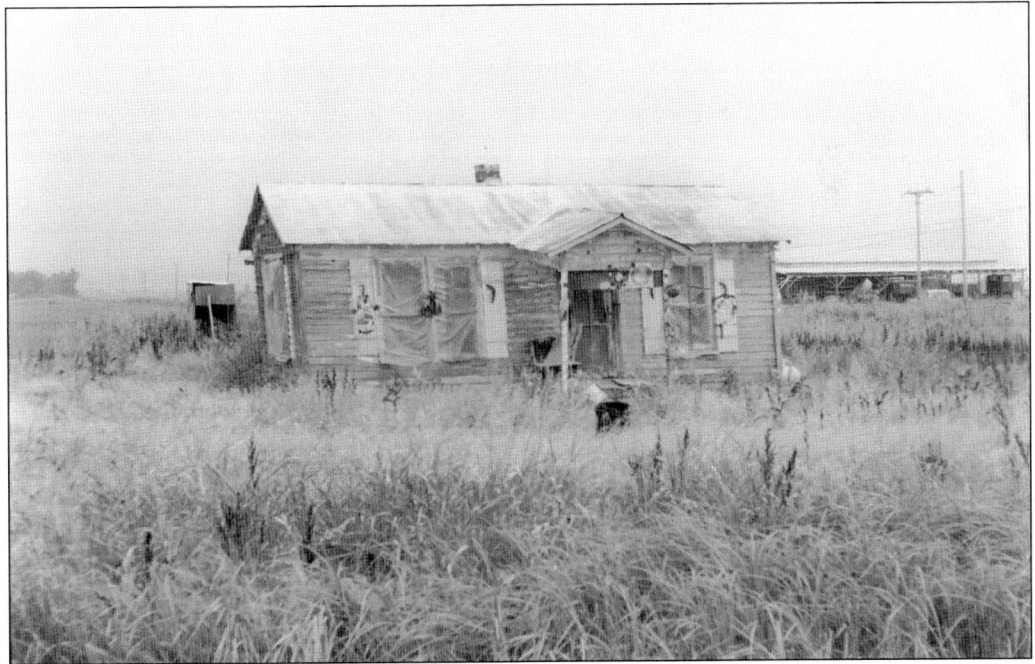

At the time of this 1970s photograph, a family still inhabited the little house. Farm workers often lived in rough conditions. Look closely at the plastic on the windows, which was used to keep out drafts.

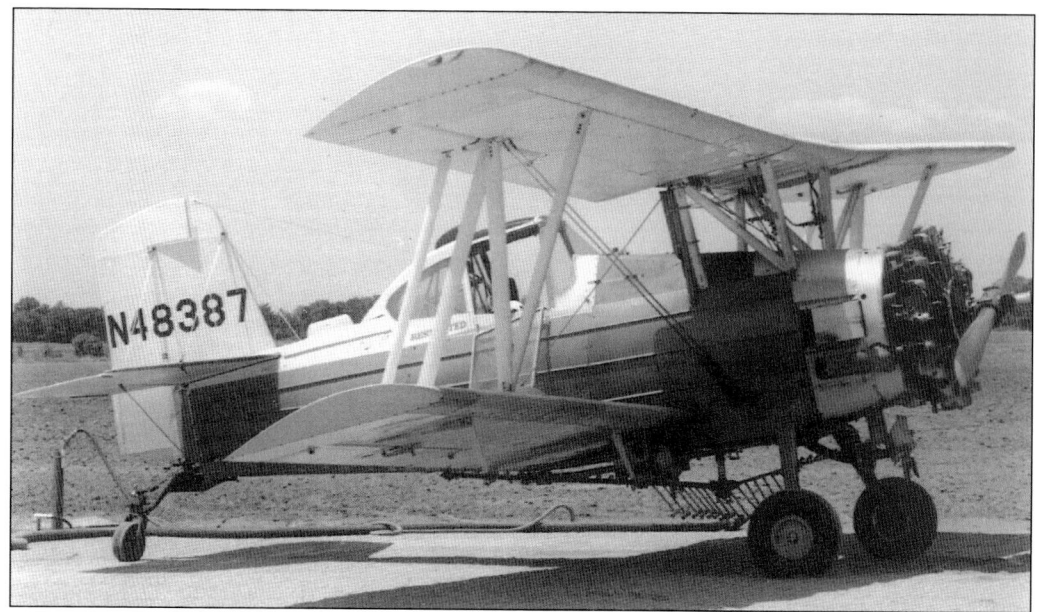

The N48387 is a 1976 model Ag-Cat aerial applicator, or crop duster. Jerald Burns purchased it from the Paul van Houten estate near Stuttgart a few days before Christmas 1985 in order to start Burns Aircraft. Jerald had flown two seasons for the Hutcherson Flying Service. Today almost all aerial applicators are turbine aircraft. Many farmers opt for ground spray rigs instead. Though more efficient, the aerial rigs make operating a small service almost impossible. The terrorist attacks of September 11, 2001, changed the crop-dusting industry perhaps more than any other. People became nervous about the possibility of a hijacked duster being used for biological warfare. The possibility of this occurrence affected standard practice, regulations, and insurance.

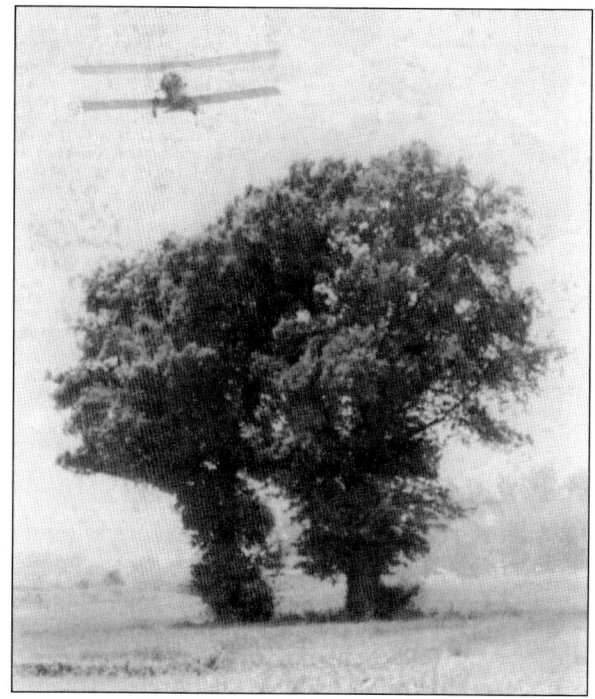

Jerald Burns fertilizes rice on the Dodson farm using the N48387 in the late 1980s. This lot lay adjacent to Highway 70 and almost at the end of the Dodson Field airstrip. Jerald's mother and uncles used the strip while piloting their L2B Taylorcraft.

Elizabeth Dodson Burns had three dreams: to have children, to learn ceramics, and to fly. She was able to fulfill each in her lifetime. Here she is shown with the L2B she shared with her brothers.

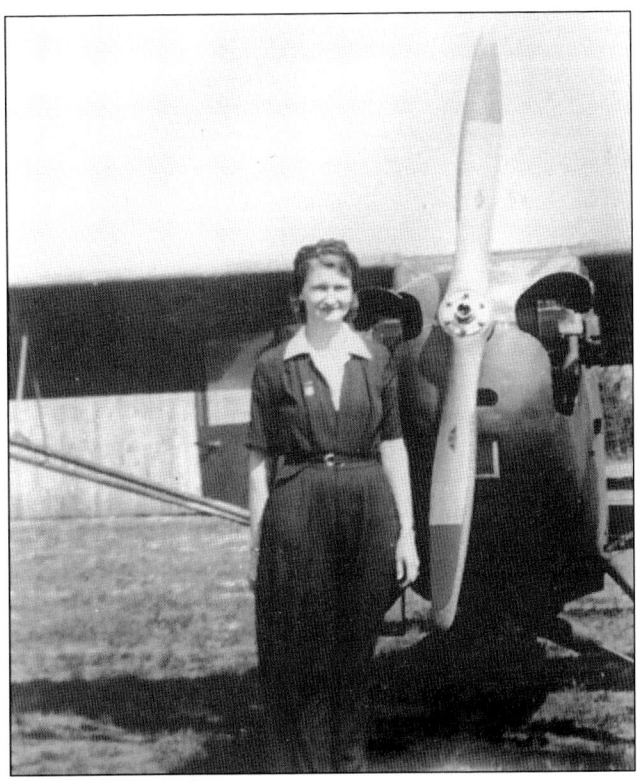

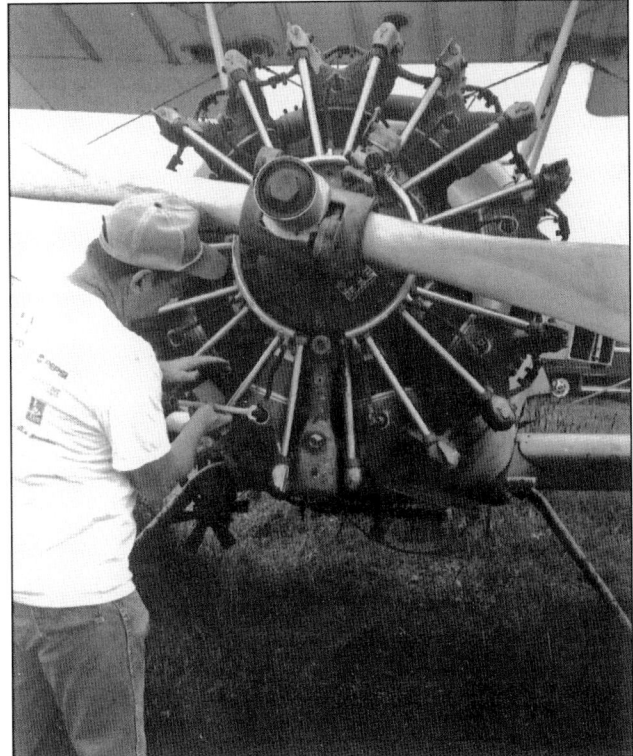

Before the turbine engine became popular for its speed and power, the crop dusters' old, slow Pratt and Whitney engines cranked out hour after hour of flying time. Many pilots carried a special fondness for these round engines, especially if they had experience working on World War II airplanes.

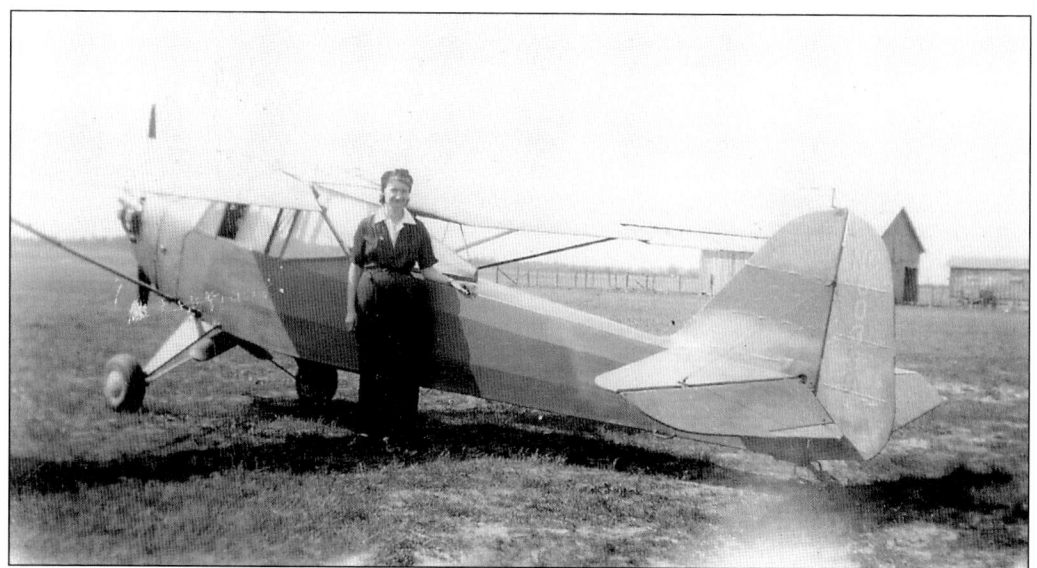

Elizabeth Dodson Burns poses here with the L2B. While she was in her 80s, one of the surefire ways to get her to smile was to ask about her time flying. One of her fondest stories was when she would tie on a bright red scarf and buzz a team of mules to scare them. Since her brother Newton had bright red hair, most people assumed it was him flying. Who would have suspected such an innocent woman? Elizabeth and her brothers sold the airplane after they each settled down and started families.

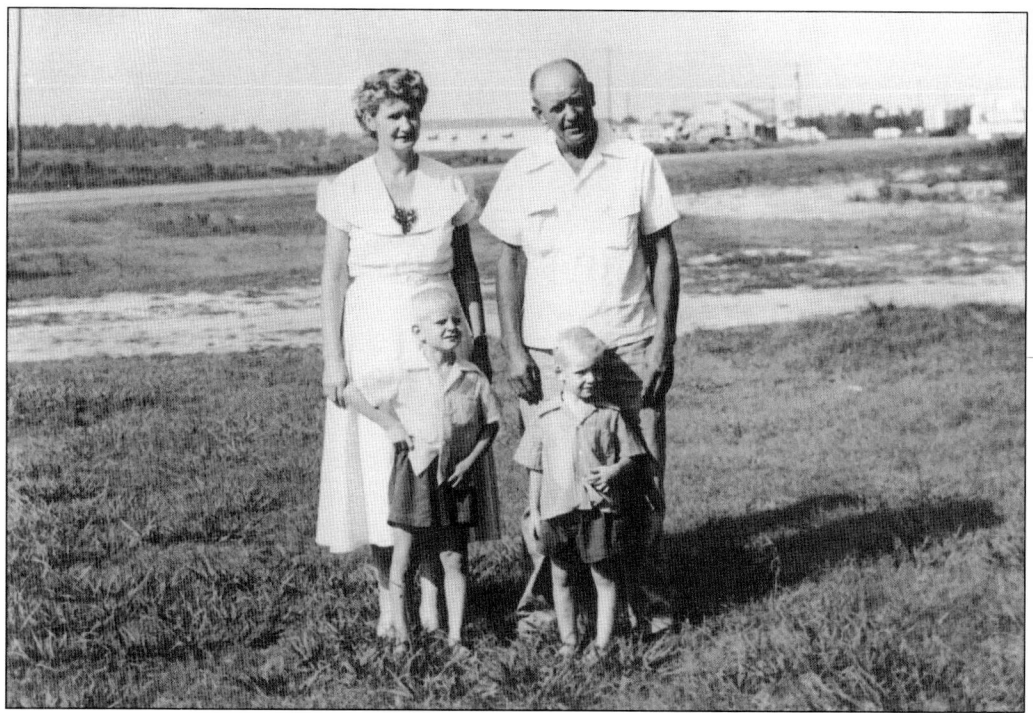

Elizabeth and Abe pose with their young sons David (left) and Jerald for a family portrait on the Dodson farm around 1953. In the background, across from Highway 70, is the Fifth Wheel Hotel and Restaurant.

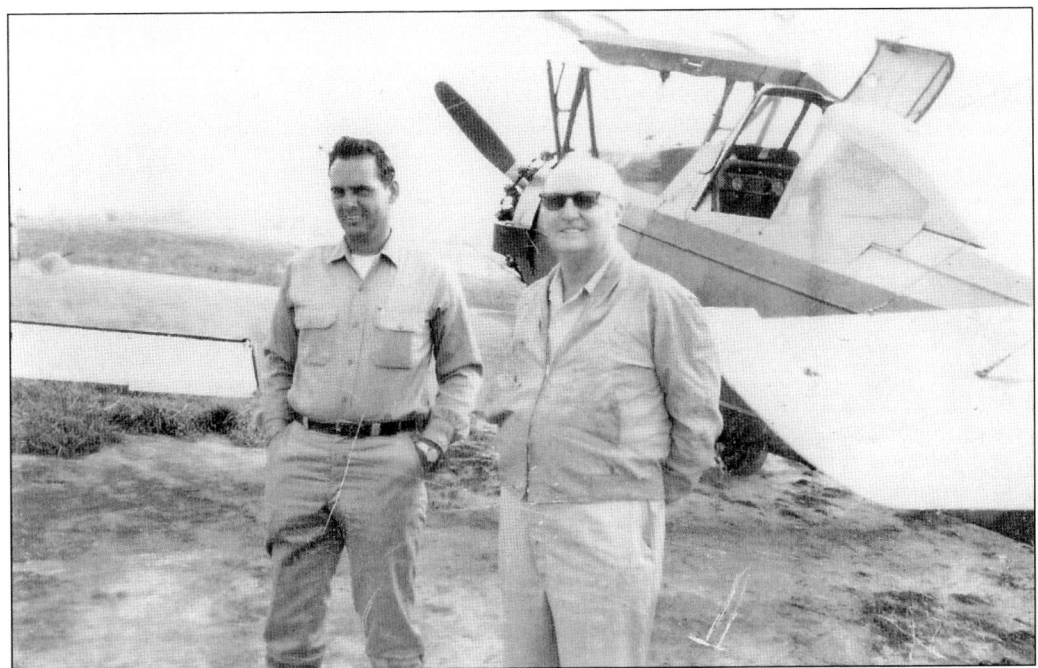

Jesse Casey (left) and George Hutcherson stand in front of an older model Ag-Cat duster. One of the first crop dusters in the area, Hutcherson founded the Hutcherson Flying Service. The company was later based at the Forrest City Municipal Airport. Today the Delta Regional Airport Authority is completing planning to construct a larger regional airport around Colt.

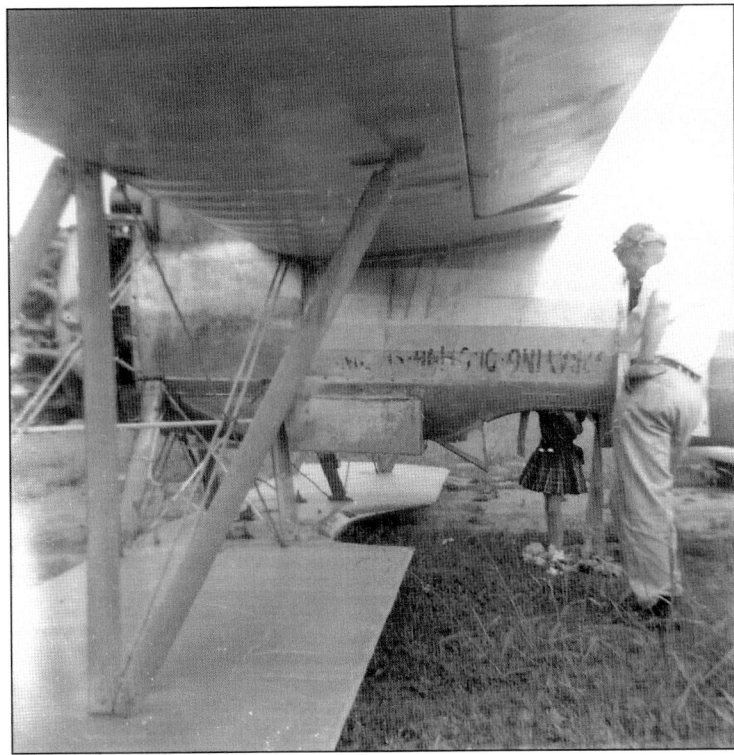

George Hutcherson's daughter Belinda checks out the upside-down Stearman duster after it has collided with the ground. The biggest danger to a crop-dusting pilot would be hitting power lines or coming too low to the ground.

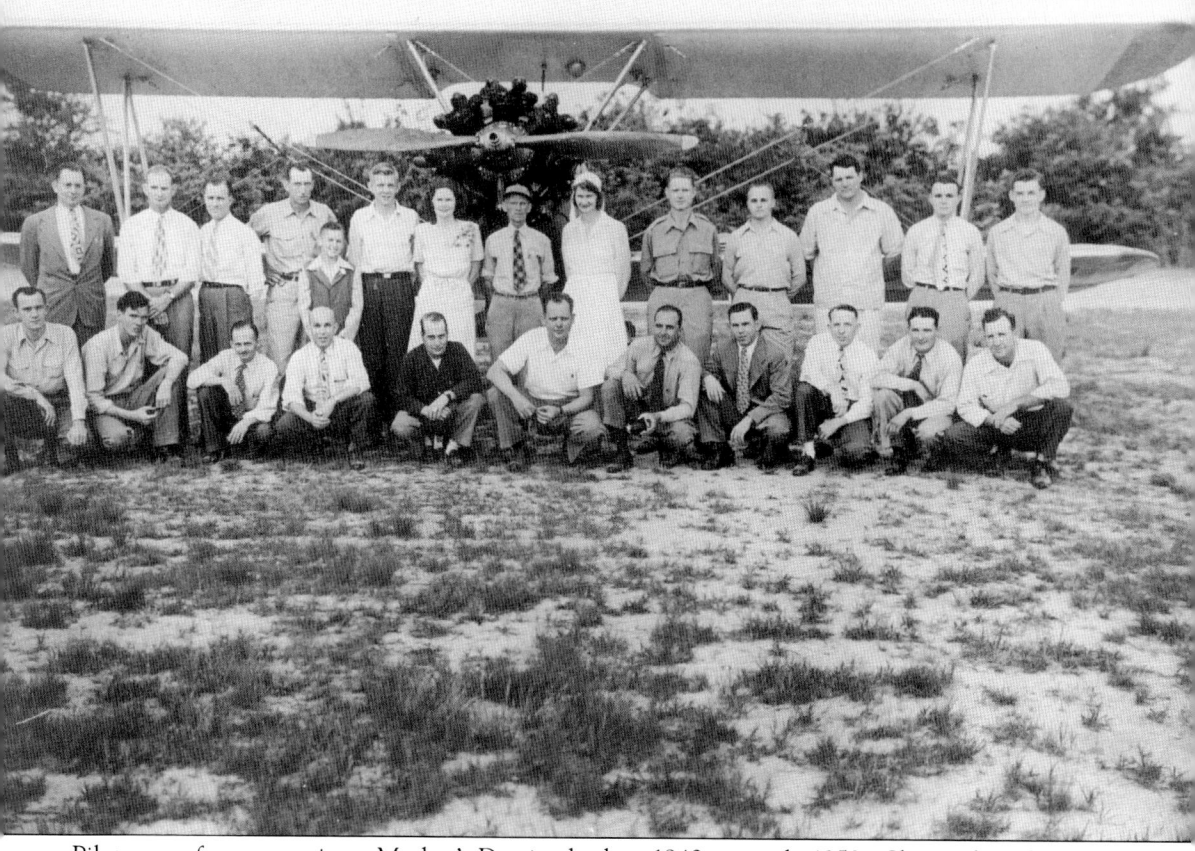

Pilots pose for a portrait on Mother's Day in the late 1940s or early 1950s. Shown from left to right are the following: (first row) Herbert Watt, Lonnie Mac Davis, Bubba Fussell, Albert Laser, Tex Harts, Walter Stevens, Don Montgomery, Sonny Harris, E. J. Butler, Carl Morris, and Fenna Stewart; (second row) E. M. Collins, Thomas Dodson, Otto Bridgforth, Newman Stewart, O. J. Gandy, Jack Gates, Virginia Moore, J. G. "Gladys" Williams, Elizabeth Dodson Burns, Newton Dodson, Marshall Fussell, John Danehower, J. C. Harbin, and Donald Williams.

Four

PEOPLE

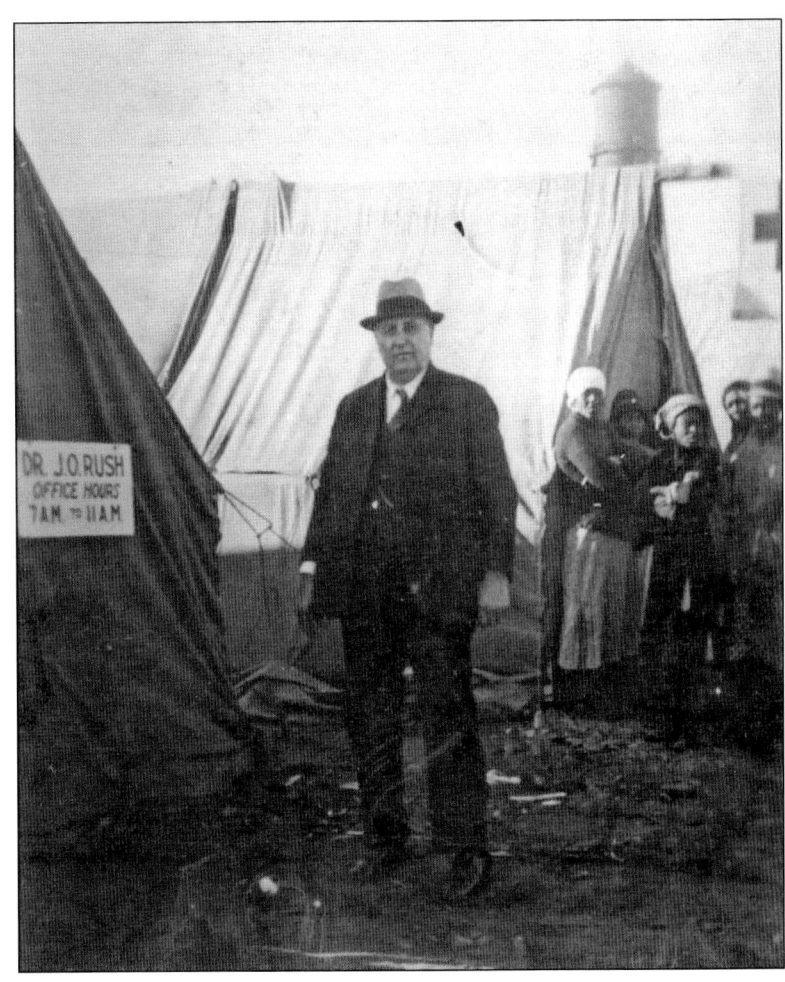

The good
Dr. J. O. Rush stands
by the entrance
to his tent office.
The sign states
his office hours.

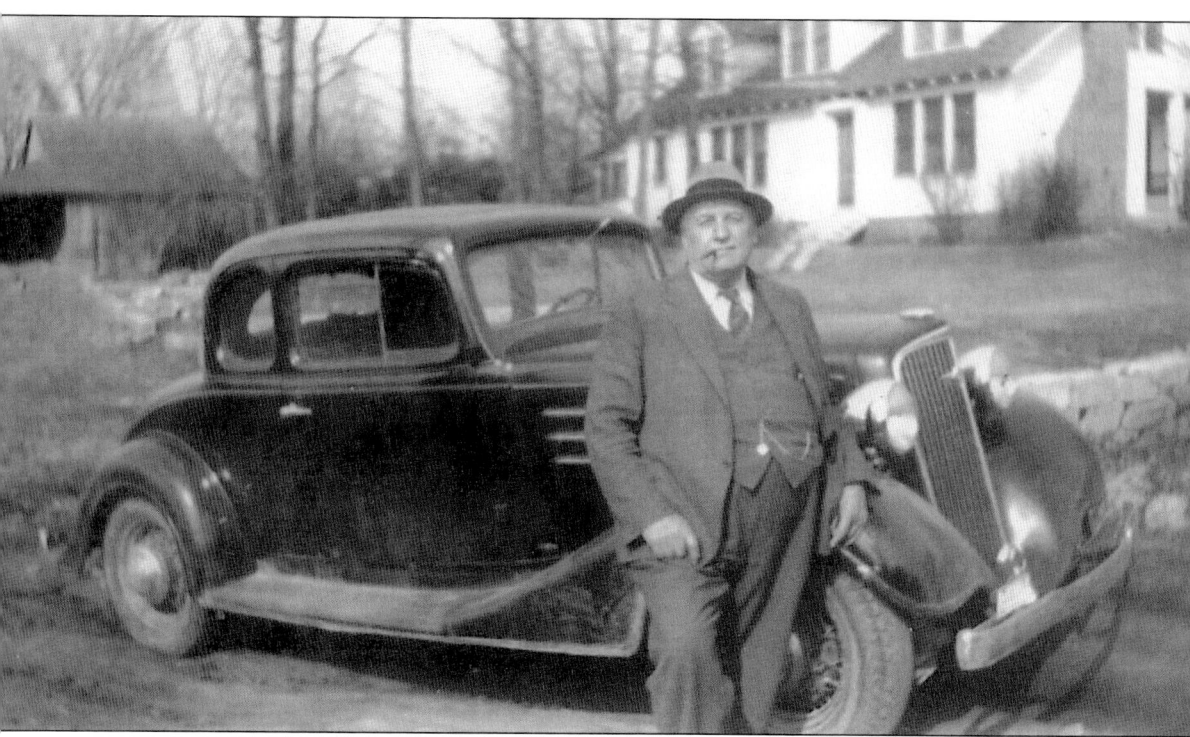

Dr. Rush made house calls by horse, by rail handcar, and then by car. He was one of the first automobile dealers in the county. Here he poses with a beautiful model in front of a house possibly located at Rushmore, his farming estate east of town.

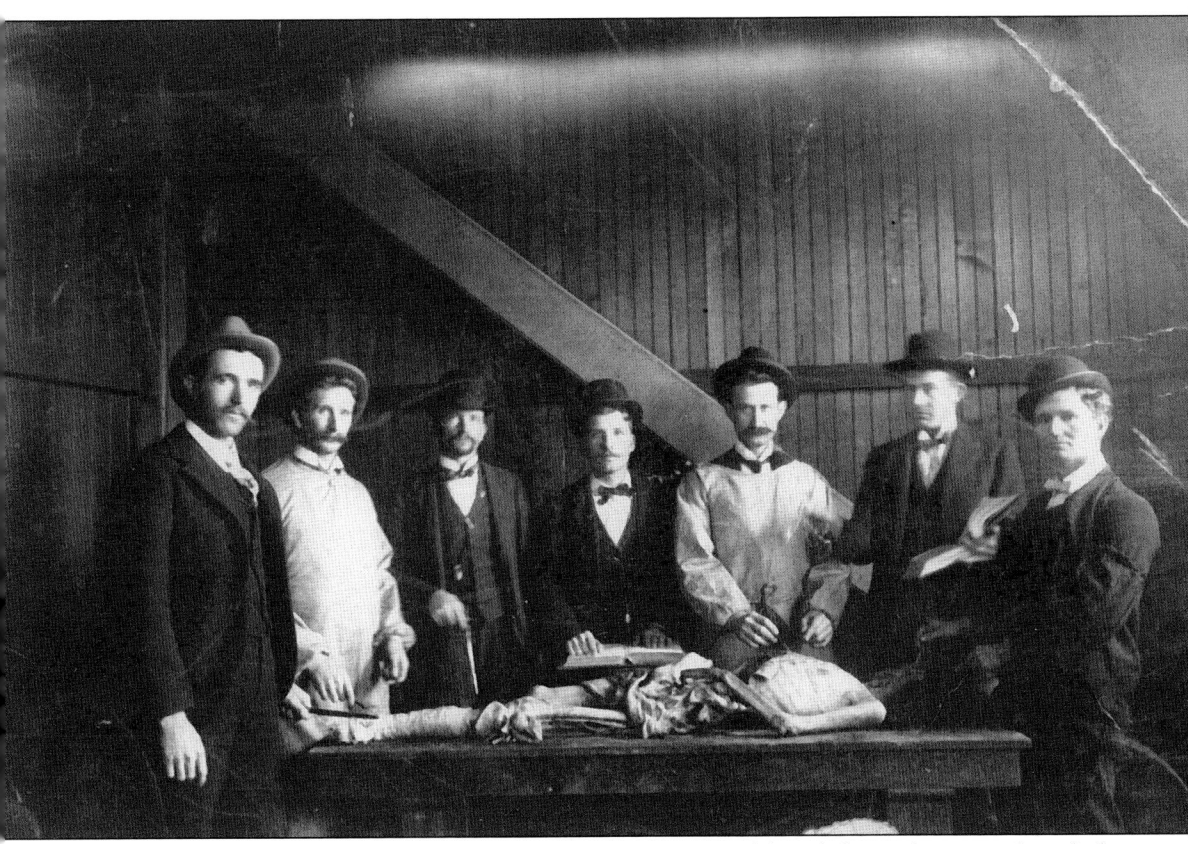
Dr. Julius Bogart and his colleagues pose with a cadaver. Pictured from left to right are unidentified; J. G. Waldrop of Grays, Arkansas; Dr. Bogart; P. A. Bazr of London, Texas; C. H. Stewart of Stickler, Arkansas; W. H. Lain of Morrilton, Arkansas; and Samuel Hancock of Blanchand, Illinois.

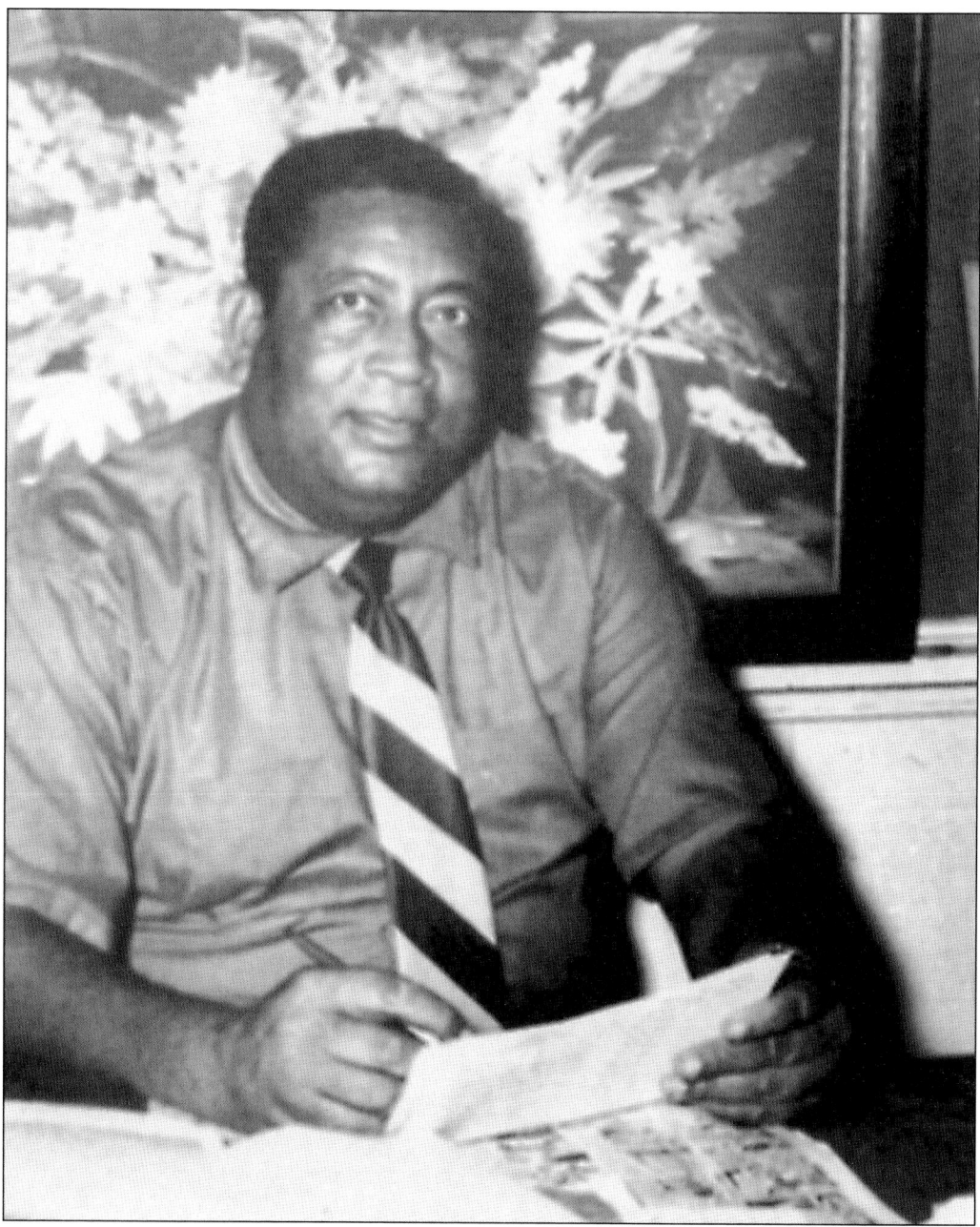
John Isom was an artist, musician, and teacher extraordinaire who taught at Lincoln High School for many years. He judged the talent show at the St. Francis County Fair the year that Elvis Presley competed. Isom was the tie-breaking vote, making Elvis as the winner. When Lincoln merged with Forrest City, he taught at that high school; he was the first African American instructor that white students remember having. Many returning natives come to the St. Francis County Museum to view Isom's paintings.

As a Forrest City dentist, Dr. John Burke served thousands of patients in his years of practice. During the time of Jim Crow laws, he was the first black doctor that many white citizens remember patronizing. His wife, Thelma, ran Burke's Mortuary, which was located on the spot where the First National Bank of Eastern Arkansas building is now.

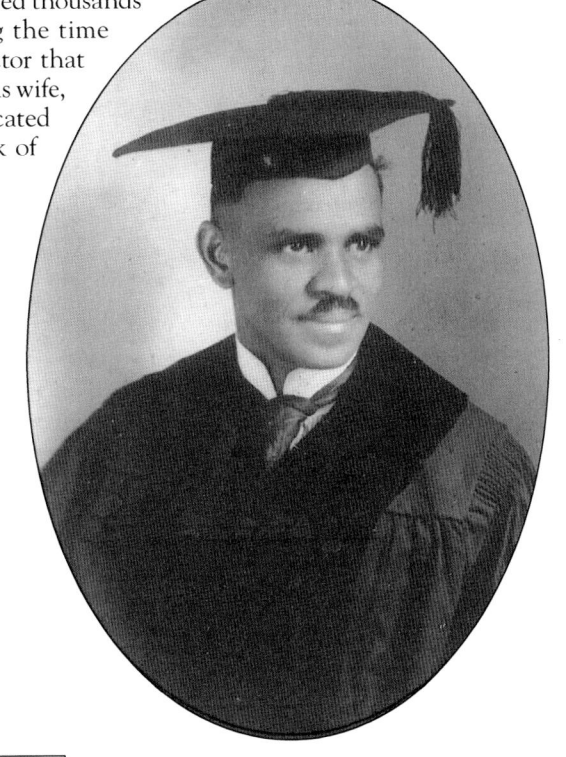

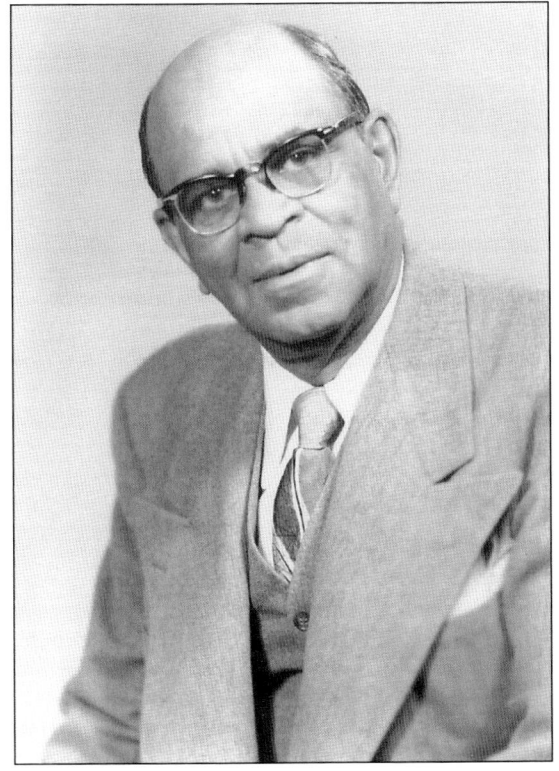

Dr. Burke had a long and successful practice in the county. In later years, he was able to find time to raise livestock and champion Great Dane show dogs.

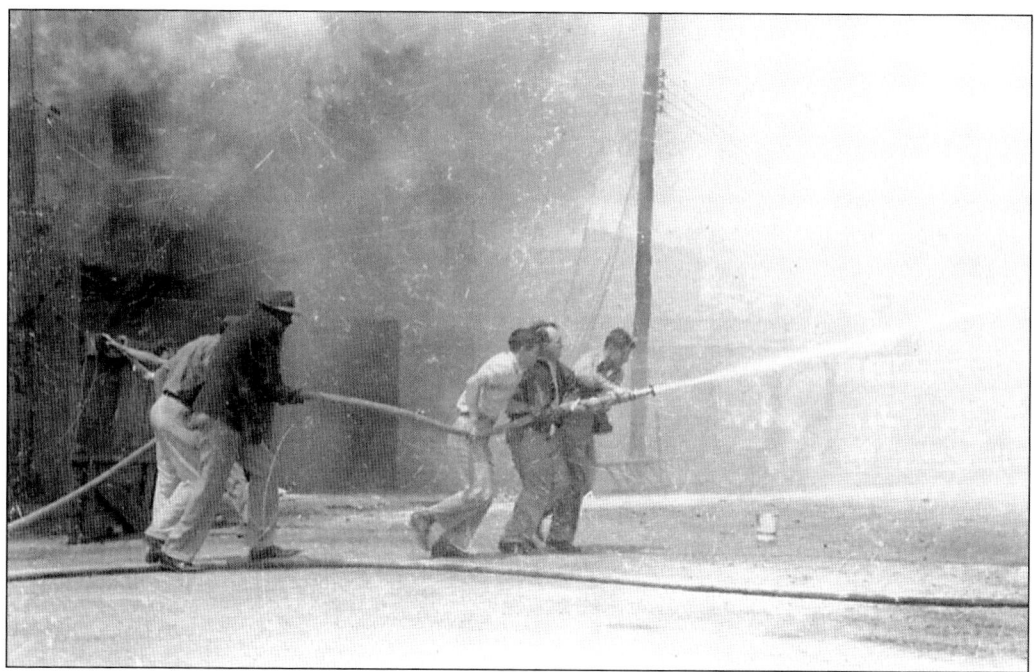
Forrest City firemen are shown in action in the 1950s. These volunteer firefighters, like those today, were ordinary people serving to protect life and property. They usually had little protective equipment.

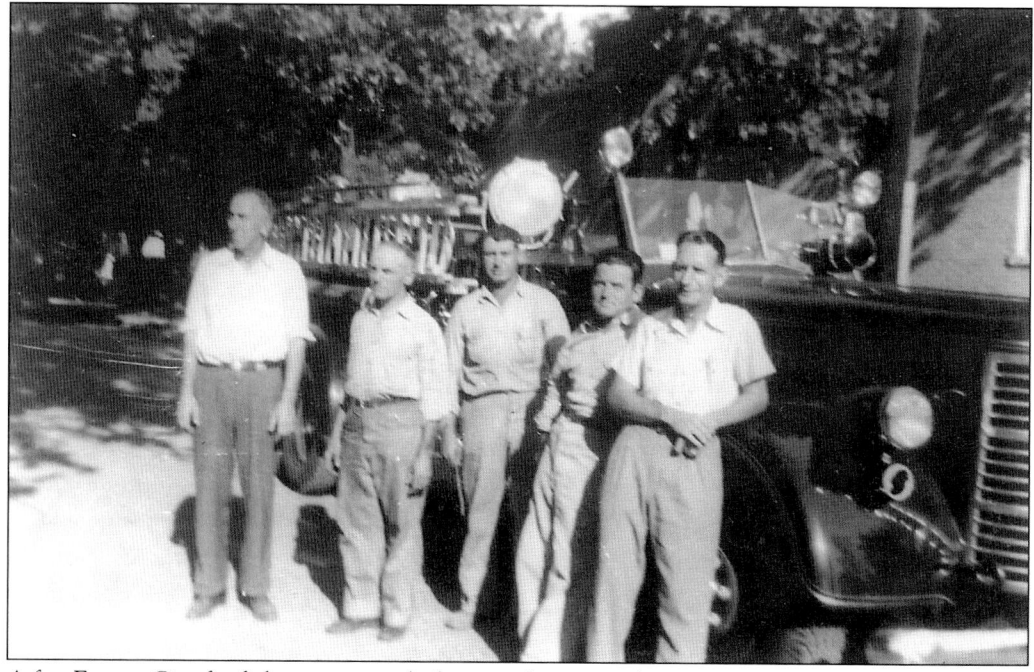
A few Forrest City firefighters pose with their newly acquired 1946 American LaFrance fire truck. It had an open cab and beautiful, sleek lines.

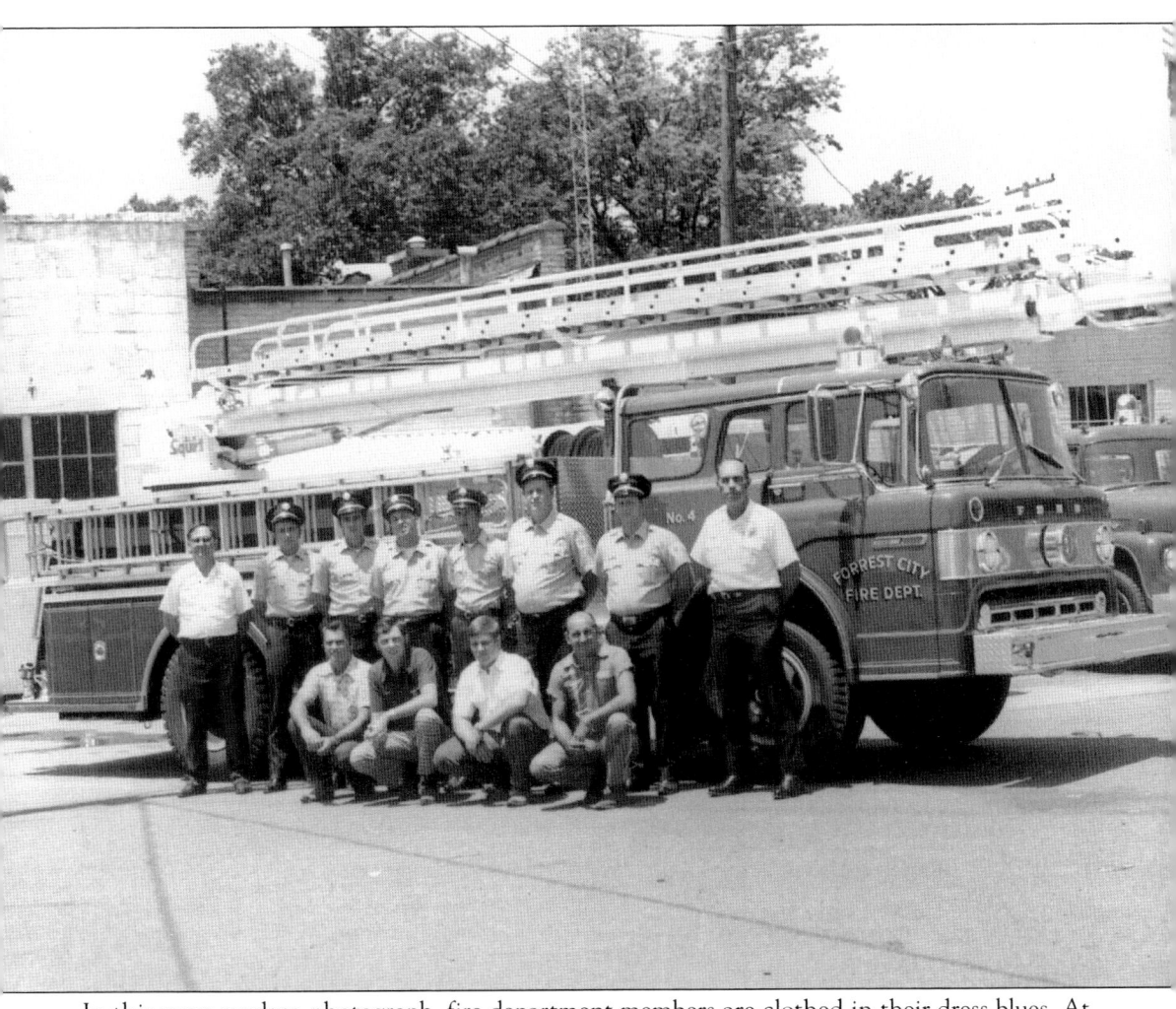
In this more modern photograph, fire department members are clothed in their dress blues. At the time of this photograph, the fire station was still located at city hall.

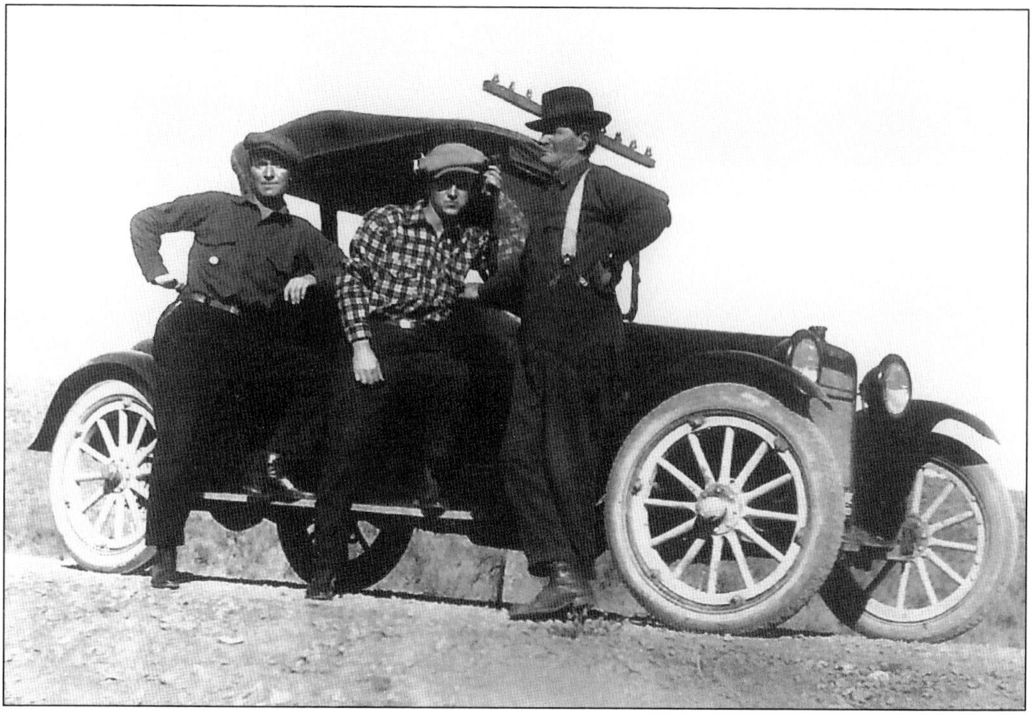

On the levee near Widener, three friends pose with Lloyd Parker's first car in the 1930s. Parker is standing in the center.

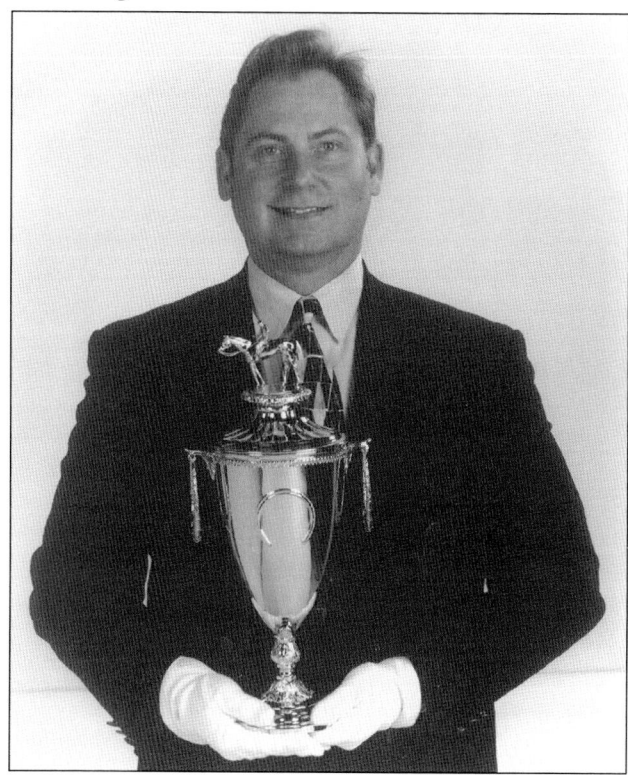

An honors graduate from Tulane, H. Wayne Parker used his bachelor's degree in business administration as a buyer for Burdins and then as director of new store openings for the Nature Company. After several years in retail, he received a master's degree in jewelry design from the Chicago Institute of Art. While serving as executive vice president of Lemon and Son's Jewelers, Wayne oversaw all aspects of the creation of the world-famous Kentucky Derby trophy. Following his 2001 retirement, he attended Hebrew Union University in Cincinnati, Ohio, to study comparative religion. He now lives in Forrest City and serves as curator of the St. Francis County Museum as well as the chair of the St. Francis County Ridgefest Committee.

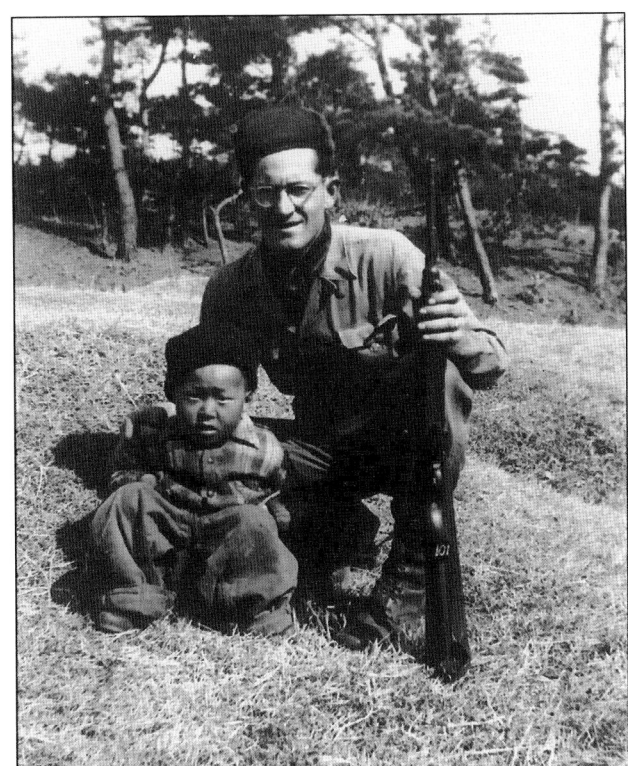

While serving in Korea, Howard Parker rescued this two-year-old boy (right) from a village where he was the only survivor. Howard petitioned the government for permission to adopt the boy and bring him back to the United States, but the request was denied. After returning from service, he settled down into a regular life, and several years later, his son H. Wayne Parker was born.

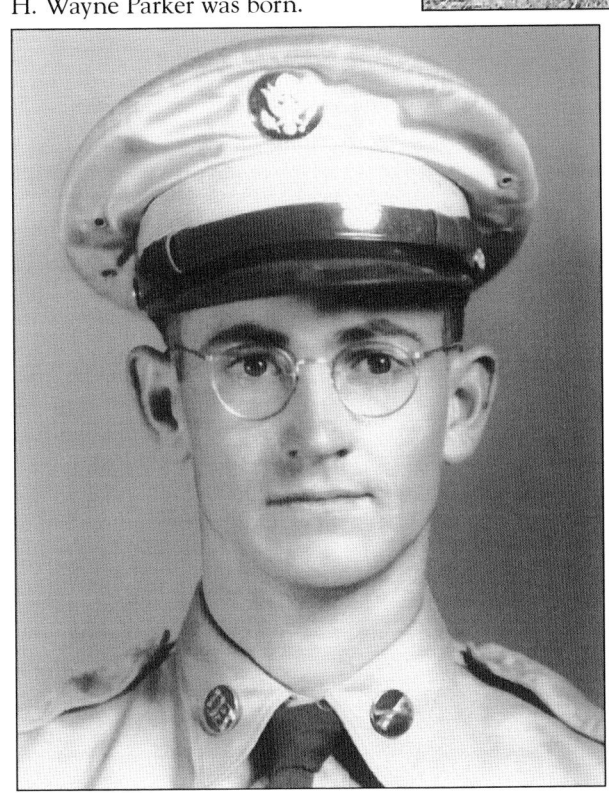

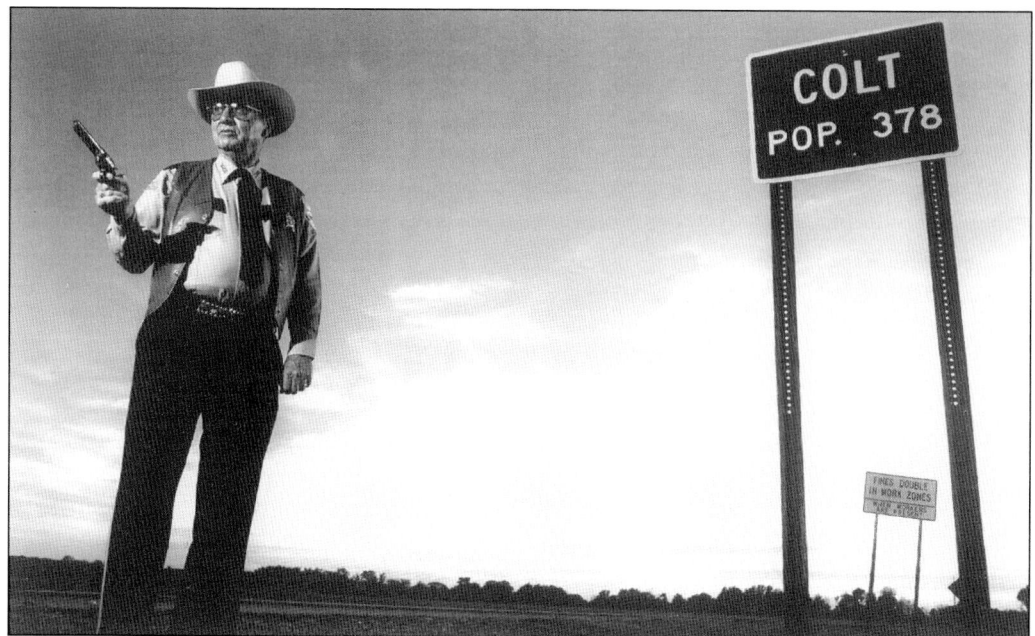

This photograph played a prominent role in the Dave Parkman Exhibit at the St. Francis County Museum in early 2008. In addition to serving as sheriff of St. Francis County for two decades, Parkman was a former Forrest City police chief, detective, and consummate politician. Upon Parkman's retirement, H. N. Green fulfilled the remainder of the term. Currently, Bobby May is the elected sheriff and collector.

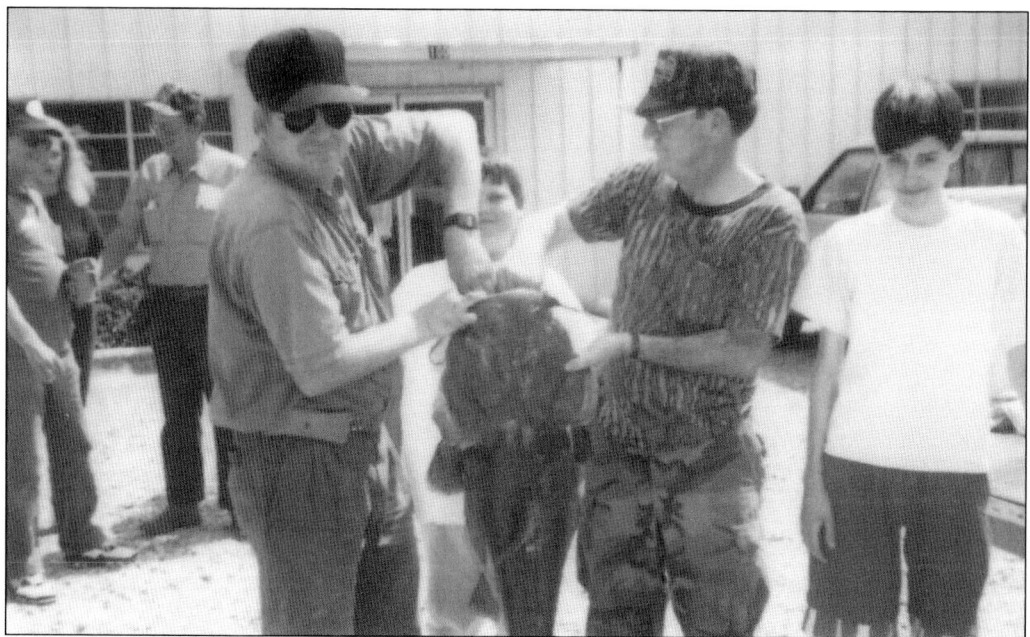

The sheriff and his deputies loved to fish during their rare time off. In front of the Palestine City Hall in the mid-1990s, Jerald Burns (county deputy 611) and Donald Parkman (county deputy 607) hold up a fish next to Allan Burns (far right), who barely outweighs the monster catfish pulled from the L'anguille River in Palestine.

The 1905 history of Forrest City introduces W. E. Williams as "the Honorable W. E. Williams, High Sheriff of St. Francis County." He was born in Maury County, Middle Tennessee, on May 16, 1850. He lost his mother at the age of two, and his family moved to Taylor's Creek, near Colt, in 1855. An orphan at the age of 12, he learned early on the importance of honesty and hard work. He had 15 children by his second wife, Eddie Mallory. Williams was elected sheriff in 1892 and retired after 10 years. He was appointed to fill the tenure of J. D. McKnight, who had died just after entering his second term.

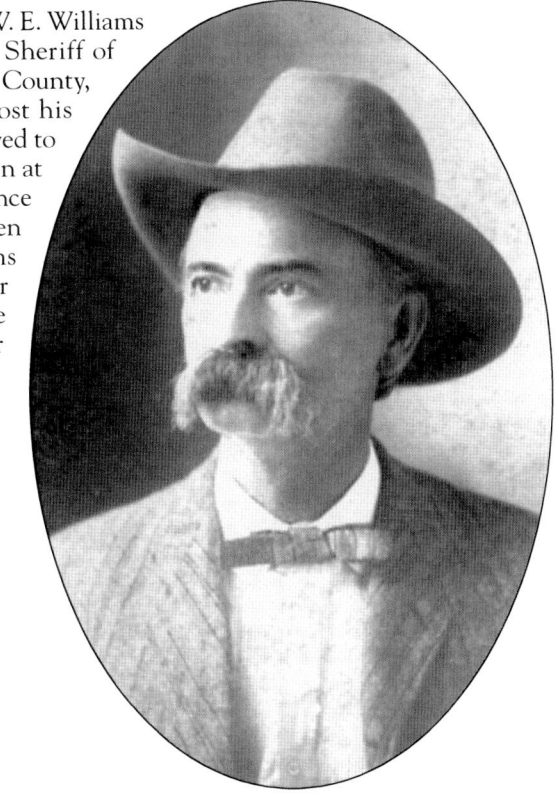

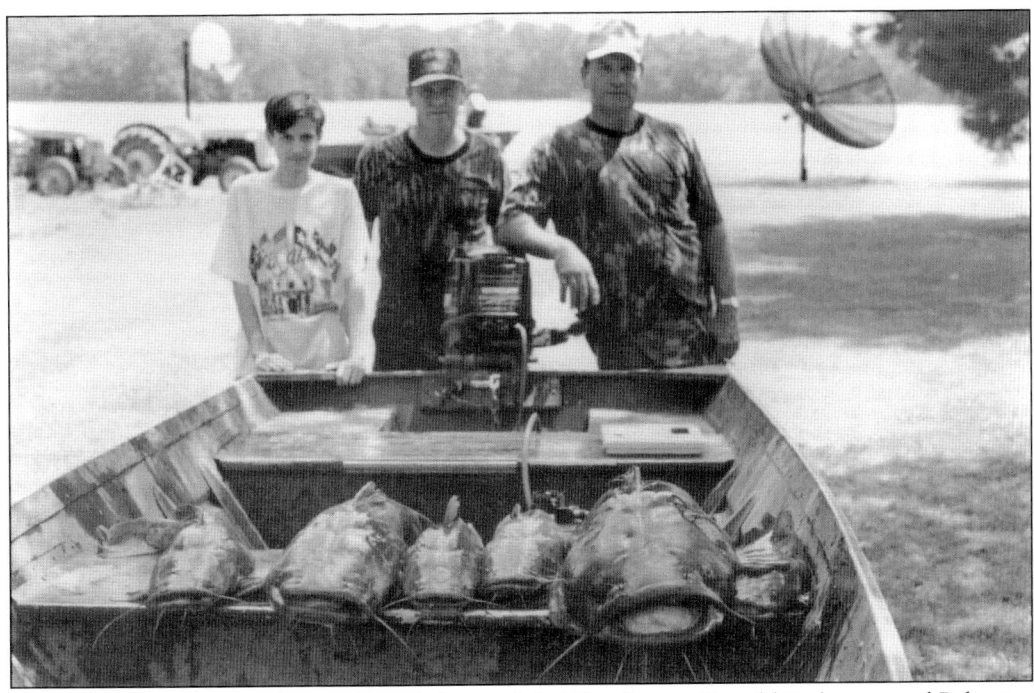

On another fishing expedition, (from left to right) Allan Burns, Donald Parkman, and Palestine policeman Gene Wingo pose with a few of the next fish to be fried.

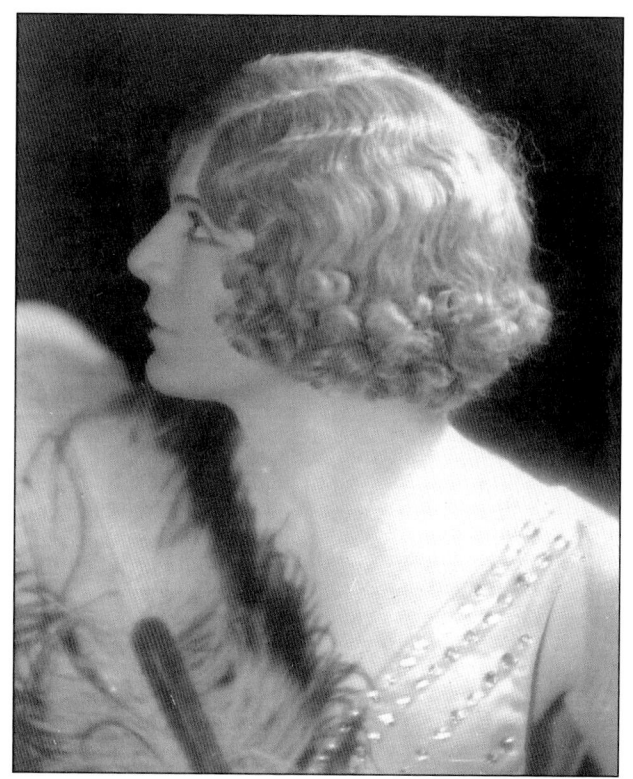

The image at left depicts Virginia Rollwage "Jackie" Collier at, according to the back, 47 Rue Eumont d'Urville. Several publicity photographs of Jackie are housed at the museum. Her career as a vaudeville performer took her all over the globe, but she eventually returned to Forrest City, where she lived until her death at the age of 103.

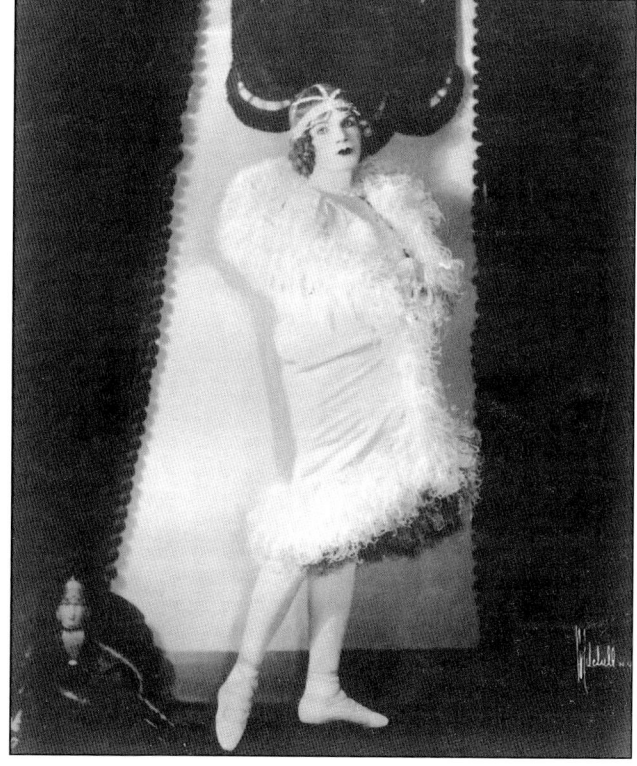

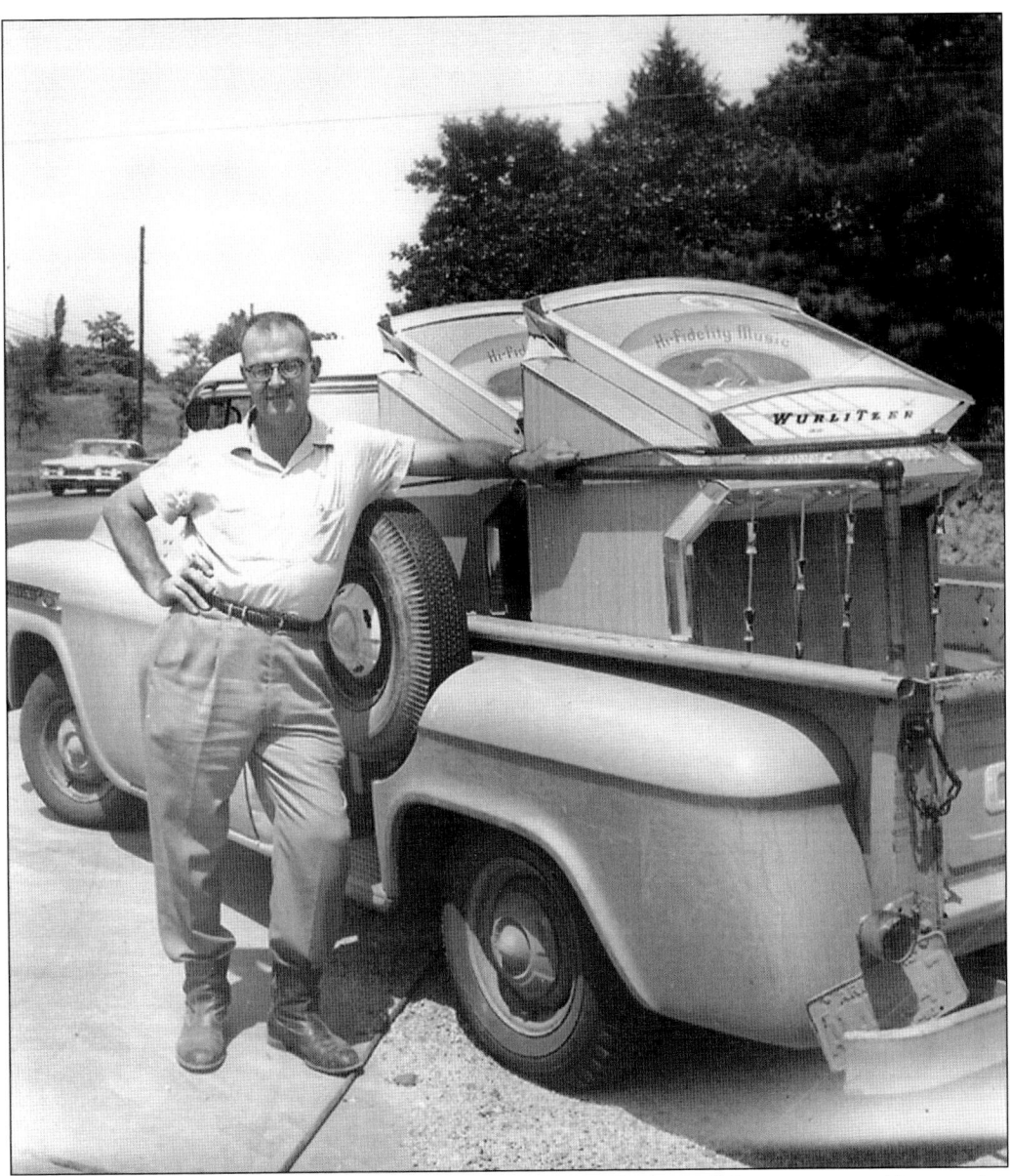

Eastern Arkansas has a rich musical heritage. From the early days of blues singers and harmonica players, Forrest City and St. Francis County have been happening places to perform. Joe Pugh was recorded by Alan Lomax, the great author and researcher of blues music. "Forrest City Joe" was known for playing the harmonica using his nostrils so he could sing at the same time. Joe, who was actually from Hughes, was killed in an automobile accident before he could become famous with a second round of Lomax recordings. B. B. King, Muddy Waters, and most of the other great blues artists played throughout the county. Madison was home to the Little Brown Jug, a music club and restaurant. Tenant farmers who worked hard all week played equally hard on Saturday nights. Al Green, Charlie Rich, and Little Beaver were a few others hailing from this area. Current up-and-coming artists include Chris Hicky, a country music video producer, and Joanna Cotton. Deana Carter now has family ties with the region, as the Hickys are grandparents to her son. J. W. Rolland is shown here with several jukeboxes.

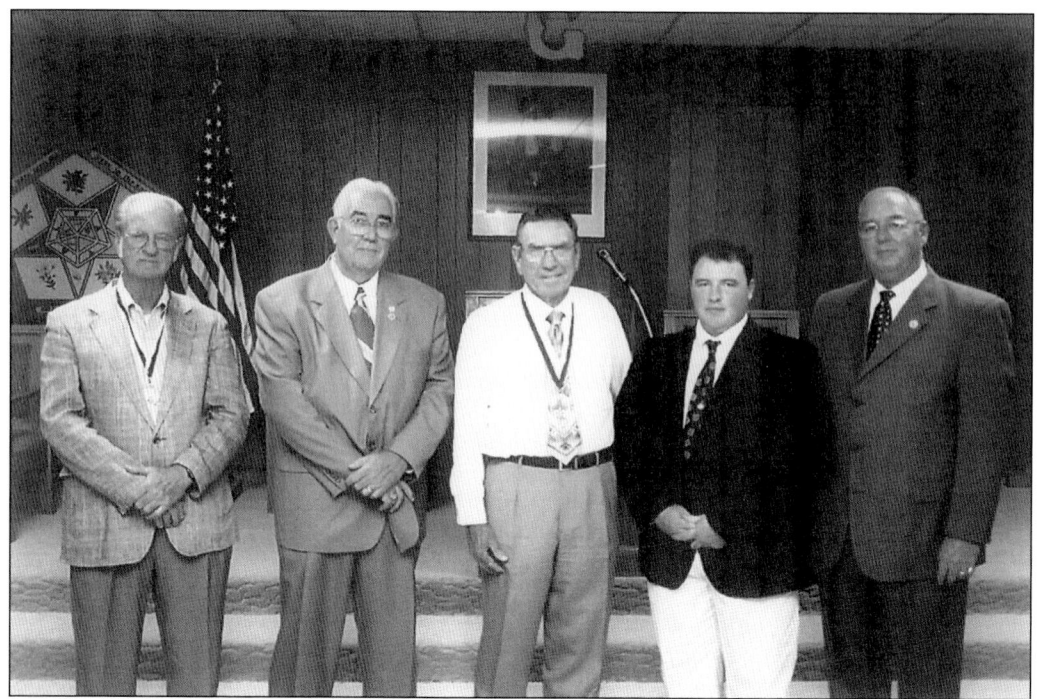

Wilburn Howton (center) of Palestine accepts the Pillar of Solomon Award at Forrest City Masonic Lodge No. 198. Howton also helped build the Hamilton-Moses steam plant shown earlier.

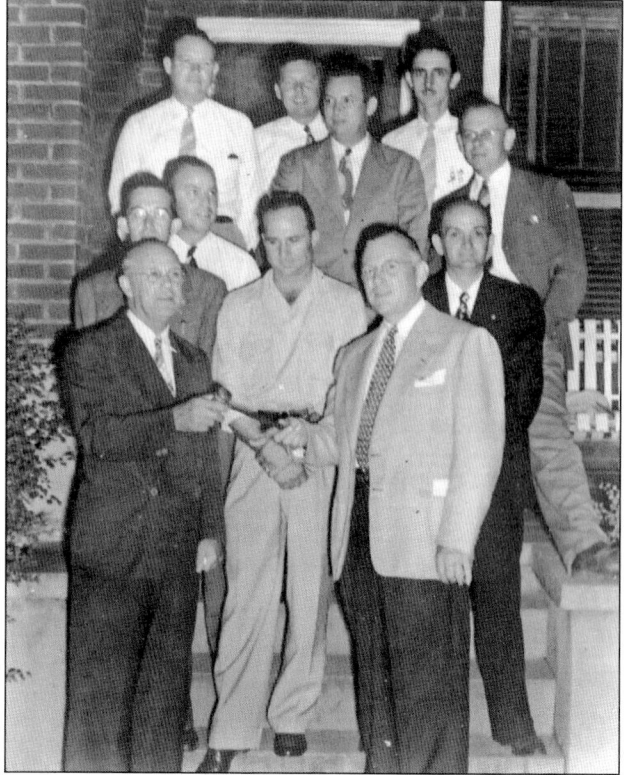

The charter members of the Forrest City Lions Club are shown here. The Lions Club is a civic organization that devotes part of its service to providing eyewear for children all over the world. The group is still active in Forrest City today.

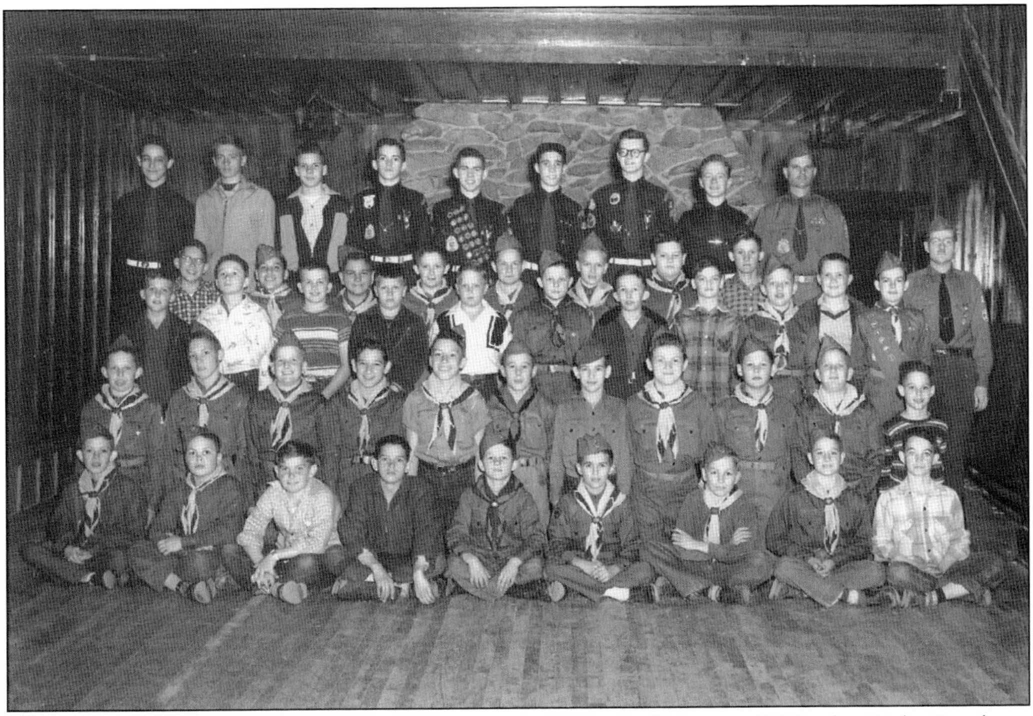

Boy Scouts are pictured in the late 1950s or early 1960s. In February 2008, the Ricky Stephens Memorial Boy Scout Exhibit debuted at the St. Francis County Museum.

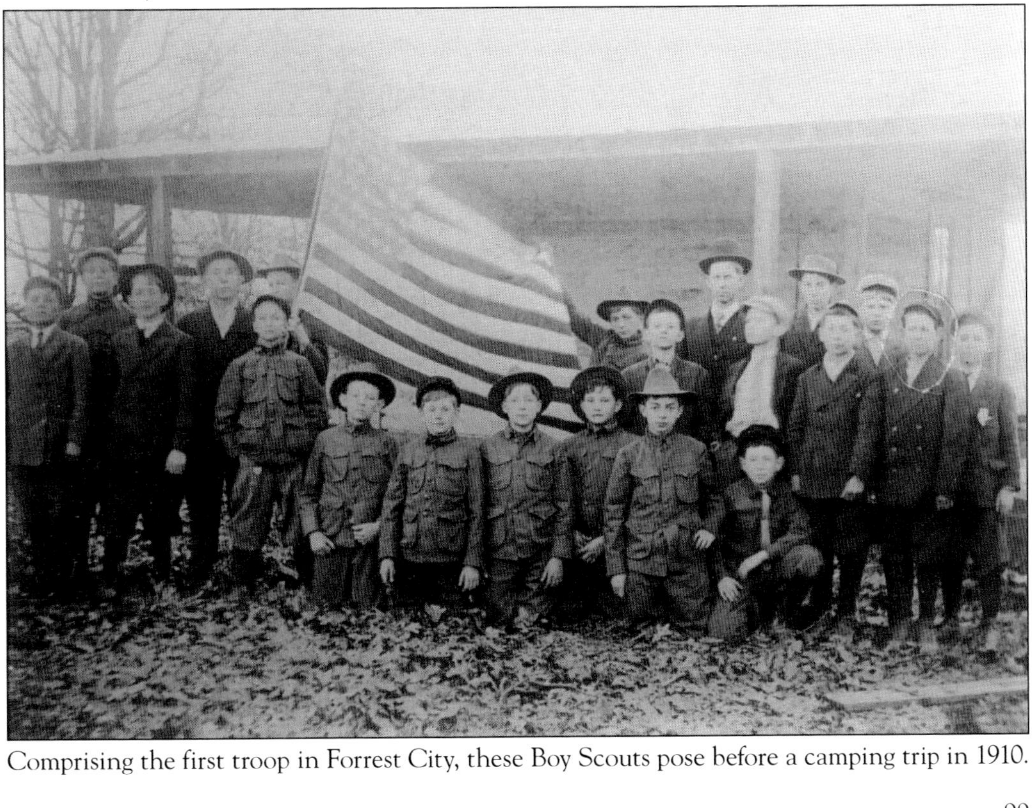

Comprising the first troop in Forrest City, these Boy Scouts pose before a camping trip in 1910.

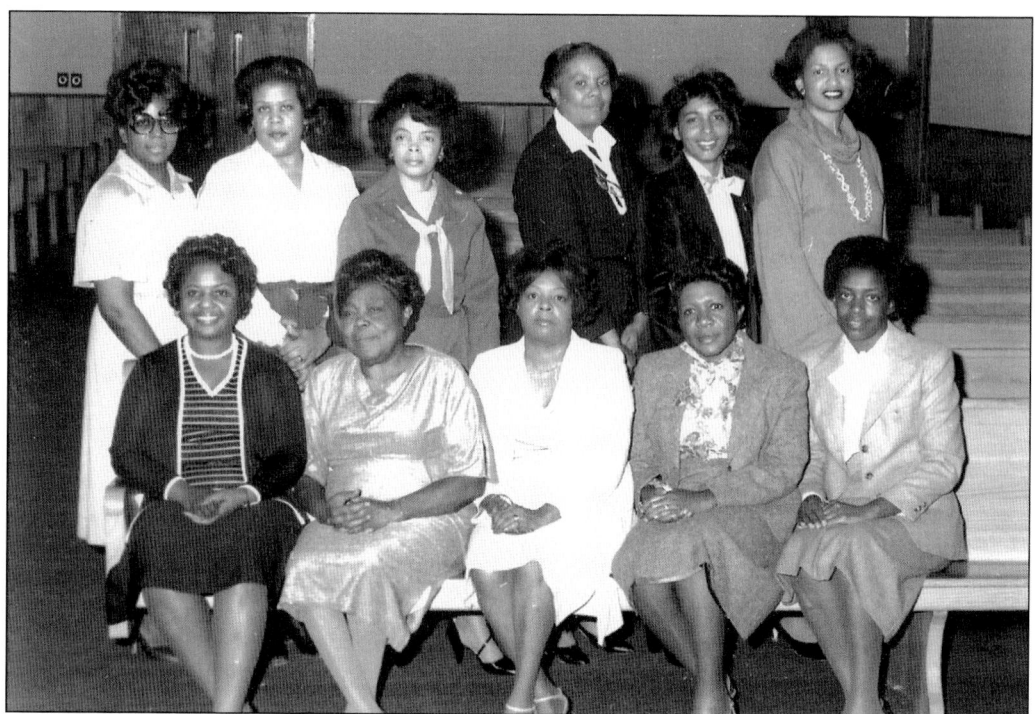

These ladies are part of the Eureka Civic and Social Club. Many have gone on to become influential members of their churches, communities, and government.

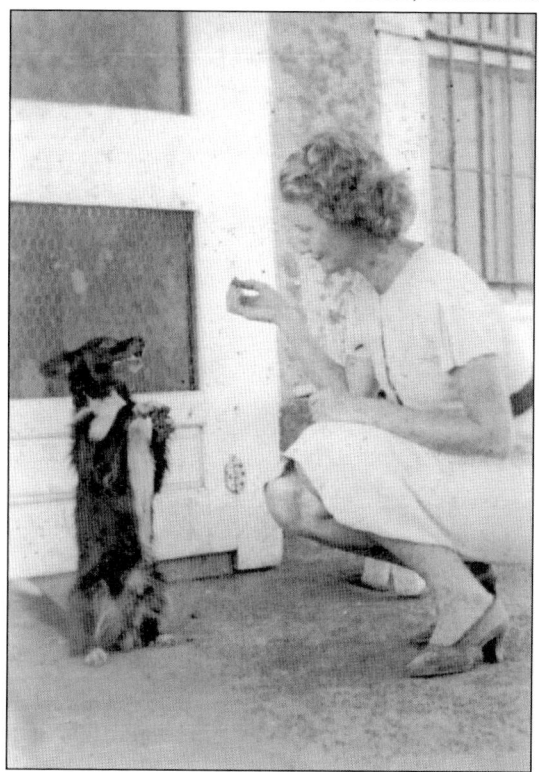

Young women in this rural society were concerned with learning how to get the most out of everything they had. Here Elizabeth Dodson is training her dog, Skippy. Many women in her time became members of the county Home Demonstration Clubs, sharing skills in cooking, crafting, home making, and leisure activities. Most of these same ladies volunteered their time in another county extension group: the 4-H youth program. It taught some of the same skills to children with fun, easy-to-learn projects. Some topics for youth included public speaking, livestock raising, and small animal training. Elizabeth Dodson was one such volunteer. Nancy Halbert, another active 4-H member, has been a leader for more than 50 years. Students remember this kind of involvement decades later.

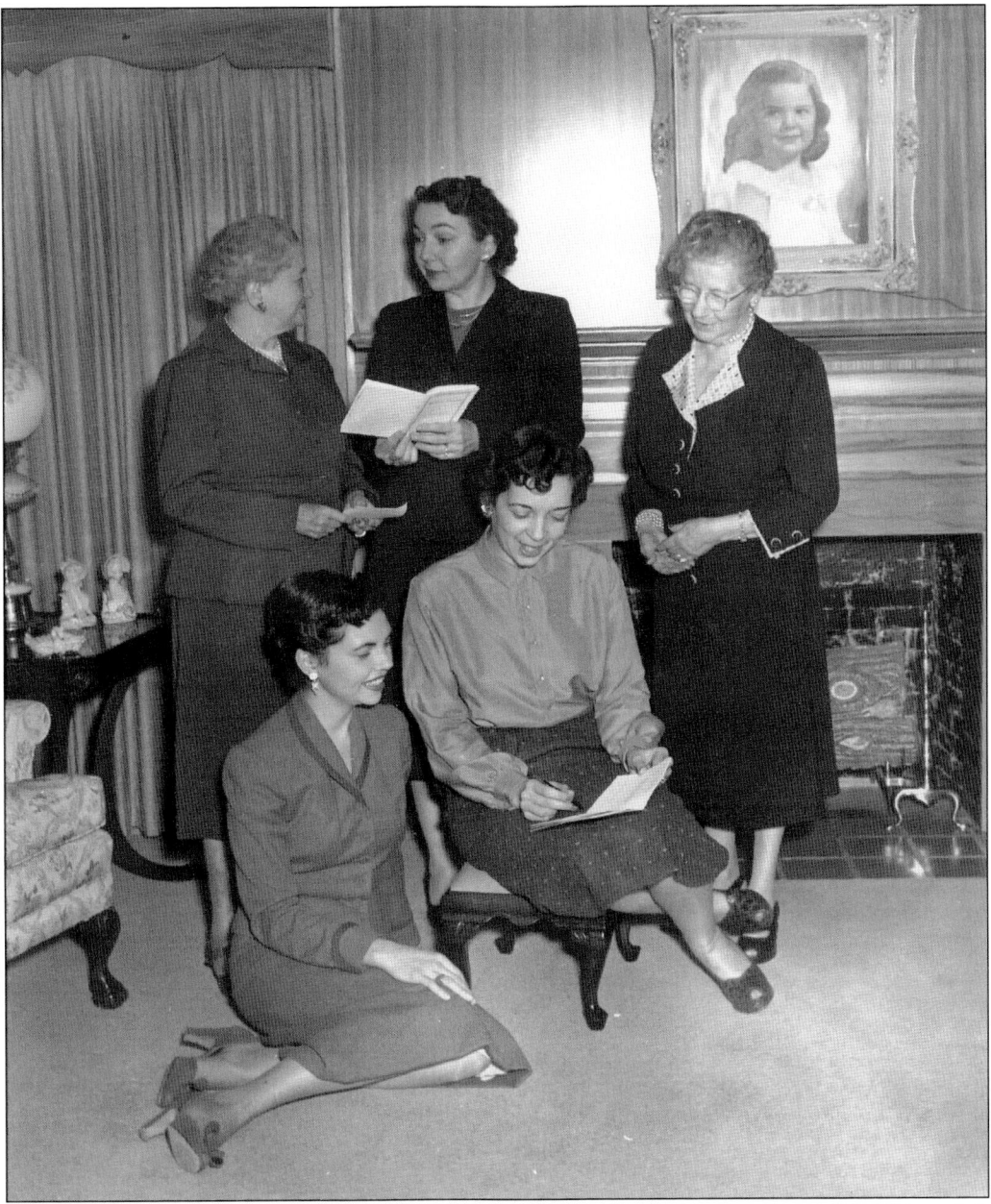
These ladies are hard at work planning their next project for the community. Pictured from left to right are (first row) Mrs. Knox (Patsy) Kinney and Mrs. Herman (Maxine) Young; (second row) unidentified, Mrs. Raymond Franks, and unidentified.

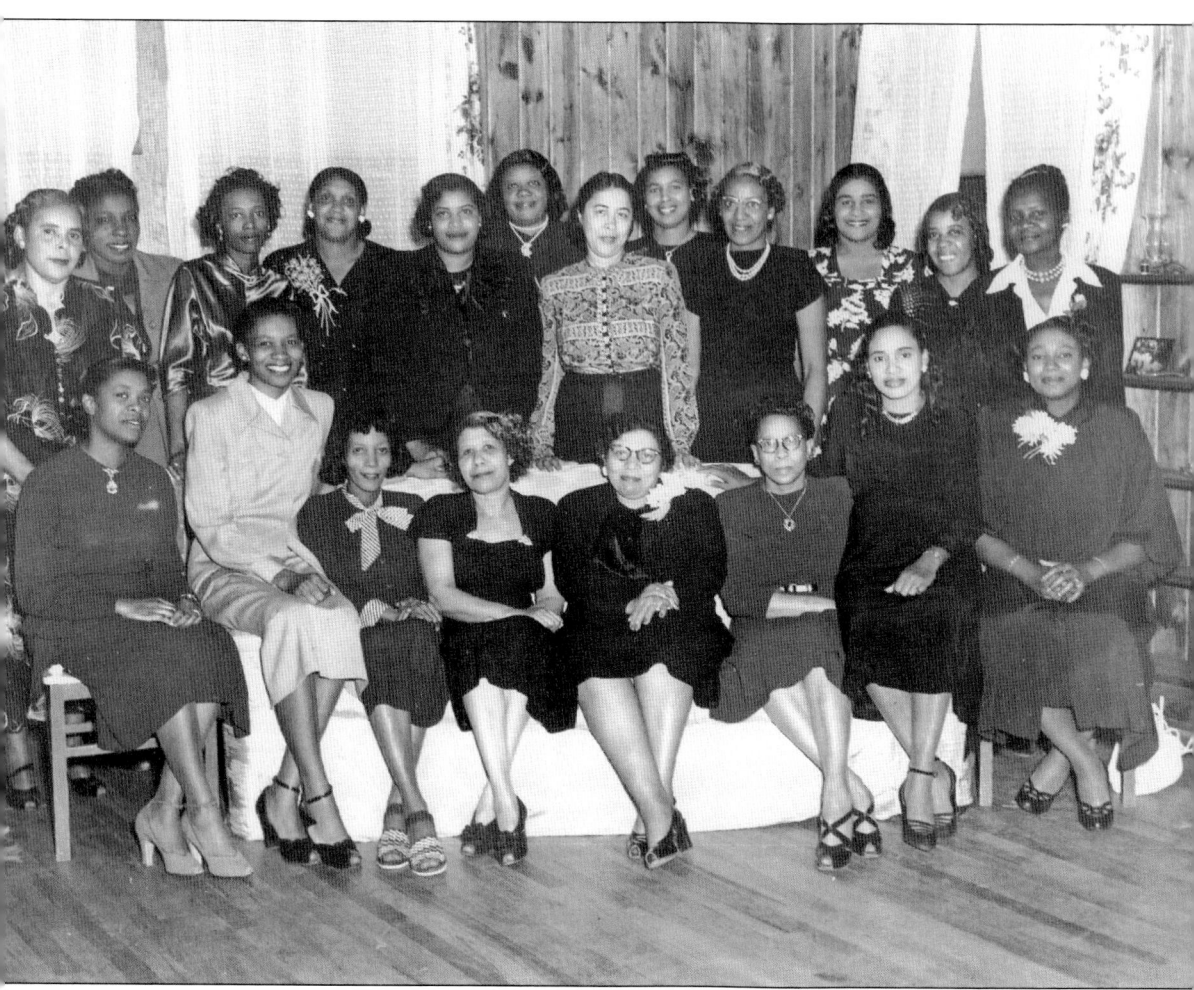

The Semper Fidelis civic organization is shown here in the mid-20th century. Both the Eureka Civic and Social Club and Semper Fidelis are still active. Other women's groups have included the Cosmos Club, which disbanded a few years ago after its 100th anniversary. The Junior Auxiliary, an active social group, recently completed a renovation of the Campbell House. The Pink Ladies are women who support and volunteer for the hospital. Beta Sigma Phi sororities of various levels meet in the county. These women all seek to serve their communities through the organizations.

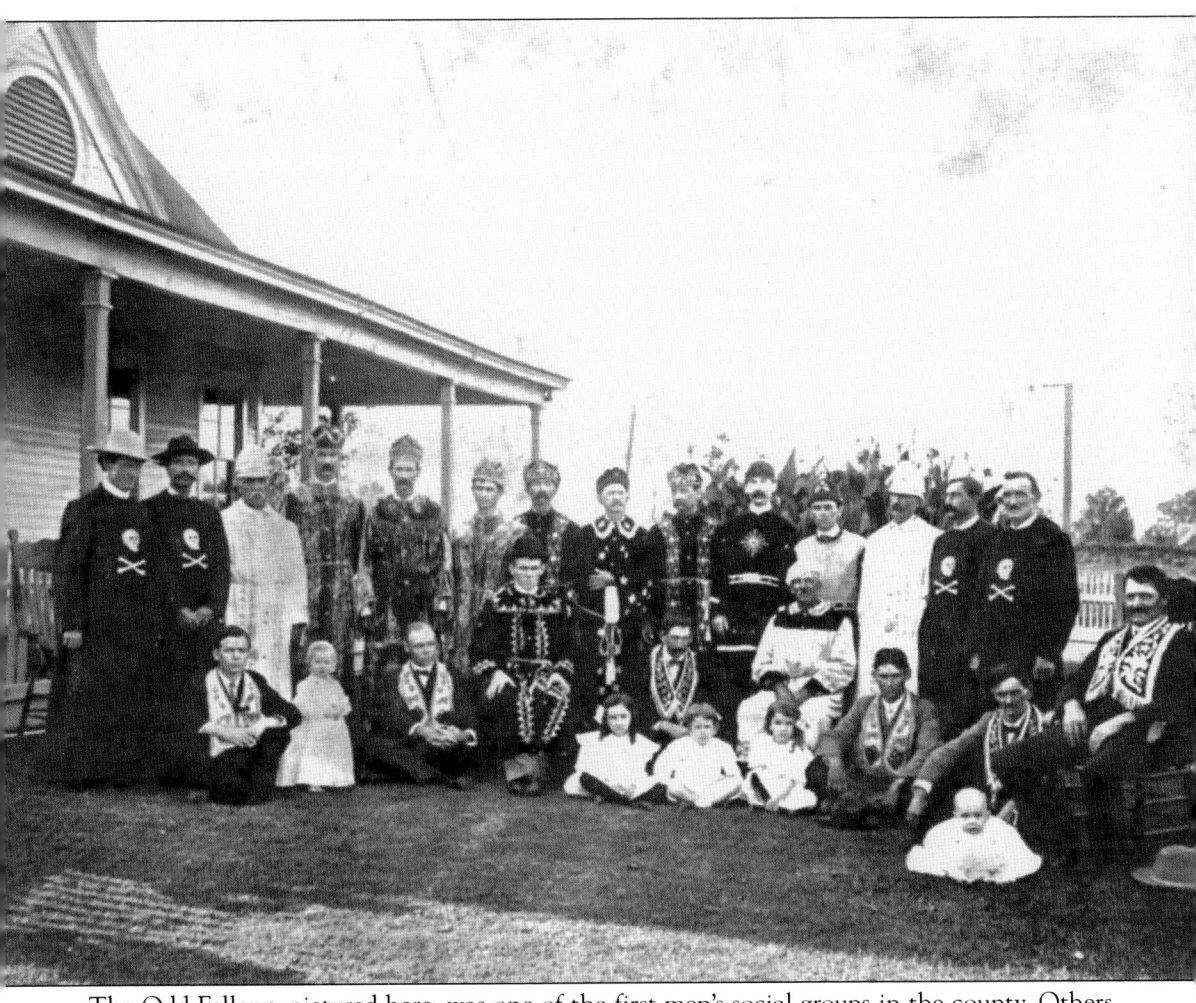

The Odd Fellows, pictured here, was one of the first men's social groups in the county. Others listed in the 1905 *Forrest City Times* art souvenir book included the Frying Pan Club.

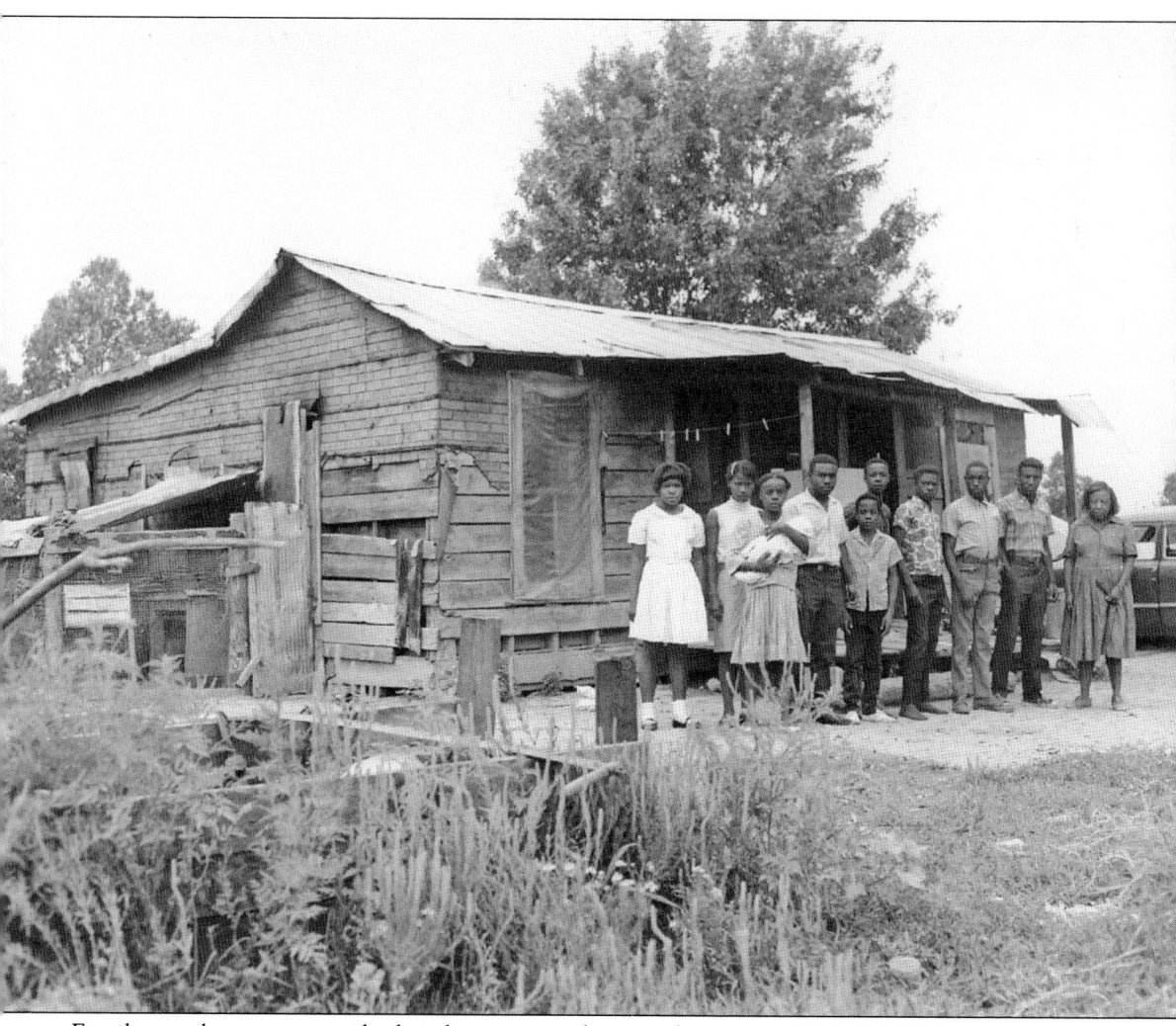

Family members pose outside their home somewhere in the county. The most important social network in the South is family. Blood is thicker than water, and that is true nowhere more than in eastern Arkansas. Homes often consist of several generations.

Five

EDUCATION

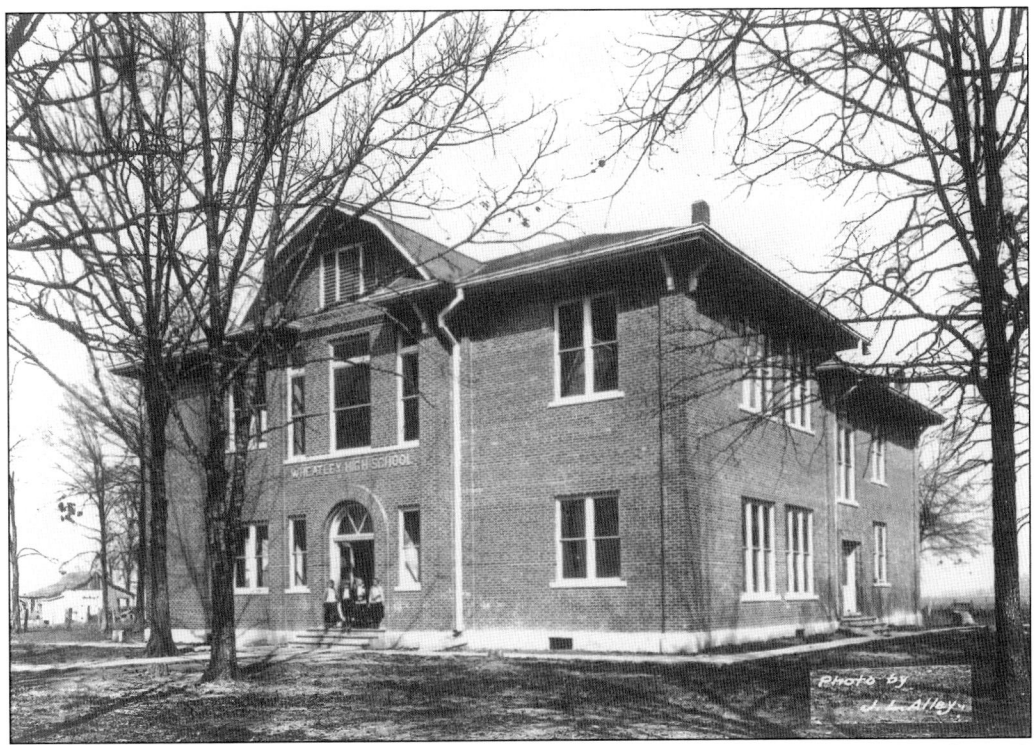

The elementary school at Wheatley is still in use, but several of the other buildings have burned. In the late 1980s, the Wheatley Pirates merged with the Palestine Red Devils to form the Palestine-Wheatley Patriots. In the district, each town has its own elementary school, but middle school students attend Wheatley and high school students go to Palestine. Wheatley High School (pictured) has been demolished.

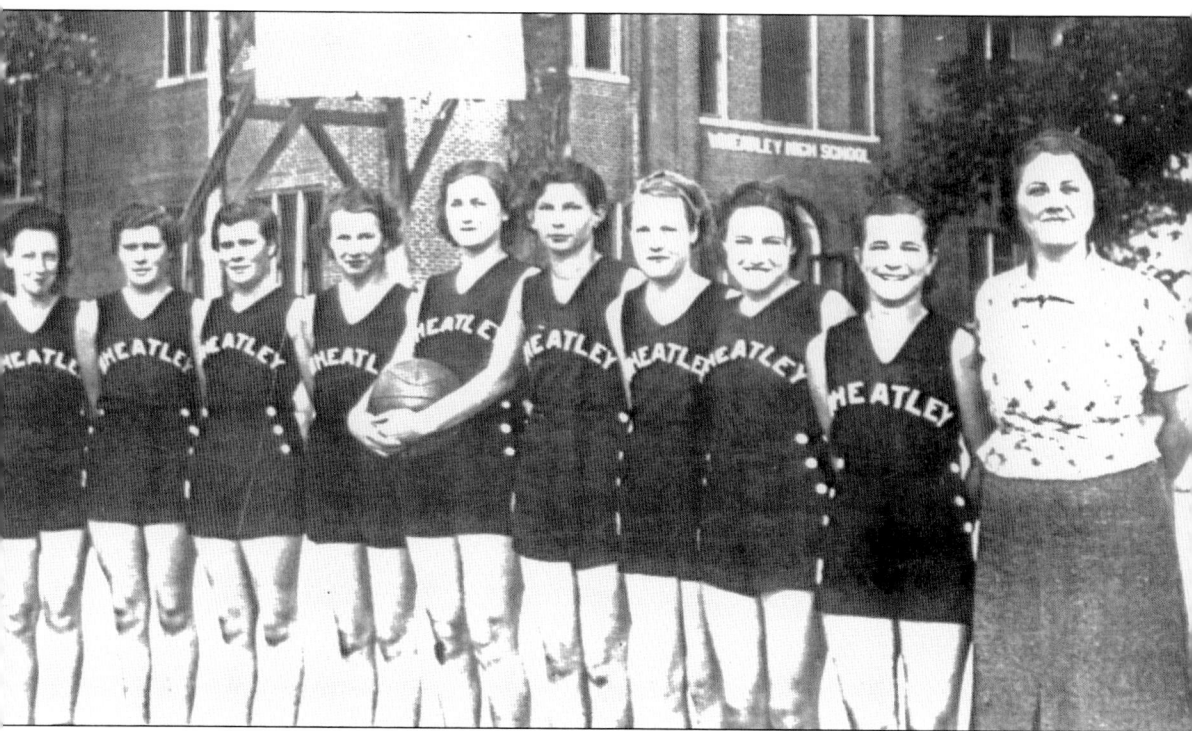

The women's basketball team is pictured at a time when all games were held outside. Wheatley and Palestine were rivals in sports, which made the merger more difficult.

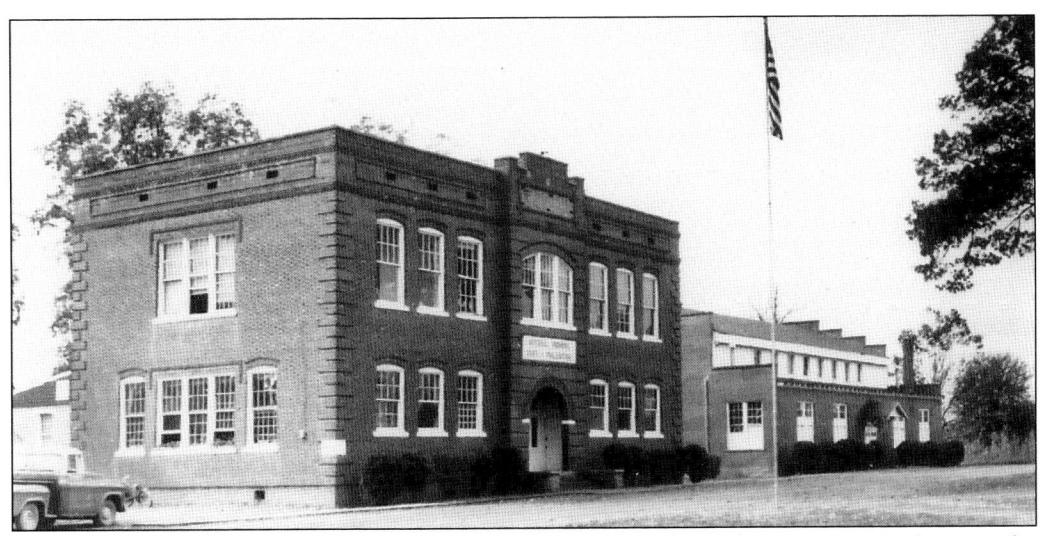
The original Palestine High School and gymnasium, seen in the mid-1960, was torn down in the 1980s. It served as a symbol of youth to many residents.

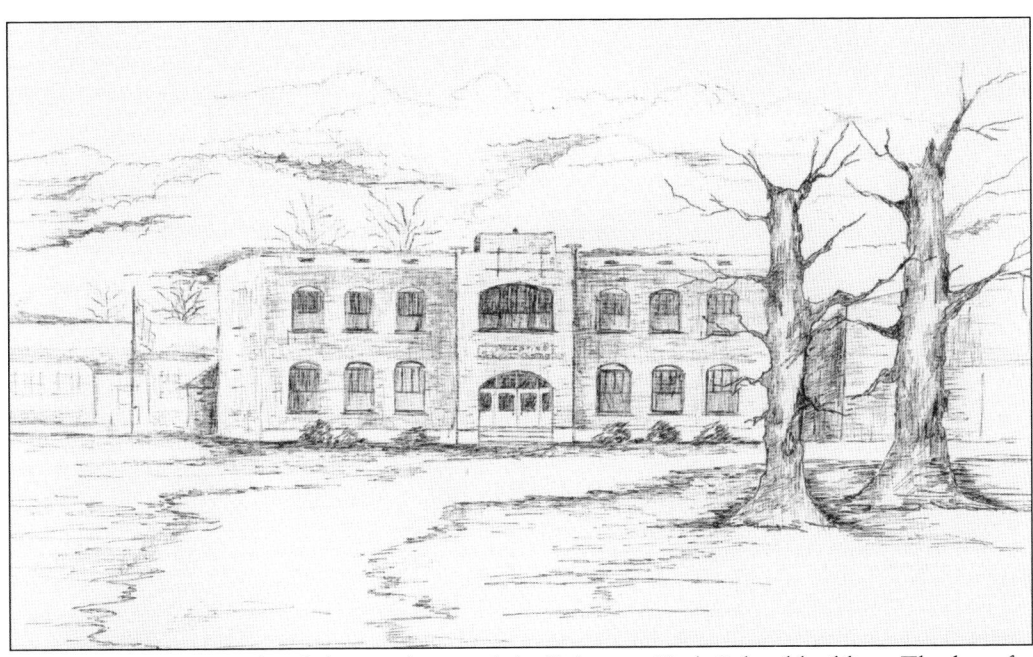
Gloria Courtney completed this rendering of the Palestine High School building. The logo for the Palestine Festival, it now hangs in the St. Francis County Museum.

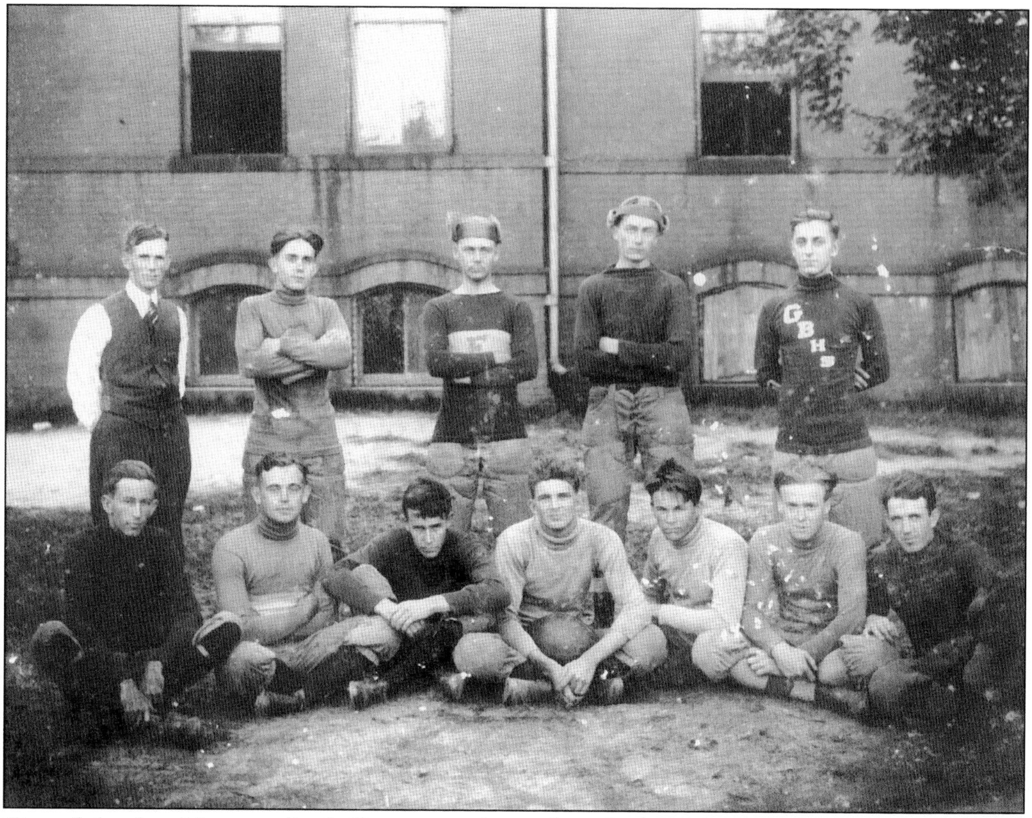

One of the first Mustang football teams is shown here looking fierce. The school behind the players is the Crowley's Ridge Institute.

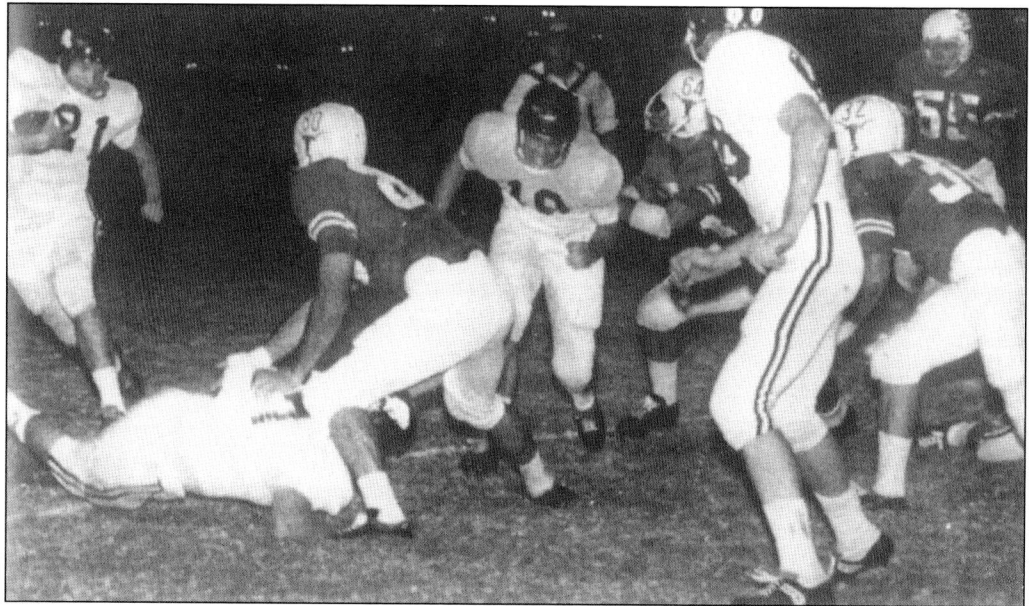

Jim Lindsey, No. 21, leads the Mustangs to victory in this *Times-Herald* photograph. He went on to compete with the Arkansas Razorbacks, where he gained fame as an outstanding player.

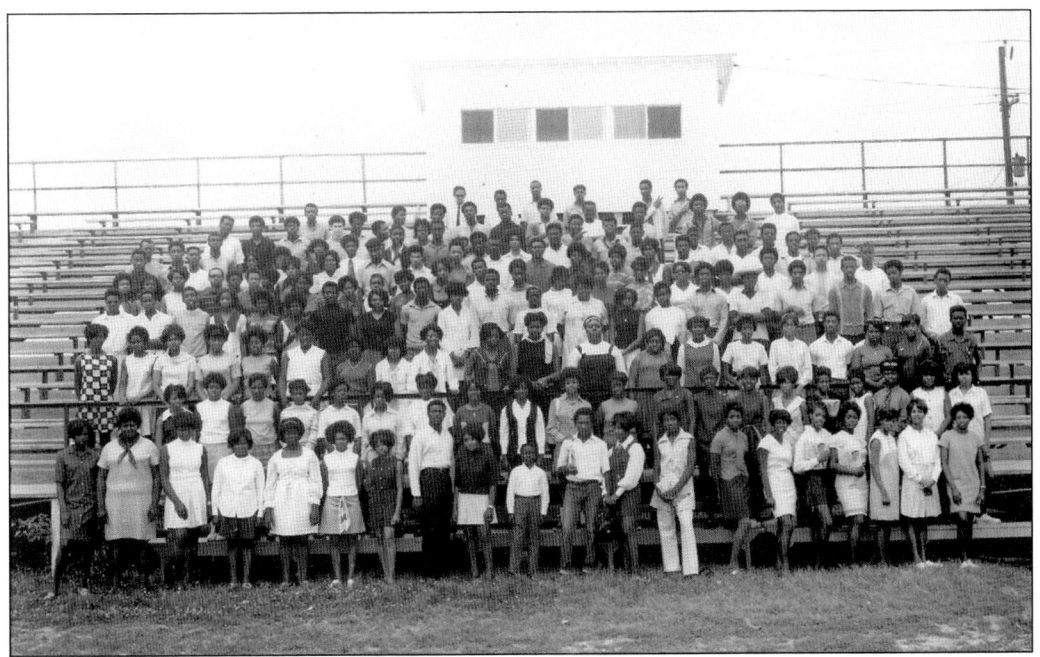

The Lincoln High School class of 1970 was the last to graduate before integration with Forrest City. For a few years, a handful of blacks went to Forrest City, so it was already technically integrated. Not until the riots nearly destroyed Lincoln did the schools completely integrate. Racial reconciliation has been a long time coming, though. The first integrated prom was not held until 1982.

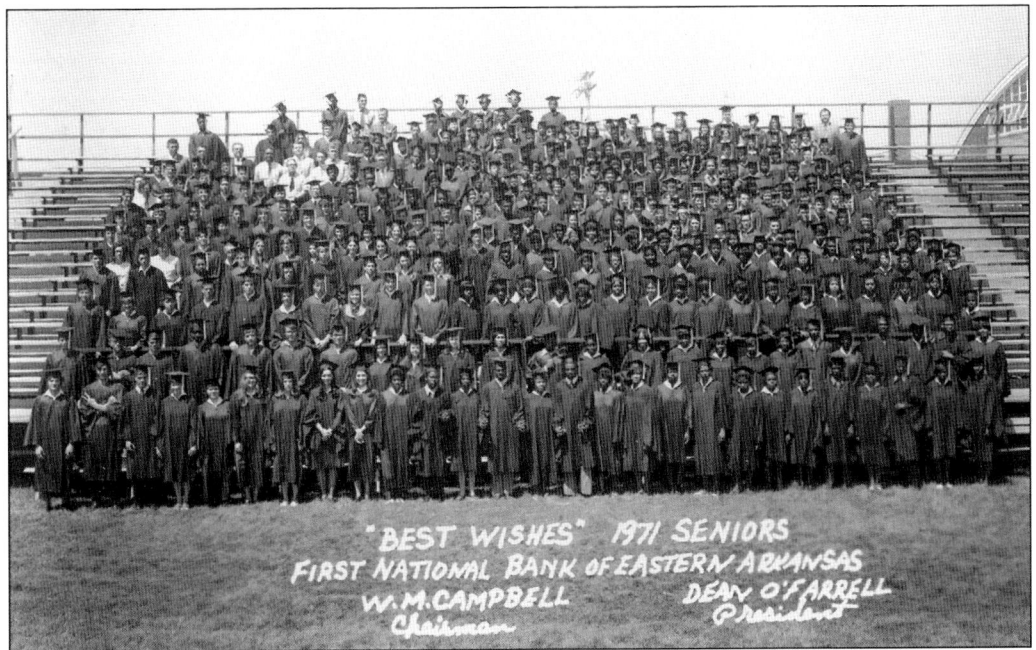

The Forrest City High School class of 1971, pictured here, marked a new era. From this point on, students went to the same building. Unfortunately, little remains from the Lincoln era besides a few trophies housed at the museum. The search is ongoing for Tiger yearbooks and memorabilia.

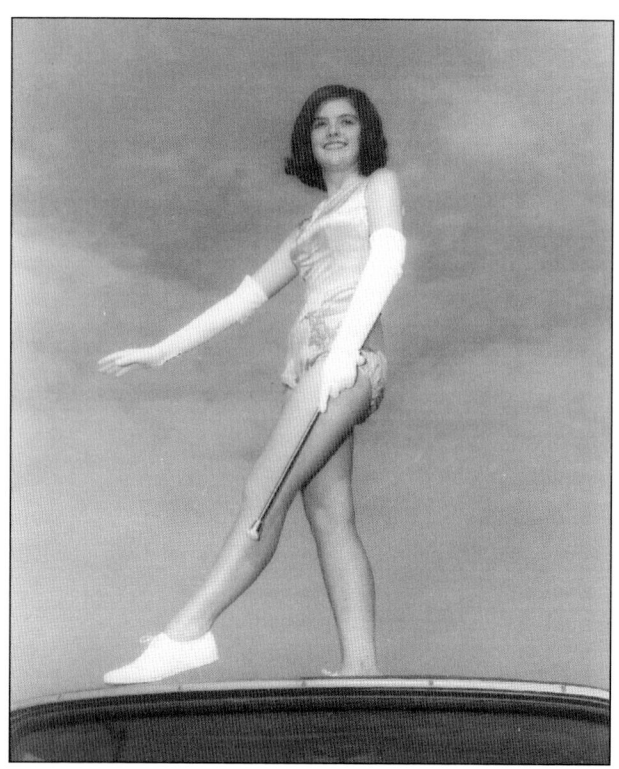

In this c. 1965 photograph, Johnnie Nell Young Carroll serves as majorette of the Forrest City Mustang Marching Band. The band continues its rich legacy today.

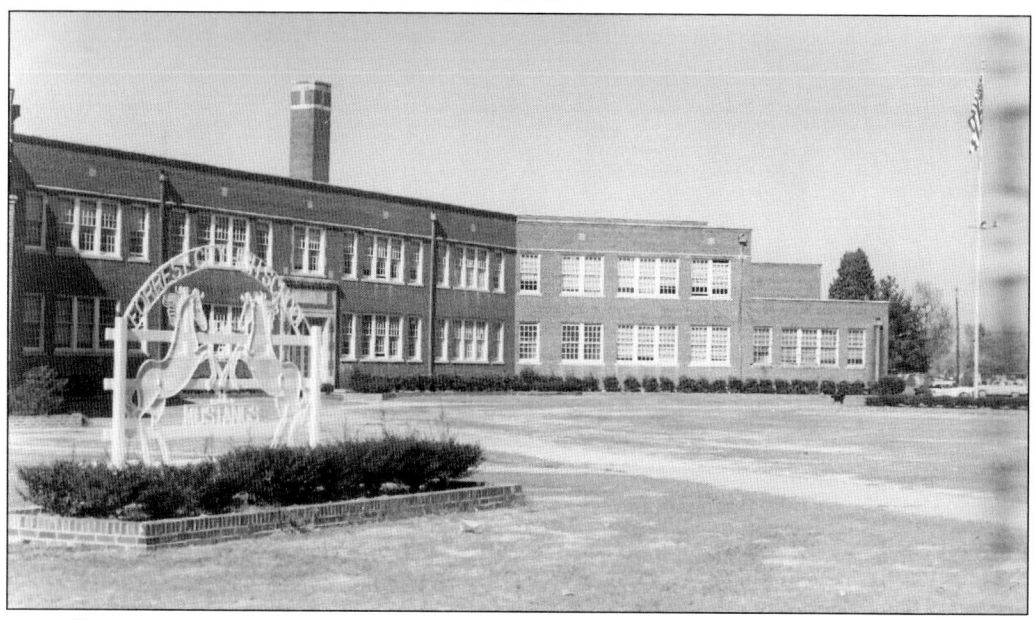

Many Forrest City alumni were devastated when the old Mustang High was demolished a few years ago. After decades of use, the building was almost uninhabitable and in need of major repair. The decision was made to save portions of the structure and replace the majority of the campus with a modern, technologically sophisticated new building. Even though the community was sad to see a part of its history go, the modern campus stands to represent a new chapter in the school's history. Today the facilities host many community events.

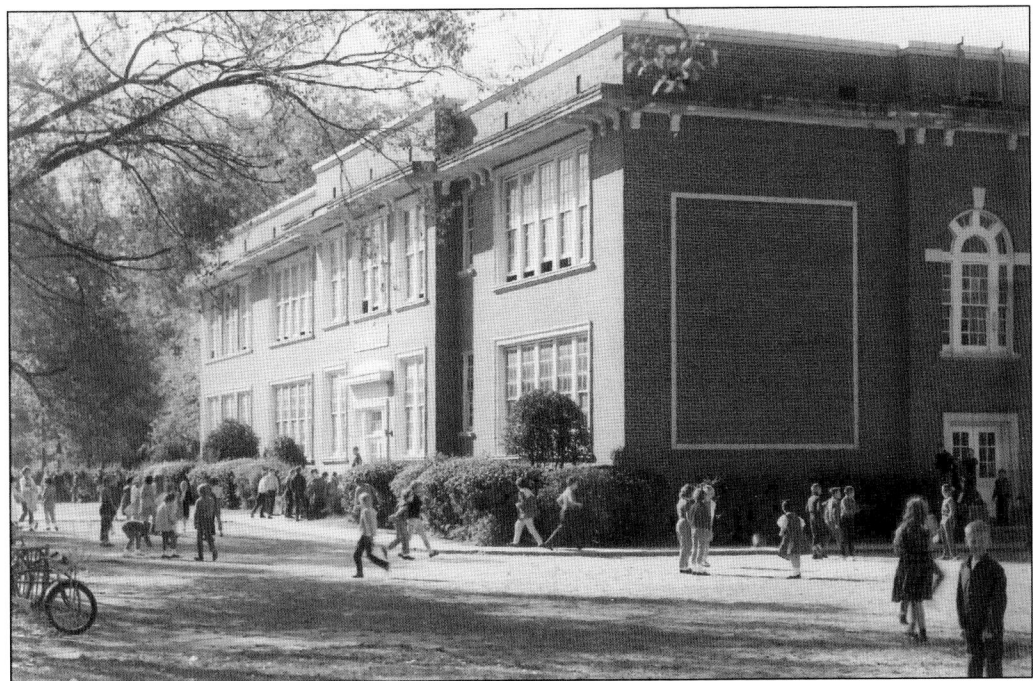

Children play outside the old Central Elementary School at recess time. The building has housed a high school, an elementary school, and now administration offices. It underwent a major renovation during the last decade.

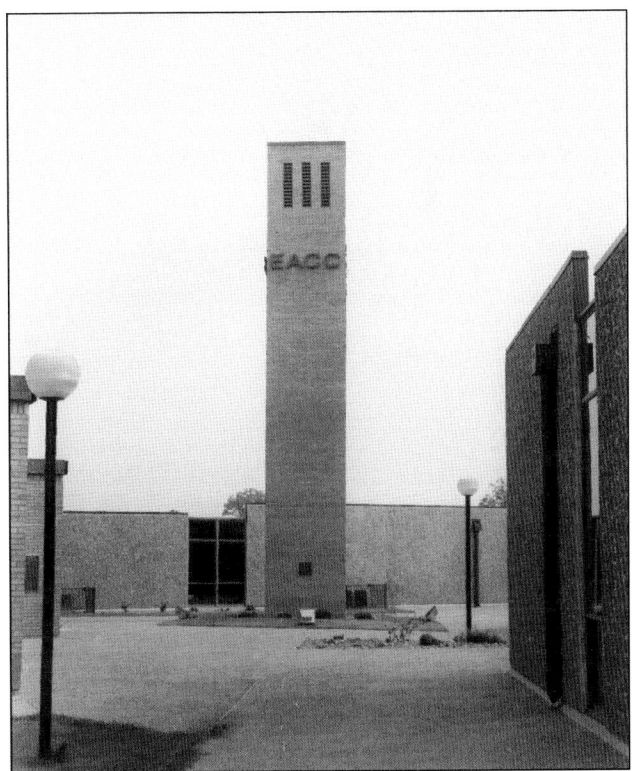

The tower of the East Arkansas Community College is shown when it was first built. The college is a two-year institute that specializes in preparing students for transfer to the four-year university in Jonesboro.

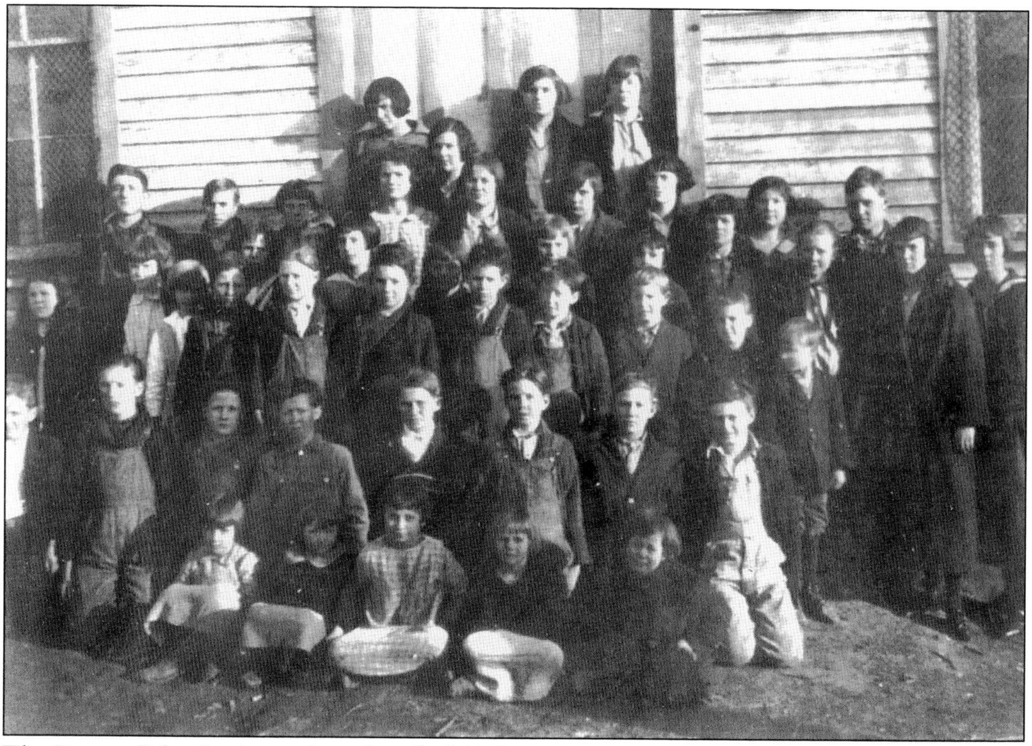

The Parrott School is located on Crowley's Ridge.

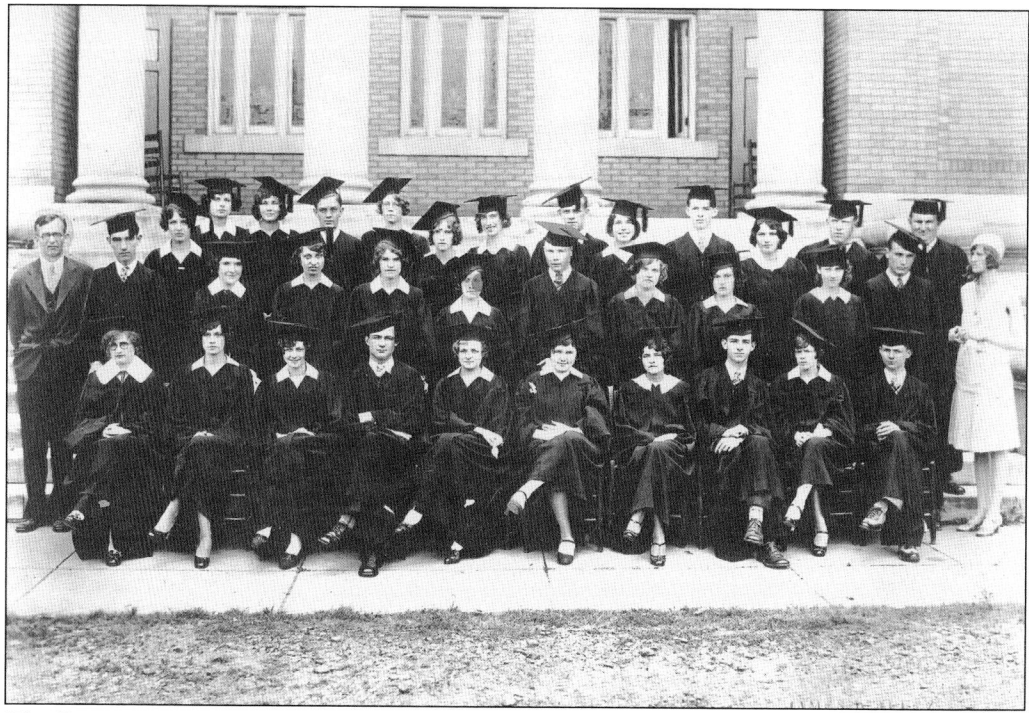

The Forrest City High School graduating class of 1929 poses for a group photograph. Margy Cannon's mother, Mrs. Carroll Cannon, appears fourth from the right in the first row.

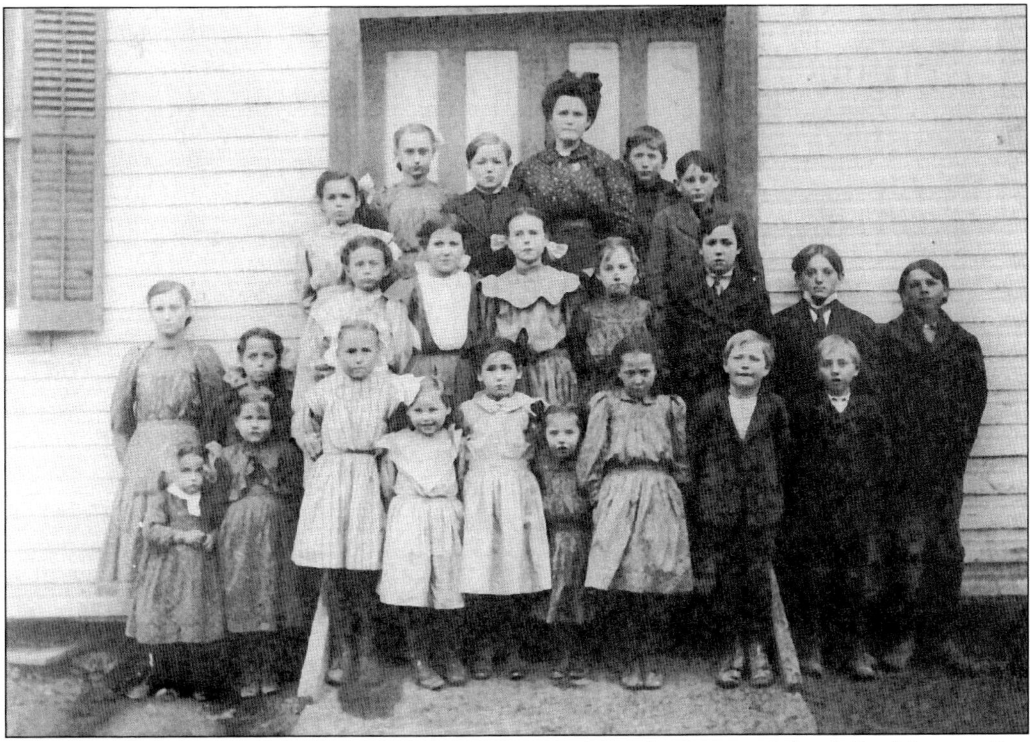

Roda Brickey Parker is in the first row of this image from the Parrott School. Roda's sister Roi stands next to her. Roi died while traveling by covered wagon to Mississippi to visit relatives.

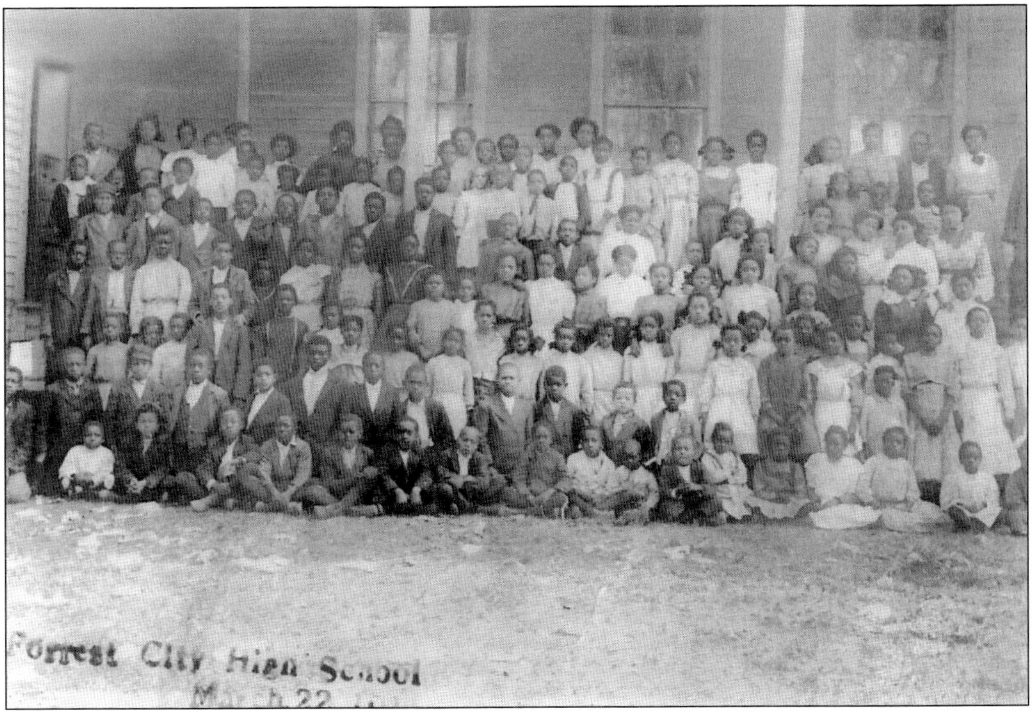

Members of the Forest City High School graduating class gather on March 22, 1911.

Here students stand in front of their schoolhouse.

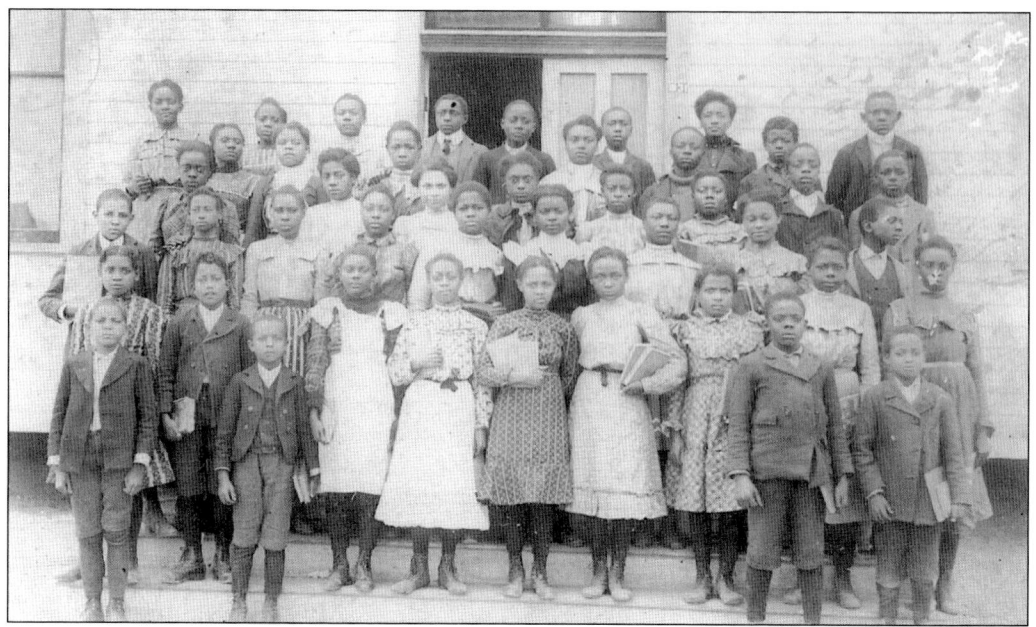

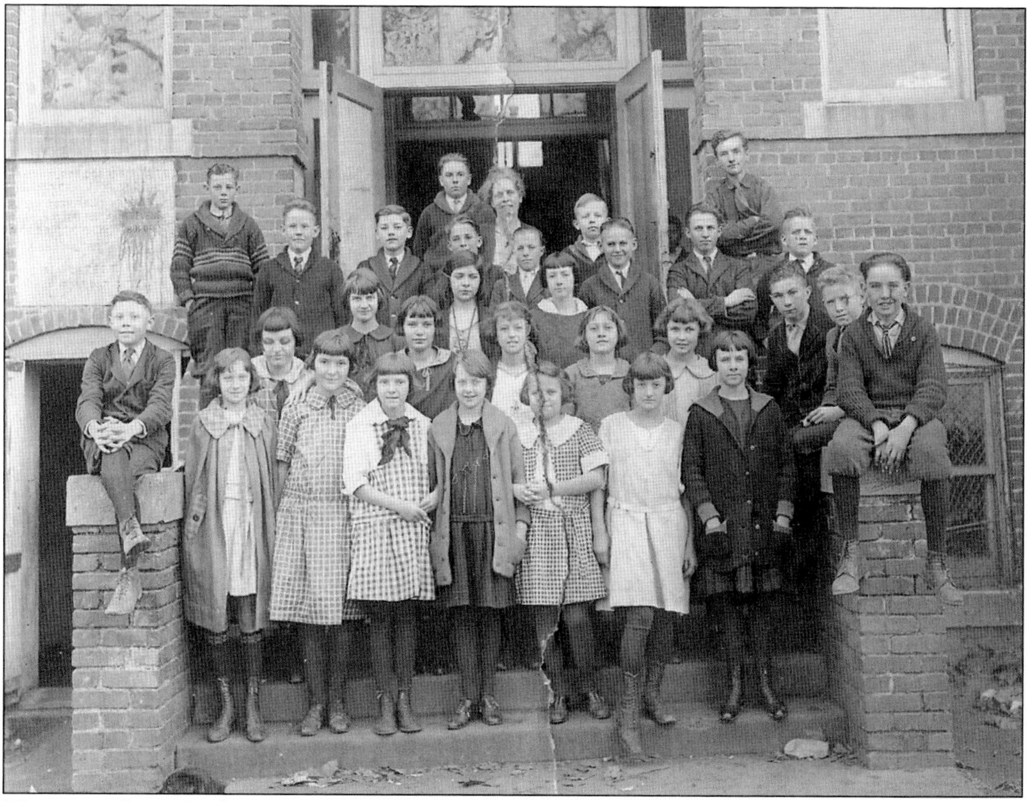

The seventh-grade class poses in front of Central Elementary School with their teacher, a Mrs. Stevens (back, center), on December 21, 1923.

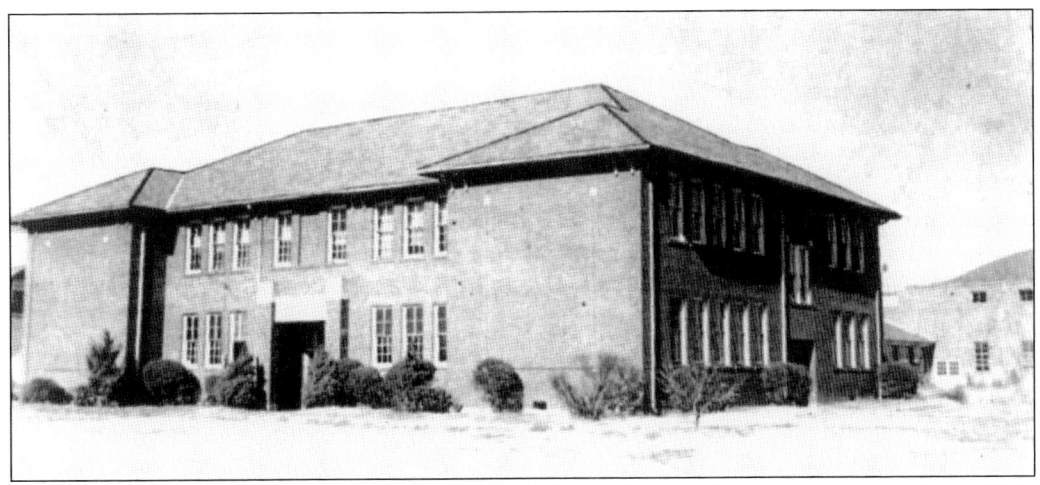

It is difficult to find artifacts from the Lincoln School. During the racial tension of the 1960s and 1970s, a riot destroyed the school. The only known trophies from the school are housed at the St. Francis County Museum, and only a few yearbooks have been traced. This building no longer exists.

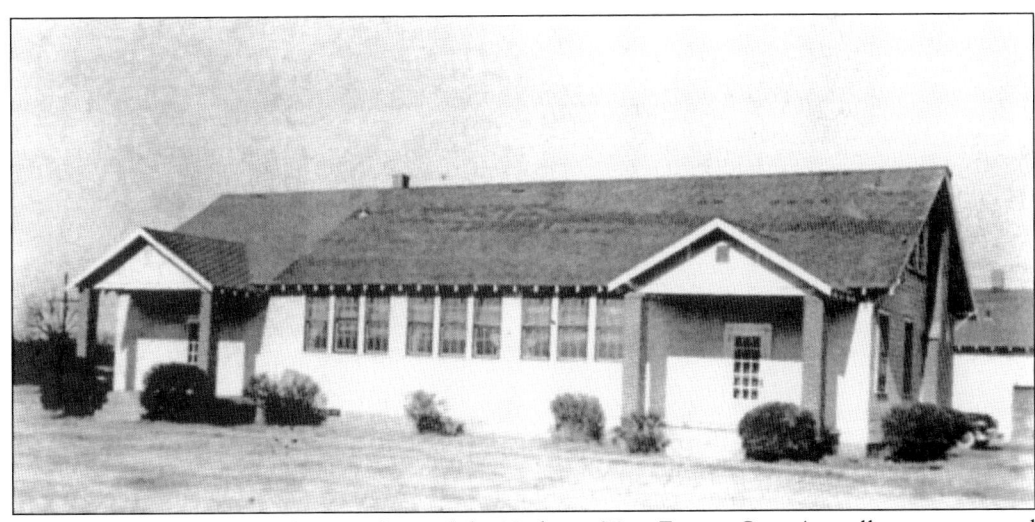

The Home Economics Building still stands by Highway 70 in Forrest City. Actually reconstructed after the Lincoln riots, it is located next to what is now called Lincoln Middle School.

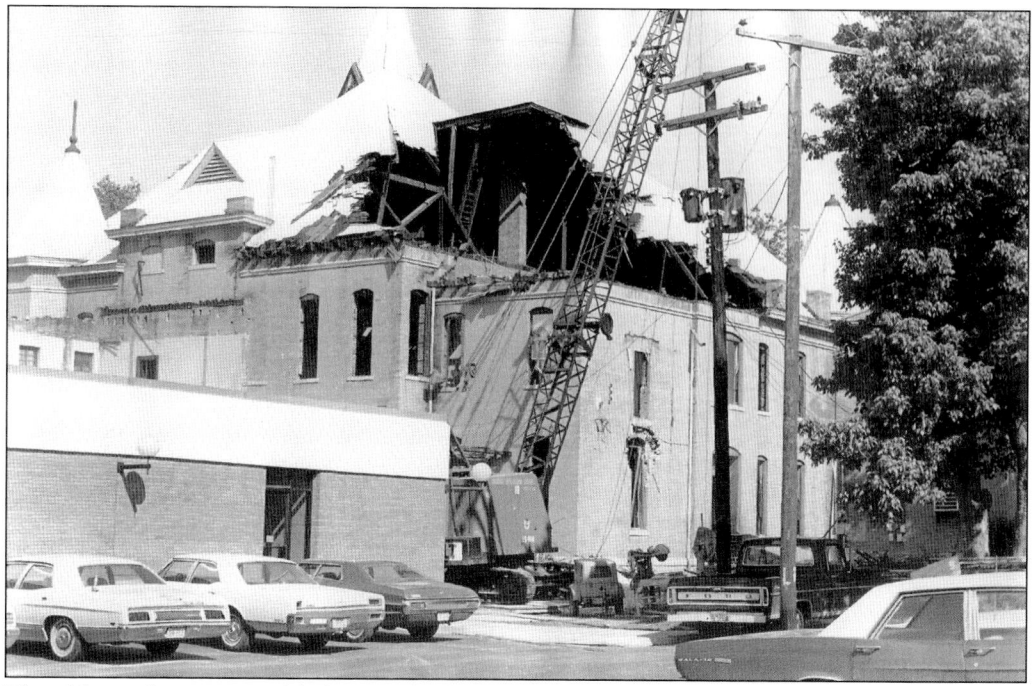

The old courthouse was a fabulous work of art by Charles Thompson, a famous architect featured in the Old State House Museum in Little Rock. The grand building fell on hard times, however, and was slated for removal. This image reveals the first phase of demolition in the 1970s.

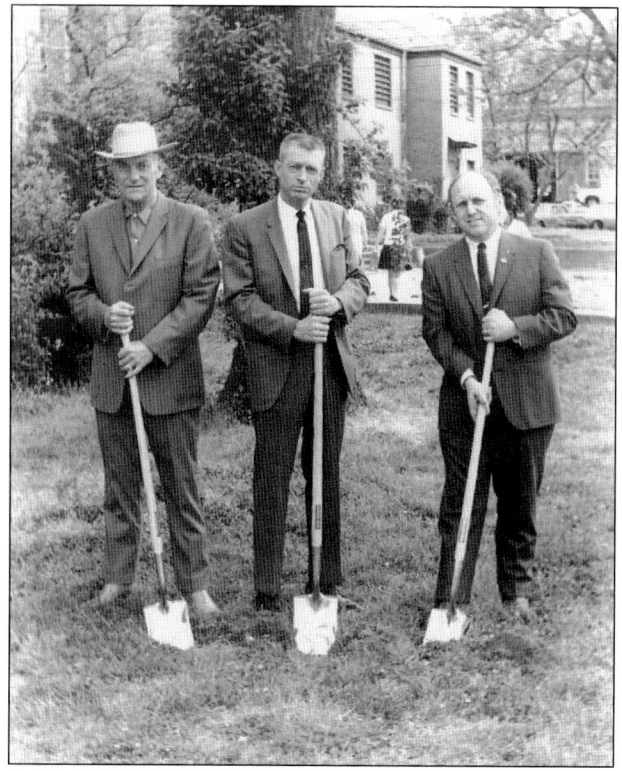

From left to right, Clarence Montgomery, Sonny Hamilton, and Gazzola Vaccaro Jr. break ground for the modern courthouse. Judge Vaccaro was instrumental in saving some of the artifacts from the old building, including portraits of Civil War heroes, the clock face, and photographs. With the founding of the St. Francis County Museum, he also made sure these items were given a proper home. Vaccaro continues in the tradition of J. O. Rush, preserving history for others.

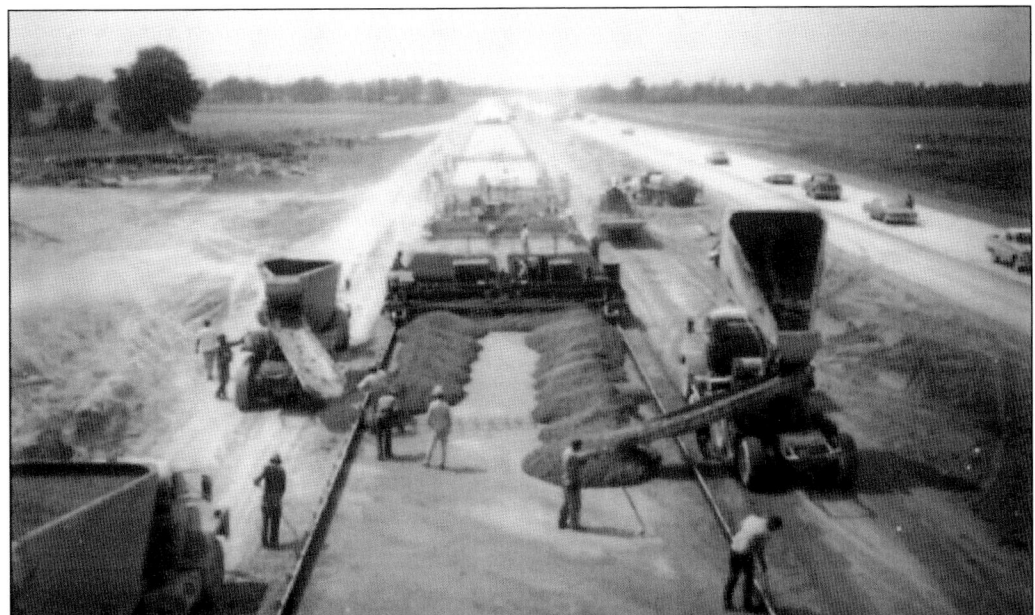

Jerald Burns reports that he was never allowed to skip school, but his family recognized the importance of the interstate coming through the farm, so his mother requested he come home from school to take a photograph. Looking west, Burns took this view to commemorate the historic event.

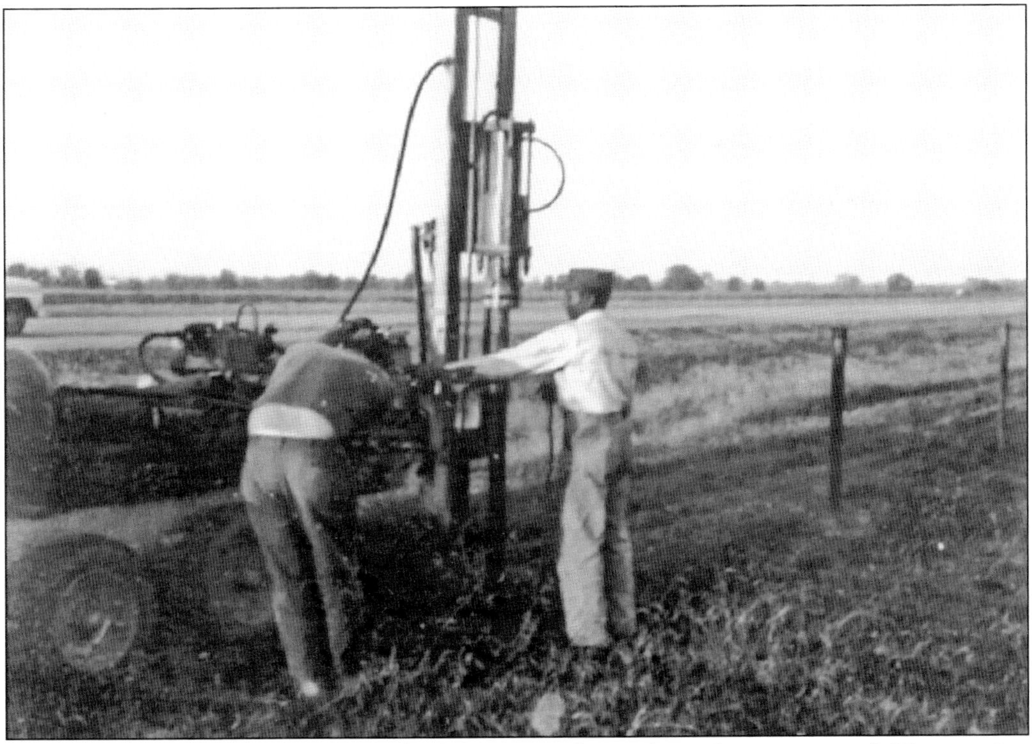

Another phase of Interstate 40 involved erecting a fence along the service road. This portion now spans the front of Burns Aerodrome in Palestine.

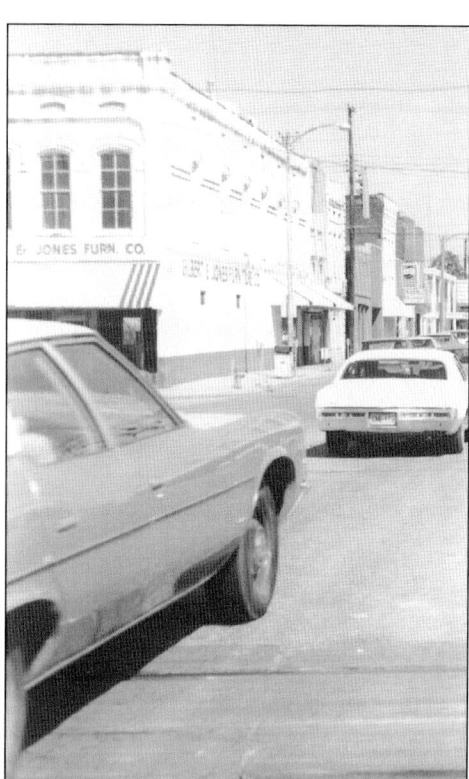

This late-1960s photograph displays South Washington Street during high traffic.

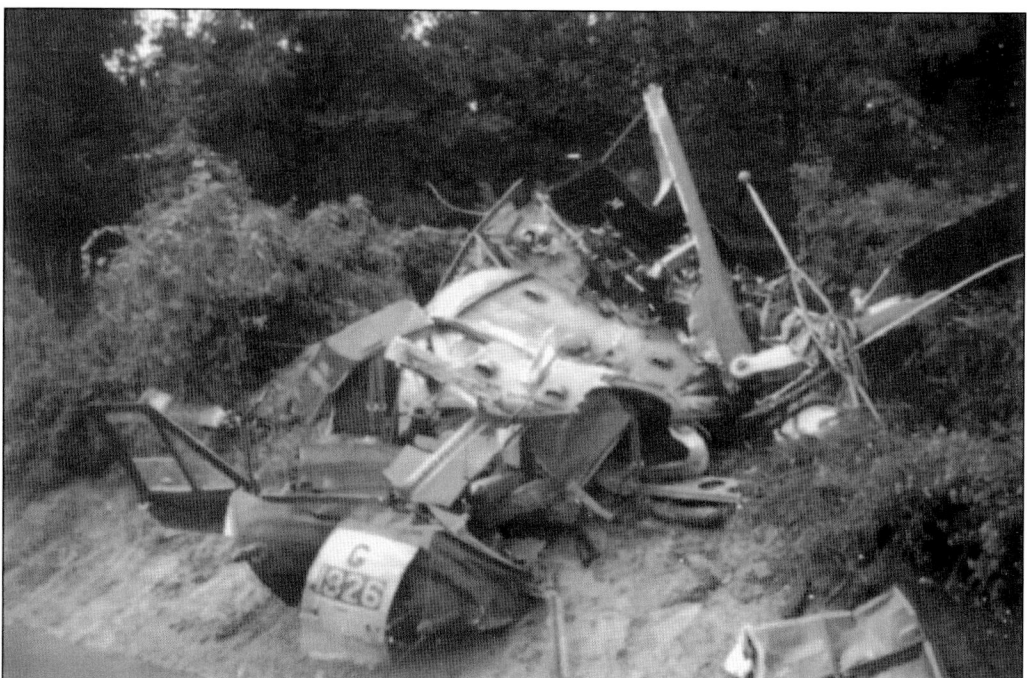

About a week after the Interstate 40 images were taken by Jerald Burns, news hit town that an army helicopter had crashed. Burns rushed to the site to document it. One crew member died, while the other broke his back but lived.

Six
Disaster Strikes

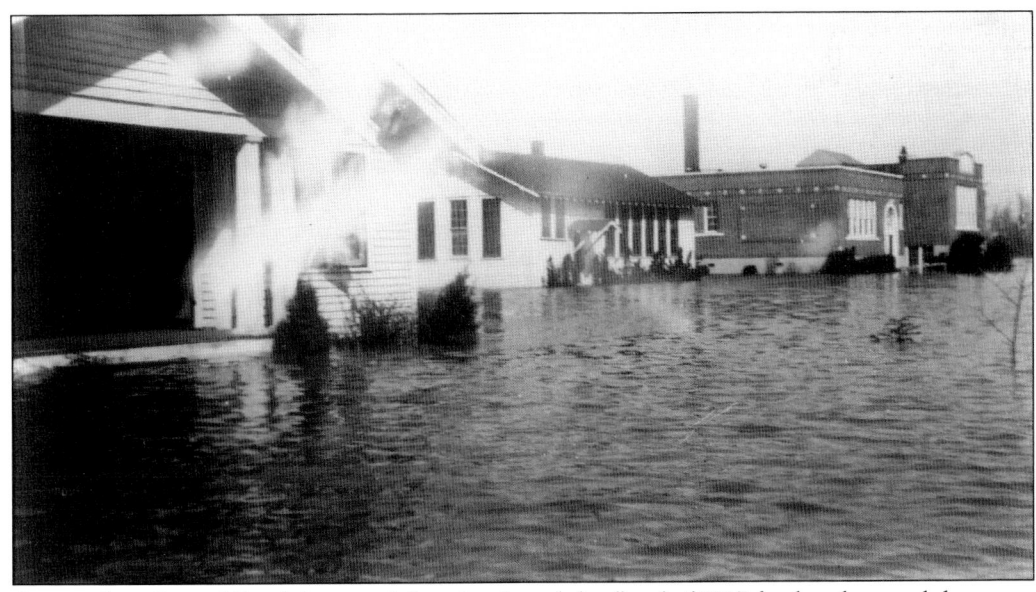
A tornado at Round Pond destroyed the school, and the flood of 1927 further damaged the town. By the 1937 flood, the little town was just not able to return to its former glory.

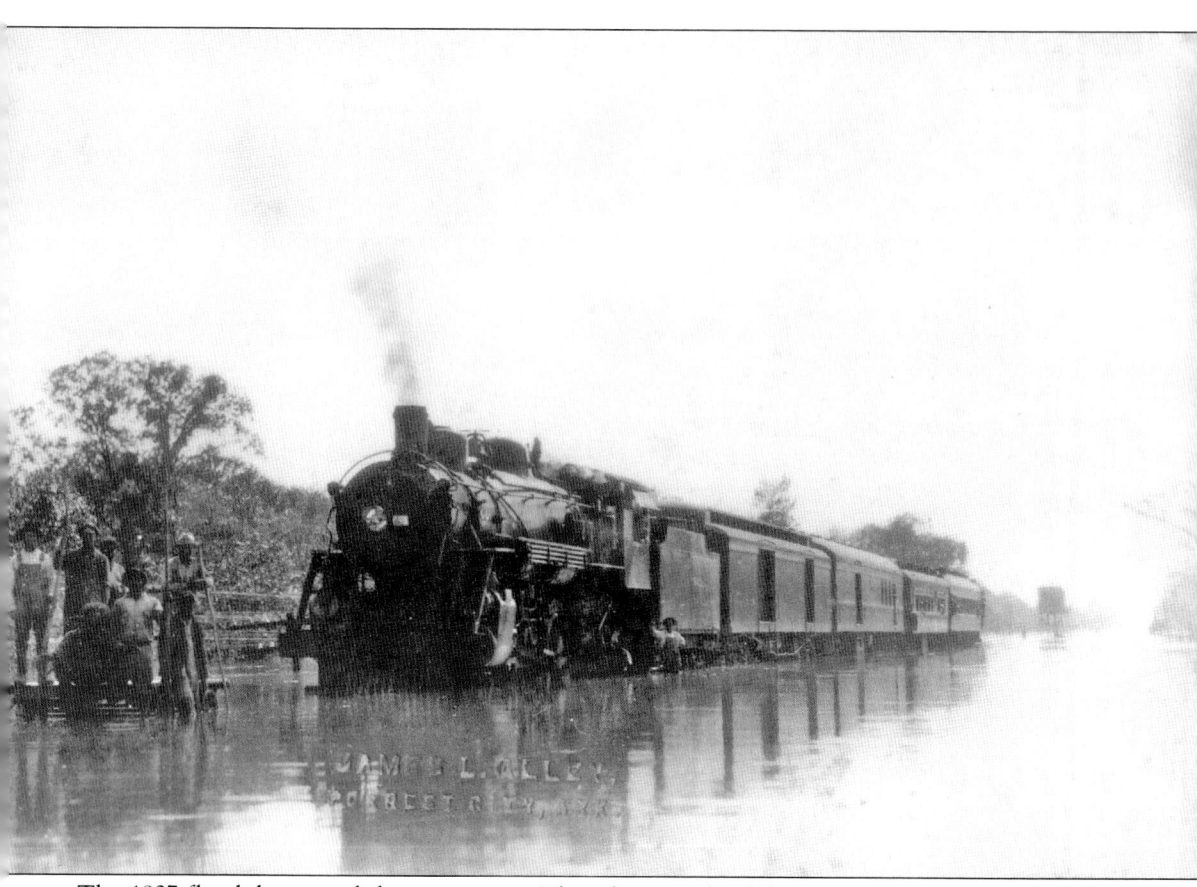

The 1937 flood devastated the entire area. This photograph of the train at Heth shows exactly how high the waters were. The region was just beginning to fully recover from the flood of 1927 when this one hit.

The first modern commercial airline disaster in history occurred in Goodwin, Arkansas, on January 14, 1936. For years, people offered the possibility of air jacking, but research has since shown that to be unlikely. The airplane followed a regular daily route from Memphis to Little Rock. The crash killed all 17 aboard, including WPA administrator W. R. Dyess; Dyess Colony, the childhood home of Johnny Cash, was renamed after him. The airplane hit so violently that no intact bodies were recovered. News photographs (right) illustrate the wreckage strewn through the trees along the whole distance of the swamp. Goodwin, located between Palestine and Wheatley, was soon inundated with ambulances, reporters, and helpers from Little Rock and Memphis. A week after the wreck, the Federal Aviation Authority sold the scrap from the plane to Hubert Hurt for $65. The author and Palestine resident Becky Lee own rings crafted from the sheet metal. Lee also has a quilt made from the crash's recovered clothing.

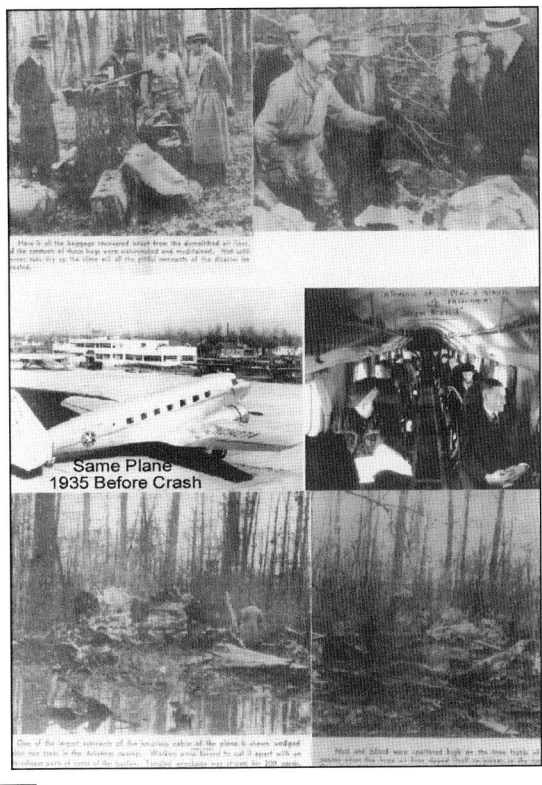

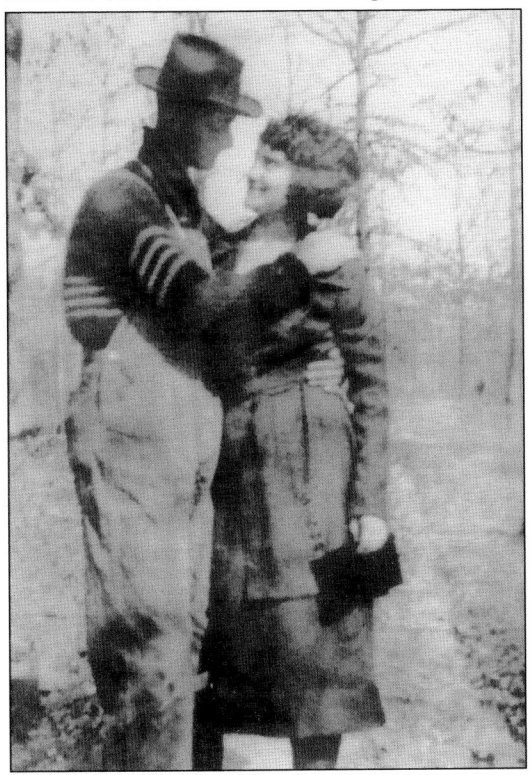

Roda Brickey was 24 years old when she married Willie Andre Parker in 1925. Willie was one of the first rescuers to respond to the scene of the Southerner crash. He passed away later that year.

121

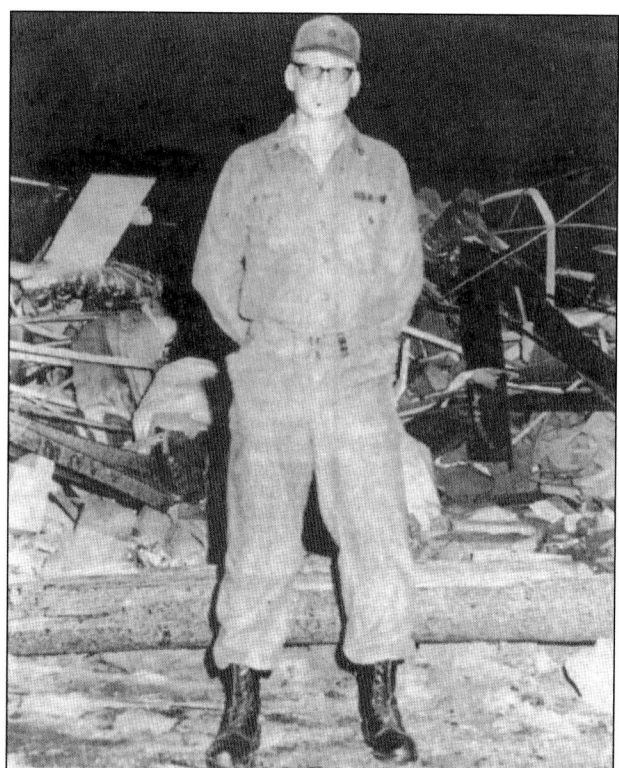

The U.S. National Guard was quickly called in to protect against looting after the 1974 tornado. Here Jerald Burns stands guard outside Proctor's Store.

The most fatalities occurred because of the collapse at the Gibson's store. Until the U.S. National Guard could be deployed, local emergency services set up communications in the Gibson's parking lot so the car radio could be used.

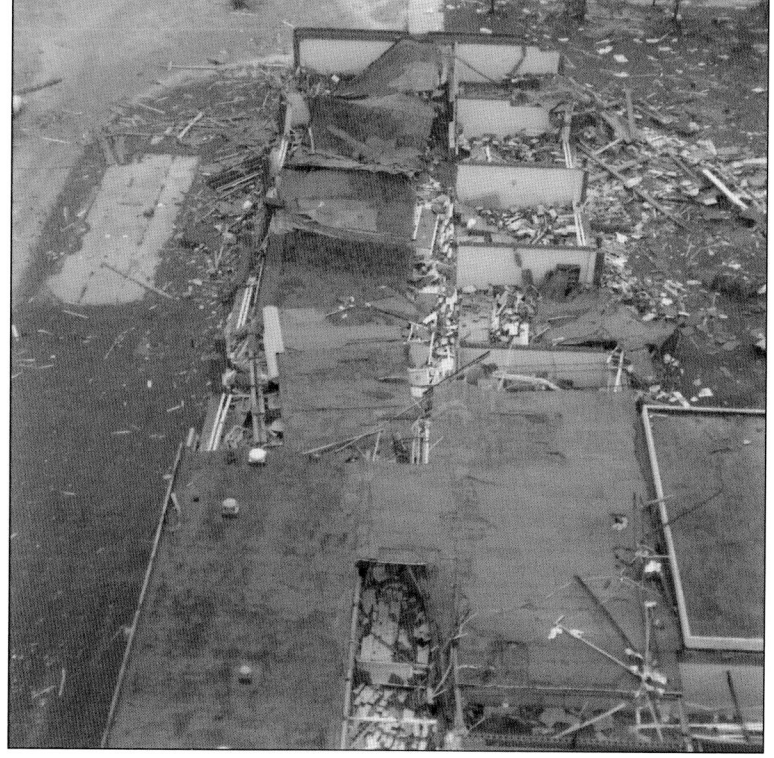

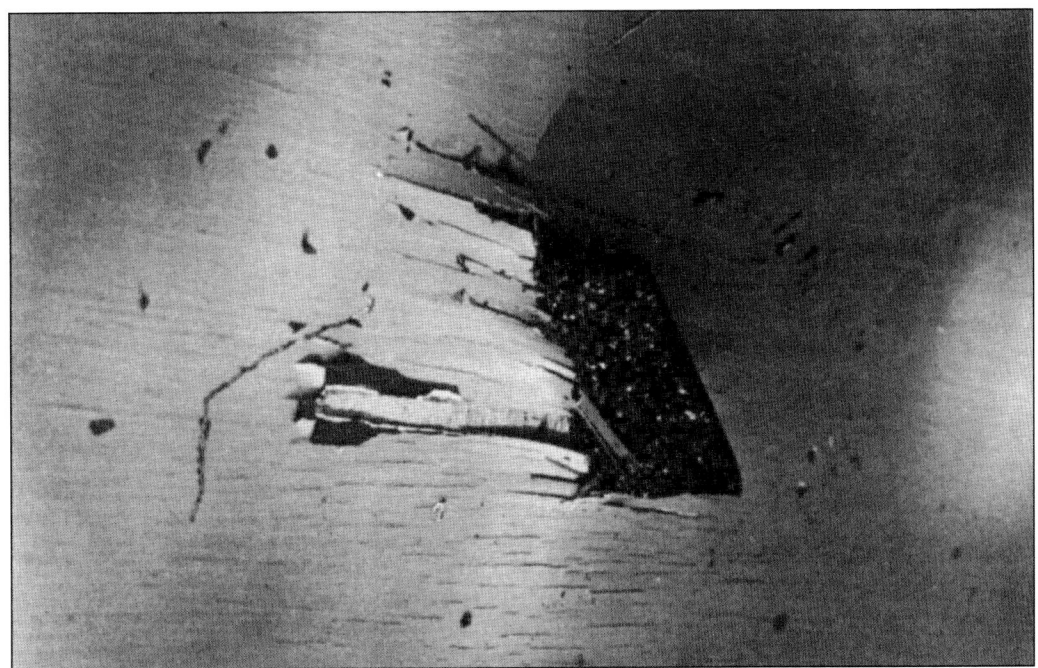

This door was once attached to the home of Gardner Smith on Welsh Street in Beech Grove. During the tornado of 1974, an asbestos shingle was driven completely through the door, composed of 2-inch-thick solid oak. Front and back views are shown. Jean Pope, who was several streets over, remembers hiding in her closet with her husband, T. C. When the couple emerged, the tornado had left the calendar still hanging on the wall in the kitchen, while just a few feet away the house was gone.

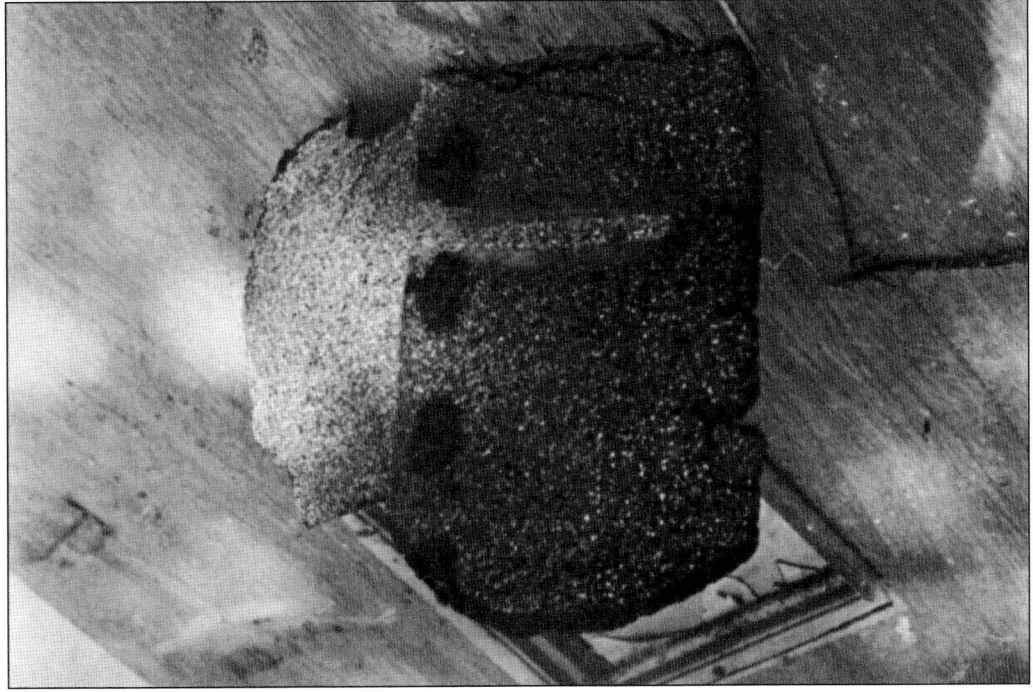

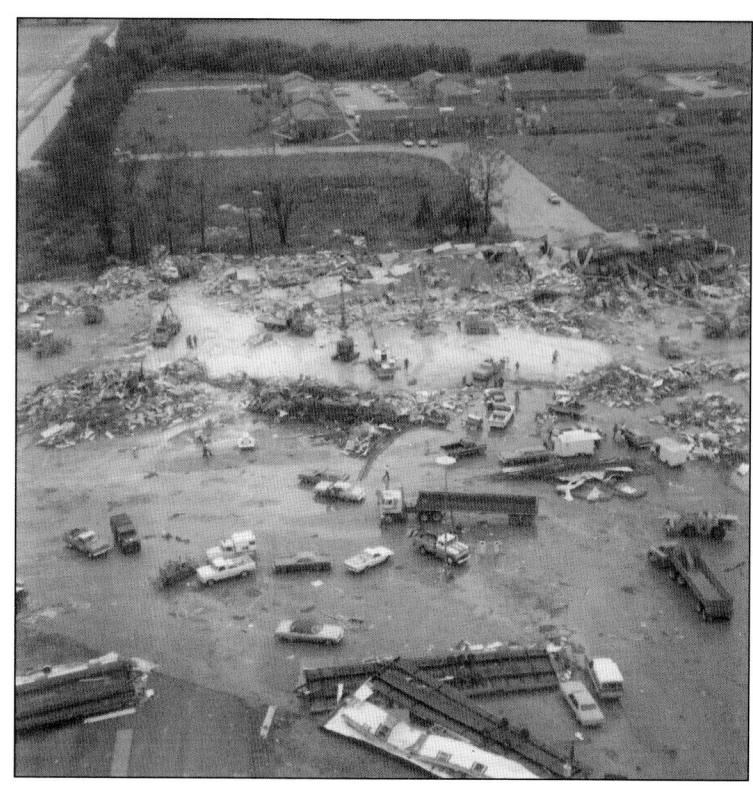

The Forrest City tornado of 1974 created some devastating images. These are just two from the tornado book organized by Claud O'Dell, who felt the event should be documented. Most natives can still remember where they were when the twister hit. As illustrated here, Gibson's and Proctor's suffered massive damage.

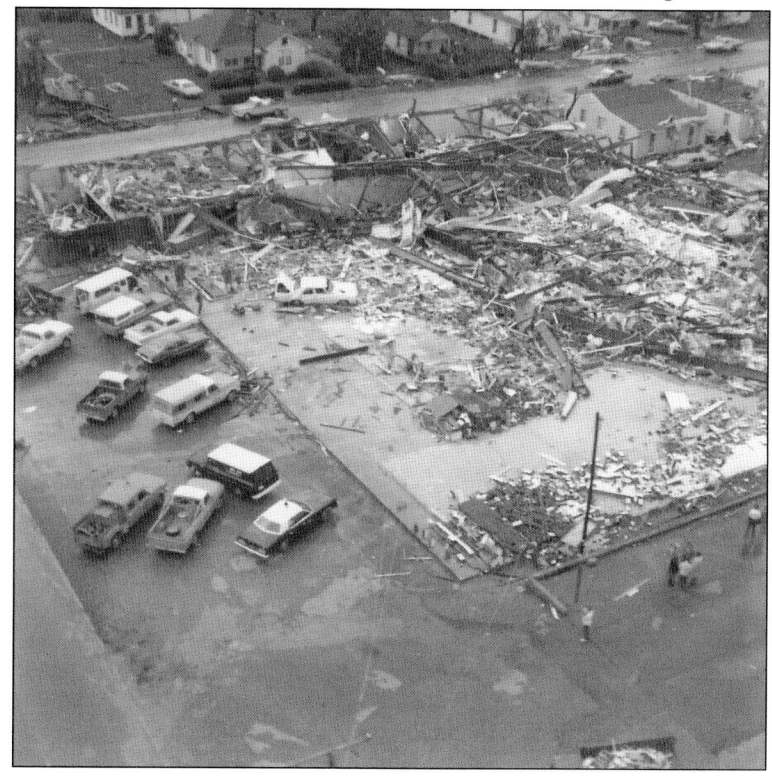

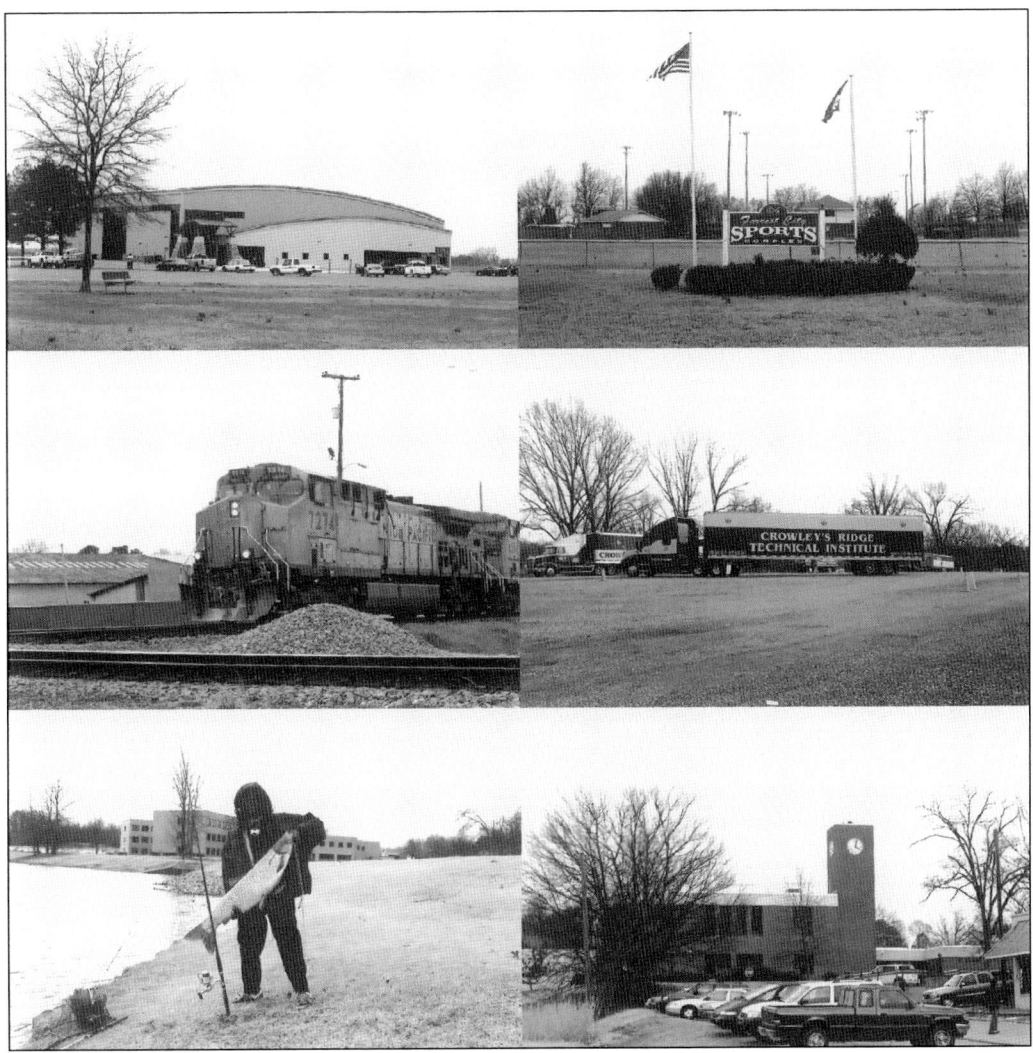

In the spirit of Claud O'Dell, St. Francis County's unofficial photographer, the book ends with a collage of current peeks into the county. Had it not been for O'Dell's insight and effort in documenting daily life, the authors would not have many memories to pass on to the reader. Many thanks to O'Dell and his family.

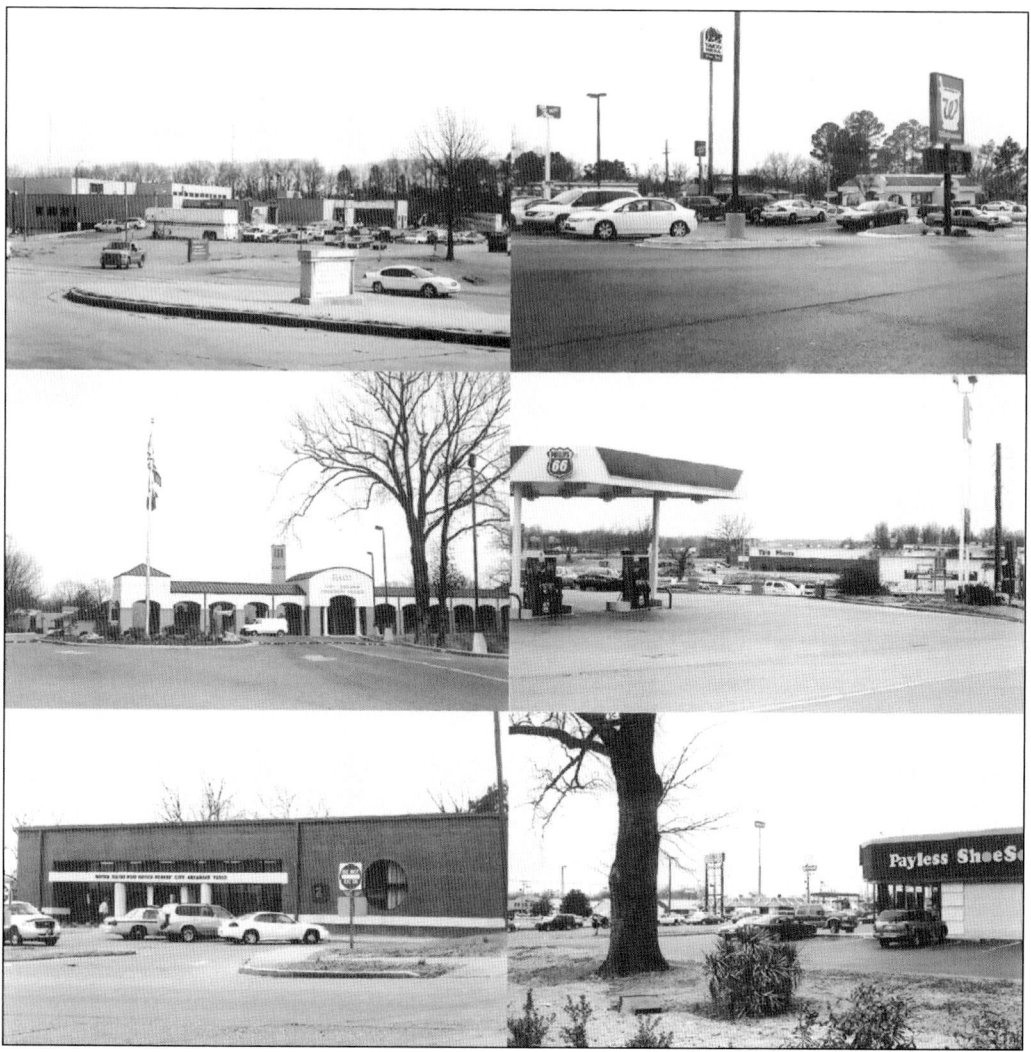
Forrest City and St. Francis County are represented in this collage of current businesses and scenes.

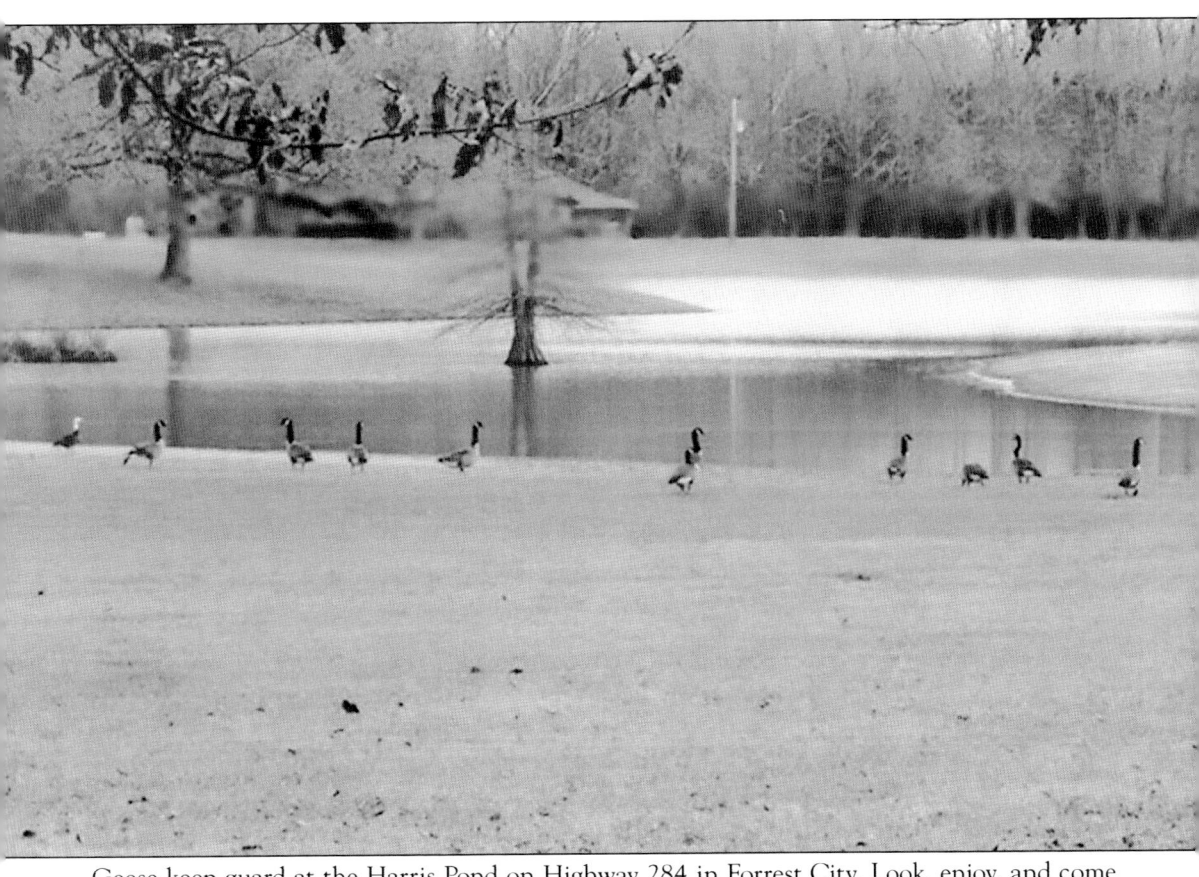
Geese keep guard at the Harris Pond on Highway 284 in Forrest City. Look, enjoy, and come visit the area soon.

Discover Thousands of Local History Books
Featuring Millions of Vintage Images

Arcadia Publishing, the leading local history publisher in the United States, is committed to making history accessible and meaningful through publishing books that celebrate and preserve the heritage of America's people and places.

Find more books like this at
www.arcadiapublishing.com

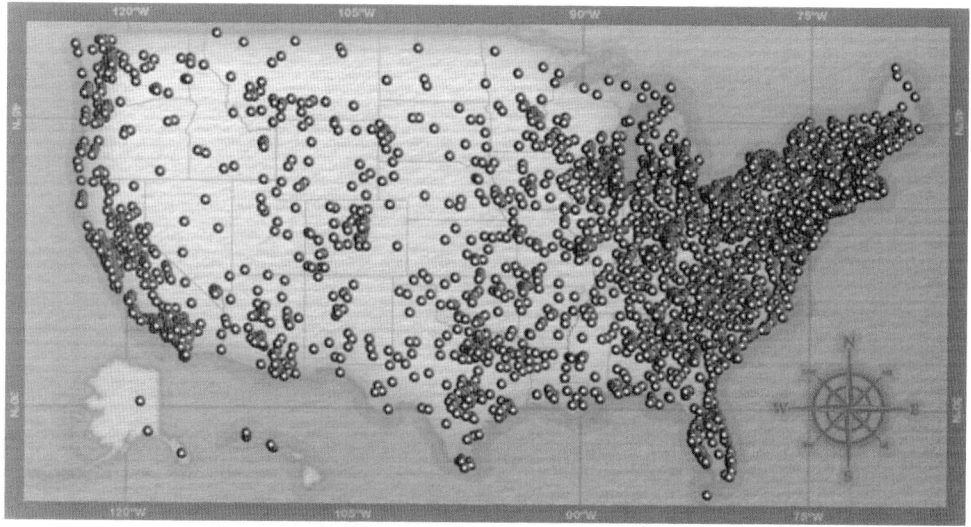

Search for your hometown history, your old stomping grounds, and even your favorite sports team.

Consistent with our mission to preserve history on a local level, this book was printed in South Carolina on American-made paper and manufactured entirely in the United States. Products carrying the accredited Forest Stewardship Council (FSC) label are printed on 100 percent FSC-certified paper.

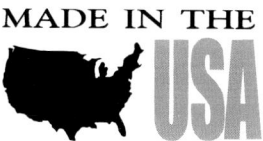